THE AGILE ENTERPRISE

BUILDING AND RUNNING AGILE
ORGANIZATIONS

Mario E. Moreira

Apress®

The Agile Enterprise: Building and Running Agile Organizations

Mario E. Moreira
Winchester, Massachusetts, USA

ISBN-13 (pbk): 978-1-4842-2390-1   ISBN-13 (electronic): 978-1-4842-2391-8
DOI 10.1007/978-1-4842-2391-8

Library of Congress Control Number: 2017936193

Managing Director: Welmoed Spahr
Acquisitions Editor: Robert Hutchinson
Developmental Editor: Laura Berendson
Editorial Board: Steve Anglin, Pramila Balen, Laura Berendson, Aaron Black, Louise Corrigan,
    Jonathan Gennick, Robert Hutchinson, Celestin Suresh John, Nikhil Karkal,
    James Markham, Susan McDermott, Matthew Moodie, Natalie Pao, Gwenan Spearing
Coordinating Editor: Rita Fernando
Copy Editor: Ann Dickson
Compositor: SPi Global
Indexer: SPi Global
Cover Designer: eStudio Calamar

Distributed to the book trade worldwide by Springer Science+Business Media New York, 233 Spring Street, 6th Floor, New York, NY 10013. Phone 1-800-SPRINGER, fax (201) 348-4505, e-mail orders-ny@springer-sbm.com, or visit www.springeronline.com. Apress Media, LLC is a California LLC and the sole member (owner) is Springer Science + Business Media Finance Inc (SSBM Finance Inc). SSBM Finance Inc is a Delaware corporation.

For information on translations, please e-mail rights@apress.com, or visit www.apress.com.

Apress and friends of ED books may be purchased in bulk for academic, corporate, or promotional use. eBook versions and licenses are also available for most titles. For more information, reference our Special Bulk Sales–eBook Licensing web page at www.apress.com/bulk-sales.

Any source code or other supplementary materials referenced by the author in this text is available to readers at www.apress.com. For detailed information about how to locate your book's source code, go to www.apress.com/source-code/.

Printed on acid-free paper

Apress Business: The Unbiased Source of Business Information

Apress business books provide essential information and practical advice, each written for practitioners by recognized experts. Busy managers and professionals in all areas of the business world—and at all levels of technical sophistication—look to our books for the actionable ideas and tools they need to solve problems, update and enhance their professional skills, make their work lives easier, and capitalize on opportunity.

Whatever the topic on the business spectrum—entrepreneurship, finance, sales, marketing, management, regulation, information technology, among others—Apress has been praised for providing the objective information and unbiased advice you need to excel in your daily work life. Our authors have no axes to grind; they understand they have one job only—to deliver up-to-date, accurate information simply, concisely, and with deep insight that addresses the real needs of our readers.

It is increasingly hard to find information—whether in the news media, on the Internet, and now all too often in books—that is even-handed and has your best interests at heart. We therefore hope that you enjoy this book, which has been carefully crafted to meet our standards of quality and unbiased coverage.

We are always interested in your feedback or ideas for new titles. Perhaps you'd even like to write a book yourself. Whatever the case, reach out to us at editorial@apress.com and an editor will respond swiftly. Incidentally, at the back of this book, you will find a list of useful related titles. Please visit us at www.apress.com to sign up for newsletters and discounts on future purchases.

The Apress Business Team

Life is about outcomes and the positive impact you make in this world including the people around you.

I dedicate this book to my three great motivators who have had a wonderful impact on my life.

To Seeme, Aliya, and Iman.

Contents

Contents

About the Author

Mario E. Moreira is an enterprise Agile consultant and master Agile coach. He helps achieve better business outcomes by increasing delivery of customer value, optimizing speed of delivery, and increasing quality. Mario specializes in transforming enterprises to Agile, bringing cutting-edge concepts and practices to help gain the business benefits that Agile brings. This includes coaching and educating executives, management, and small-to-large distributed teams in Agile mindset, concepts, and practices (Scrum, XP, Kanban, Lean, VFQ, Story Mapping, Value Stream Mapping, and more).

Mario has worked as an executive, advisor, manager, and hands-on team member so he understands the importance of what is needed for various roles at each level of an Agile and business transformation. He has experience leading within organizations such as Fidelity Investments, CA Technologies, Walmart, Emergn, and Vistaprint.

In addition to his Agile experience, Mario is seasoned in software configuration management, portfolio management, product management, business strategy, requirements, architecture, IT governance, technology, development, delivery, innovation, quality assurance, and more.

Mario is the author of several business and technology books including The *Agile Enterprise: Building and Running Agile Organizations*, *Being Agile: Your Roadmap to Successful Adoption of Agile*, *Adapting Configuration Management for Agile Teams*, *Software Configuration Management Implementation Roadmap*, and *Agile for Dummies*. He writes regularly for his Agile Adoption Roadmap blog at cmforagile.blogspot.com.

About the Contributors

David Grabel (co-author of Chapter 12) is an enterprise Agile coach at Vistaprint, bringing Agile beyond engineering to the entire business unit. He has introduced Scrum, Kanban, XP, and SAFe at both small and large organizations. As a consultant, his clients included Vistaprint, Trizetto, Bose, and PayPal. He has helped these clients adopt Agile at the team and enterprise level. He is certified as CSM, CSP, and SPC. He is a board member and former president of Agile New England, a non-profit group dedicated to accelerating the adoption of Agile throughout New England. He has spoken at many conferences including Agile 2015 and 2016, Lean Kanban North America, and Mile High Agile.

JP Beaudry (co-author of Chapter 16) is an engineering leader and Agile coach. JP is currently director of technology with Cimpress, where he leads the enterprise Agile transformation and technical operations for the billion-dollar Vistaprint line of business. Before Cimpress, JP led various engineering organizations at Cisco Systems. In 2013, his business unit won the Cisco Pioneer Award on the strength and depth of its Agile practice. JP is certified by the British Computer Society (BCS) as an Agile practitioner and by Emergn as a Value, Flow, Quality (VFQ) expert coach.

Acknowledgments

I want to especially thank Rita Fernando at Apress for her patience and encouragement in keeping me focused on my writing as other work and life adventures were occurring. I want to thank Robert Hutchinson and Laura Berendson at Apress for their editorial efforts in helping me make this book a reality.

To JP Beaudry and David Grabel for being strong Agile advocates and the co-authors of two chapters of this book. You helped make this journey fun, and your contributions were greatly appreciated.

To those Agilists in Emergn and Vistaprint—thank you for being part of my Agile family, both inspiring me in my Agile work and supporting my ideas.

To all my readers who are both Agile champions and enthusiasts—thank you for making a commitment to learn what it means to establish an Agile enterprise and embrace the many concepts, mindset, and methods that are needed to achieve an Agile transformation that is customer-value-driven.

Getting Started

An Agile enterprise has Agile occurring end-to-end and top-to-bottom.

—Mario Moreira

Imagine an enterprise where everyone focuses on the highest customer value, an enterprise that methodically yet quickly adapts toward high value and cuts the tail of lower-value work.

Imagine a company where employees are trusted to use 100% of their brain power to self-organize around the work and think of better ways to work, a company where employee satisfaction comes from within the employees themselves for a job well done.

Imagine an organization where ideas—from strategies to tasks—are transparent so everyone knows if their work is aligned with strategy and high-priority ideas, an organization where budgeting is given to the highest-value ideas.

Imagine an enterprise where a discovery mindset wins over certainty thinking, an enterprise where experimentation with increments and feedback helps define the way toward customer value.

Imagine a company where managers are coaches, mentors, and leaders who encourage people with inspiration, vision, and trust; a company where there is a singular focus on putting the enterprise first instead of individual egos.

Imagine an enterprise where customers embrace the ideas being built because they are engaged in the building of the work all along the way, an enterprise where customers become your partners providing continuous feedback.

© Mario E. Moreira 2017
M. E. Moreira, *The Agile Enterprise*, DOI 10.1007/978-1-4842-2391-8_1

If you can imagine this type of enterprise, then this book can help you realize it. This book provides insightful and pragmatic knowledge and activities to help you visualize what an effectively running Agile enterprise looks like. You will learn more about the importance of engaging customers and gaining their feedback. Fully embrace the importance of engaging employees, ensuring they have ownership and can self-organize around the work. Embrace the idea of leading your Agile transformation with education and focusing on the behavioral changes prior to the mechanical changes.

Have you realized that there is much more to Agile than following a process? Are you yearning to explore an effective culture where the discovery mindset brings you closer to customer value? Have you come to the conclusion that Agile is about building a holistic enterprise culture that is optimized for being agile and delivering customer value?

This book will share many cutting-edge concepts, mindsets, and practices to answer these questions. It will help you adapt to the culture, roles, and practices that you will need to be a customer-value-driven enterprise. If you are committed to customer success and realize that it does take a whole enterprise to achieve it, then this is the book for you.

Agile should not be done for the sake of Agile. Instead, Agile helps you deliver more value to customers and achieve better business outcomes. This is why, every step of the way, every activity should be viewed as how it is optimizing for customer success. This book will lead you down this path.

Innovations of This Book

As this book helps you apply Agile values and principles in the form of concepts, mindsets, practices, and techniques across an enterprise to be the most effective and successful that you can be, it introduces you to three innovations in the way Agile is approached.

The first innovation this book provides you is a holistic top-to-bottom and end-to-end view of an Agile enterprise where everyone is engaged. Get introduced to the Agile Galaxy in your customer universe shown in Figure 1-1. It is designed to help you better understand your Agile landscape of today and what you want your future to look like.

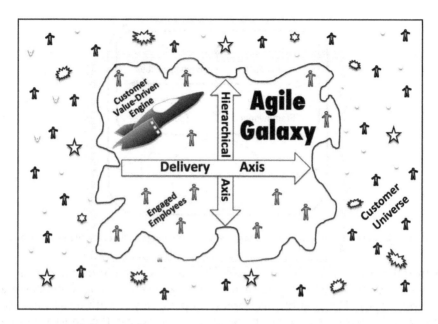

Figure 1-1. Your Agile Galaxy in your customer universe

The second innovation this book provides you is the customer-value-driven (CVD) enterprise, the CVD framework, and its corresponding engine of customer value that emphasizes the importance of customer feedback. An Agile CVD framework is a business and delivery system that is driven by customer value, where you capture and prioritize ideas based on customer value, continuously validate customer value throughout with customer feedback, and deliver customer value in a timely manner, all for the purpose of optimizing the delivery of what the customer finds as value. This includes engaging employees in the pursuit of customer value.

The third innovation of this book is a packaging of many cutting-edge Agile concepts, mindsets, practices, and techniques that it will reveal regarding the adoption of Agile throughout an enterprise, from idea to delivery and from the team level to the executive level. In a sense, this is the iPod of Agile books (in other words, your iAgile) as shown in Figure 1-2. The iPod wasn't innovative because it was yet another mp3 player. Instead it was innovative by how it brought together many cutting-edge concepts, technologies, and processes that enabled the highest value to the customer. (See Figure 1-2.)

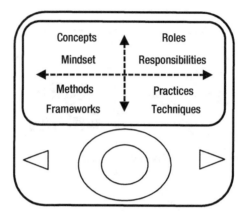

Figure 1-2. This book is your iAgile, packed with cutting-edge Agile elements in one place

While there are many Agile processes, frameworks, and practices out on the market, not all of them may fit perfectly into your environment and cover all of your needs. The goal of this book is to provide you with insight into the many Agile elements that can be applied in and across the end-to-end and top-to-bottom enterprise landscape so that you may more intelligently and adaptively determine what works better for your context.

This book is your guide to adapting to an Agile and CVD culture that starts the moment an idea gets recognized to the moment it gets delivered and only ends when you receive market feedback of what was learned (in other words, how successful the idea is).

On the one hand, this book will provide you a vision of where you can go. On the other hand, this book is a pragmatic guide to help you through your journey. This book is neither exhaustive nor prescriptive, but it will hopefully inspire you to think out-of-the-box and beyond the more traditional and common Agile elements and processes. The guidelines in this book can be applied equally to whether you are just starting your Agile journey or continuing to improve your Agile universe.

What You Will Learn

This book provides a landscape of options designed to help you consider, understand, deploy, and adapt an Agile culture, mindset, methods, and practices throughout an enterprise, from executives to Agile teams, and everyone in between. More importantly, it will help you narrow the gap between what the customer really wants and what you deliver. It is not surprising, given the mediocre success of many products and services, that those who claim to be customer-focused are optimizing less for the customer and more for the organization's bureaucracy, sub-optimizing for a division or personal goals.

What you will learn is that it does take an enterprise from as early as ideation through reflection after delivery (left to right) and executives to team (top to bottom) to make an Agile value-driven enterprise work.

What you will also learn is many of the latest modern concepts, mindsets, practices, and techniques that can help you on your journey so that you can run your enterprise in a customer value-driven manner.

This book maps the bottom-to-top and idea-to-delivery ways to operate in an enterprise Agile manner and gain the benefits that you desire from an Agile transformation. The topics that this book focuses on include the following:

- Becoming a **customer-value-driven** enterprise that optimizes its culture and processes for **customer value**

- Approaching Agile from an **outcome** perspective to gain better business results

- Establishing a **top-to-bottom view** of the **roles** in an Agile enterprise including the **executive role** for sponsoring your **Agile galaxy**

- Evolving into an Agile culture where the mindset embraces **Agile values and principles** and the **pluralistic-green** and **evolutionary-teal** paradigms

- Constructing an **end-to-end** view that visualizes an **idea pipeline** of the work following the **six R model** from recording the idea to reflecting on the results

- Building **high-performing teams** (for example, **lightning-bolt shaped teams**, collaboration, **teamocide avoidance**)

- Evolving management, HR, finance, portfolio, PMO, and other **roles** to work effectively in an Agile enterprise

- Building an enterprise where **customers matter**; **personas** are used to help with **user stories**, testing, and **demos**; right customer for right **feedback**; and **customer feedback vision**

- Building an enterprise where **employees matter, self-organizing** teams are applied, **Agile roles** are established, **motivations** are understood, and **bounded authority** is defined

- Building an Agile **discovery mindset** focused on **hypothesis thinking, feedback loops, innovation, divergent thinking**, and **incremental thinking**

- Seeing **uncertainty** as a smart starting point and removing **pretend and arrogant certainty**

- Establishing a **prioritization** framework to identify high-value work at the idea level via **cost of delay** and other prioritization methods

- Building a culture of **challenging assumptions** to increase confidence in decisions and reduce risks of releasing something the customer doesn't want

- Establishing **work-based Agile education** on a learn-apply-share model focused on **Agile values and principles** led with **value, flow, and quality**

- Powering your employees through **self-organizing** teams, an **Agile education vision**, and **gamification** while supporting an **Agile community**

- Understanding the importance of **Agile budgeting** and its benefit to **supply and demand**

- Constructing **Agile success measures and dashboard** focused on the value of the work, lead times, delivery pace, and quality

- Applying a **lagging to leading metric path** where leading indicators help you get to the (lagging) outcomes you are looking for

- Establishing a **requirements tree** to understand the hierarchy of how **strategy, ideas, increments, epics, user stories**, and **tasks** work together

- Connecting **idea pipeline** to team backlogs while managing **dependencies** and utilizing **velocity, WIP**, and **pull systems** to manage the flow of work

- Learning **ideation** with **Lean Canvas**, for capturing ideas and their assumptions, value, target audience, and to better understand the idea

- Applying an **incremental mindset** by introducing **decomposition** techniques such as **story mapping** to thin-slice ideas into increments and epics

- Writing effective **user stories** and the importance of **collaboration, acceptance criteria**, and how they relate to progress

- Reinventing HR as promoters of Agile, supporting Agile roles, focusing on employee motivation, adapting reward systems, obtaining **continuous employee feedback,** meeting **team-based goals, and exploring self-management**
- Adventuring through an **Agile enterprise story** that shows you how an enterprise may **transform** to Agile in an incremental manner using the materials in this book

Who This Book Is For

The primary readers for this book are

- executives and senior management
- sponsors of Agile transformations
- Agile coaches, consultants, and champions
- portfolio management teams
- project management offices (PMOs)
- product owners, product managers, and business analysts
- business and finance departments
- human resources (HR) departments
- marketing and sales departments
- investors and entrepreneurs
- ScrumMasters and Agile project managers
- cross-functional engineering/Scrum teams including developers, quality assurance (QA) analysts and testers, technical writers, user experience (UX) engineers, configuration management (CM) engineers, and more

How to Navigate This Book

You can read this book in various ways depending on your purpose and prior knowledge. You are welcome to read the book from beginning to end. Since chapters are relatively short, it is feasible to read a chapter in one sitting. You can also customize your path through the book to suit your knowledge level, specific challenge, or theme of interest.

The first four chapters set the conceptual groundwork for an effective customer-value-driven enterprise. The remaining chapters provide you with concepts, mindsets, practices, and techniques to help you make a value-driven Agile enterprise real. There are specific ways to navigate this book via theme, topic, or challenge. The following list shows chapter clusters that pertain to certain themes to help you focus on particular topics per your current need.

- Agile as it relates to the customer: Chapter 2 (Envisioning a Customer-Value-Driven Enterprise), Chapter 3 (Achieving Better Business Outcomes), Chapter 6 (Embracing Customers), Chapter 13 (Capturing Ideas with Lean Canvas), Chapter 14 (Incorporating Customer Feedback), and Chapter 18 (Collaborating on User Stories)

- Agile as it relates to the employee: Chapter 3 (Achieving Better Business Outcomes), Chapter 4 (Building Your Agile Galaxy), Chapter 7 (Embracing Employees), Chapter 8 (Evolving Roles in an Agile Enterprise), Chapter 9 (Building a Learning Enterprise), Chapter 10 (Applying a Discovery Mindset), and Chapter 21 (Reinventing HR for Agile)

- Building a customer-value-driven Agile enterprise: Chapter 2 (Envisioning a Customer-Value-Driven Enterprise), Chapter 6 (Embracing Customers), Chapter 10 (Applying a Discovery Mindset), Chapter 11 (Visualizing the Enterprise Idea Pipeline), Chapter 12 (Prioritizing with Cost of Delay), Chapter 13 (Capturing Ideas with Lean Canvas), Chapter 14 (Incorporating Customer Feedback), Chapter 15 (Establishing Your Requirements Tree), Chapter 18 (Collaborating on User Stories), Chapter 19 (Promoting Agile Budgeting), and Chapter 20 (Applying Agile Success Measures)

- Agile culture and mindset: Chapter 4 (Building Your Agile Galaxy), Chapter 5 (Activating an Agile Culture), Chapter 6 (Embracing Customers), Chapter 7 (Embracing Employees), Chapter 9 (Building a Learning Enterprise), Chapter 10 (Applying a Discovery Mindset), and Chapter 21 (Reinventing HR for Agile)

- Running an Agile enterprise: Chapter 5 (Activating an Agile Culture), Chapter 8 (Evolving Roles in Your Agile Enterprise), Chapter 9 (Building a Learning Enterprise), Chapter 10 (Applying a Discovery Mindset), Chapter 11 (Visualizing the Enterprise Idea Pipeline), Chapter 12 (Prioritizing with Cost of Delay), Chapter 13 (Capturing Ideas with Lean Canvas), Chapter 15 (Establishing Your Requirements Tree), Chapter 17 (Connecting the Idea Pipeline to Backlogs), Chapter 19 (Promoting Agile Budgeting), Chapter 20 (Applying Agile Success Measures), Chapter 21 (Reinventing HR for Agile), and Chapter 22 (Sharing an Agile Enterprise Story)

- Establishing your requirements relationships and decomposing requirements from idea to task: Chapter 11 (Visualizing the Enterprise Idea Pipeline), Chapter 13 (Capturing Ideas with Lean Canvas), Chapter 15 (Establishing Your Requirements Tree), Chapter 16 (Decomposing Ideas with Story Mapping), Chapter 17 (Connecting the Idea Pipeline to Backlogs), and Chapter 18 (Collaborating on User Stories)

Pit Stops, Exercises, and References

Sprinkled throughout the book are what I call "Agile pit stops." These pit stops are meant to provide you with insights in a chapter if you are browsing. They also act as anchors to let you know what topic that part of the book is currently covering. Figure 1-3 is an example of an Agile pit stop.

■ **Agile Pit Stop**   Pay particular attention to the Agile pit stops throughout the book. They illuminate ideas or highlight important points.

Figure 1-3. Example of an Agile pit stop

This book also provides you with exercises that you may try or mentally ponder to get you to more deeply experience a topic. Sprinkled throughout each chapter, you will find these exercises.

Finally, at the end of some of the chapters, a reference section is included to provide you with more material about some of the topics discussed in that chapter. I hope you have a great Agile journey and hope you gain beneficial information from this book leading to a more effective Agile transformation and greater business success!

Envisioning a Customer-Value-Driven Enterprise

The hyperfocus of a customer-value-driven enterprise is incrementally learning what the customer wants and delivering it.

—Mario Moreira

What is a customer-value-driven enterprise? It is a company that optimizes for what the customer considers valuable and more specifically what the customer is willing to buy and use. It is also a company that optimizes its internal organizational processes toward a focus on customer value. This type of company attempts to remove any organizational processes or activities that do not directly link to customer value. As a simple example, a status report requested by manager that has little or no direct benefit to what the customer finds as valuable should be eliminated since this task takes time from focusing on customer value.

© Mario E. Moreira 2017
M. E. Moreira, *The Agile Enterprise*, DOI 10.1007/978-1-4842-2391-8_2

The core of a customer-value-driven enterprise is a mindset that understands the importance of discovery and incremental thinking that is continuously injected with customer feedback. The mechanics that support a customer value-driven enterprise is a CVD framework. This framework serves to develop products and services around the engagement of customers in each aspect of the customer journey from identification and recording the idea, revealing it for priority, refining it, realizing it, releasing it, and reflecting on its value for the customer. This is why it is important to be truly engaged with customers and continuously get their feedback along the journey.

The CVD framework also relies on applying a discovery mindset to learn what is valuable to the customer. It leverages current Agile processes, practices, and techniques by emphasizing the importance to delivering incrementally and frequently so that you are minimizing the risk of delivering something that the customer doesn't want. A CVD framework also applies the adaptive Agile budgeting framework, which ensures budget goes to both the highest customer-value idea and the team(s) that can build the idea into a working product, enabling you to stay in touch with the customer and marketplace in a timelier manner.

■ **Agile Pit Stop** The Customer-value-driven (CVD) framework focuses on applying customer feedback along the way to ensure what is delivered is considered valuable to the customer.

Not only should you identify processes that are not directly assisting with identifying or creating customer value, you should also shed those processes that are constraining change. While some processes are unrelated or distantly related to customer value, there are others that actively restrict, delay, or ignore the signals that help us understand what is valuable to the customer.

At the heart of the CVD framework is establishing an engine for customer value. This engine emphasizes the importance of getting closer to the actual customer and of having a discovery mindset with experimental thinking. It highlights the detriment of having too much certainty within an organization, while regaling the benefits of challenging assumptions to better understand initial perceived value and shedding those enterprise processes that are weighing down the organization.

I will not specifically call out the CVD framework from this point on as the intent is to place more focus on the culture and mindset of engaging customers and collecting their feedback. The goal is to build an organization that runs on a customer engine that optimizes for what customers consider valuable and optimizes its internal organizational processes toward a focus of delivering customer value.

The Engine of Customer Value

The goal of a company is to have the willingness to truly engage the customer in every step, from idea to delivery and into reflection. The thrusters within this engine include activities focused on learning about the current customers or potential customers via personas, capturing ideas from customers, getting continuous feedback from customers as the product is built, delivering to customers, receiving actual customer outcome data (in other words, sales or usage), and reflecting on the status of the customer value once it is in the marketplace to better understand the next steps of value. This is what I refer to as the CVD engine that runs your business (See Figure 2-1).

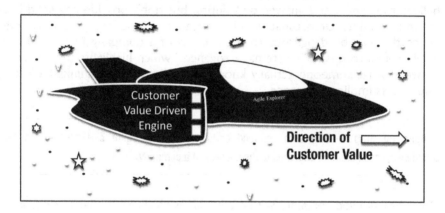

Figure 2-1. Customer-value-driven engine

To keep this engine running well, you need two important contributors—the engaged customer and the engaged employee. Engaged customers ensure you move in the direction of customer value. Engaged employees maintain the engine so the value is delivered with high velocity and quality. If all thrusters are firing well, the engine purrs, which increases the chances for a successful delivery of customer value. If one of the thrusters is sputtering or missing, it reduces the success of the engine and, hence, reduces the potential value being delivered to customers.

What you are also trying to avoid is having an engine whose horsepower is diverted to many weighty systems that have little to do with the delivery of customer value. Effectively, what you are looking for is building an engine where every unit of horsepower is focused primarily on delivering customer value.

Moving Away from Certainty

In many organizations, there is a need to act as if you are certain. In fact, the higher up you go in an organization, the compulsion of acting with certainty becomes greater and greater. Statements like "That's why we pay you the big bucks" are used to imply that the higher you are in an organization, the more you are expected to know all the answers. Certainty is an anti-pattern in getting to customer value and the polar opposite of what is needed to fuel a CVD engine.

Some people think they must act with "pretend certainty" for the benefit of their careers. Others have convinced themselves of "arrogant certainty"; they believe they know the answer or solution but don't provide any solid basis for this certainty. Unfortunately, this arrogance can be interpreted as confidence that can be dangerous to the success of a company. Nassim Nicolas Taleb[1] refers to this as "epistemic arrogance," which highlights the difference between what someone actually knows and how much he thinks he knows. The excess implies arrogance.

■ **Agile Pit Stop** People with "pretend certainty" and "arrogant certainty" exhibit false confidence, which can be dangerous to the success of a company.

What has allowed certainty within companies to thrive is that there is a distance between the upfront certainty and the time it takes to get to the final outcome. There lacks an accountability trail between certainty at the beginning and the actual results at the end. Often the difference is explained away by the incompetence of others who didn't build or implement the solution correctly.

The truth is somewhere in between. Unfortunately, the concept of certainty is dangerous to an enterprise since it removes the opportunity of acknowledging the truth and allowing the enterprise to apply a "discovery" mindset toward customer value via customer feedback loops and more.

You also want to avoid the inverse, which is remaining in uncertainty due to analysis-paralysis. A way to avoid this is to apply work in an incremental manner with customer feedback loops to enable more effective and timely decision making. Customer feedback will provide you with the evidence for making better decisions. Applying an incremental mindset will enable you to make smaller bets that are easier to take and allow you to adapt sooner.

---

[1] *The Black Swan*, Second Edition, by Nassim Nicolas Taleb, Random House, May 11, 2010

Adapting toward Value

A healthier and more realistic approach is to have leaders who understand that uncertainty is actually a smart starting position and then apply an approach that supports the gaining of certainty. The reality is that the earlier you are in the lifecycle of the work product, the less customer information and certainty you have. It is, therefore, incumbent upon you to have an approach that admits to limited information and certainty and then apply a discovery and fact-building approach toward customer value. This is why you must learn more about the customers and their needs for the new idea or feature you are building for them.

■ **Agile Pit Stop**   As a leader, hire people who have a discovery mindset, who understand that customer, technical, and marketplace certainty is only derived by hypothesizing, testing, and adapting toward value.

MENTAL CERTAINTY IDENTIFICATION EXERCISE

Identify who among your staff leans more toward the "pretend certainty" or "arrogant certainty" mindset and who leans toward the discovery and incremental mindset. What you are looking for is building a culture where certainty is something to strive for and not a starting position.

Challenging Assumptions

When ideas that are valuable to customers are identified, there are often some expressed and many unexpressed assumptions. It is important to tie assumptions to the idea that is perceived to be customer value and rigorously explore the assumptions. It is often faulty assumptions that lead you to believe something is perceived to be more valuable of an idea than it really is. This can lead to work that is actually of low value to the customer, closing off options for change too early or ignoring valuable customer feedback along the way.

Challenging the assumptions of perceived customer value helps you rationally discuss the progression of how you got to the conclusion of value. It separates what you think you know from what you actually know. By discussing the assumptions, major uncertainties at the time are uncovered. By highlighting these uncertainties, it provides you with information that helps you think about how to validate the assumptions. By having a conversation around assumptions, it helps those involved with an idea have a better understanding of possible customer value and the work ahead.

■ **Agile Pit Stop**   Challenging assumptions helps you discuss the progression of how you got to the conclusion of value. It separates what you think you know from what you actually know.

Earlier I discussed pretend and arrogant certainty. A good way to uncover where the certainty is coming from is to challenge the assumptions that lead to certainty thinking. It can be quite dangerous for an enterprise to ignore the signals of too much expressed certainty. This can lead a company to select lower-value work.

```
ASSUMPTIONS AWARENESS EXERCISE
```

Observe those involved in discussing the value of a piece of work. Listen for any discussion on the assumptions and any engagement in challenging the assumptions of value. If there is little discussion of assumptions, it can mean several things. The first is that it can mean that people are not engaged. This can be the result of people either just going through the motions of their work, people being fearful to speak up, people not wanting to "rock-the-boat," or people not being aware that they should be actively discussing the assumptions. It is recommended to understand the root cause of this lack of assumptions discussion. I will discuss how the process of challenging assumptions helps you and ways to assertively yet amicably challenge assumptions in Chapter 12.

Shedding Enterprise Weight

As part of being a value-driven enterprise, it is important to remove any organizational processes or activities that do not directly link to customer value. The goal is building a customer-value engine that focuses on delivering customer value—not the weight of non-value added activities. This can be particularly challenging when those within the organization sub-optimize for internal processes or, more dangerously, for themselves.

It is important to gauge what your organization is optimizing for. As you look across your organization, do you see processes that are too heavy? I have seen groups whose functions are no longer central to the delivery of customer value yet continue to enforce their processes on others. I have seen multiple levels of management approval where only one (or none) should be necessary.

■ **Agile Pit Stop**   Is it important to gauge what your organization is optimizing for? Is it the customer or internal processes and status quo?

How many of you have witnessed situations where the customer feedback clearly told you that you were moving in the wrong direction of customer value, yet because of in-house governance and processes, feedback was inhibited or ignored and the original plan was followed anyway. Even when you spoke up, those "in-charge" choose to optimize for the process and not customer value. This is why the value "responding to change over following a plan" found in the Agile Manifesto is so important.

Do you see people who are focused primarily in building their own kingdom? Are you (or those within the organization) internally sub-optimizing for the preservation of the status quo, for ensuring bonuses, or for maintaining power positions rather than for satisfying the customer? Some people are so entrenched in their internally sub-optimized culture that they do not allow themselves to see the need to change until it is too late. However, they presumably have been allowed and even rewarded to continue this behavior, so changes are critical to this mindset.

When adapting Agile, there is often a lack of awareness of the amount of non-value-added work occurring. Value-added work is requested and validated by customers to produce working product. Non-value-added work is work not directly adding value as perceive by the customer. Some non-value-added work is even less valuable that others. While not all non-value-added work can be removed, attempts should be made to make it as lean as possible. As illustrated in Figure 2-2, when shedding weighty organizational process and non-value-added work, you can turn your cumbersome organization into a faster and leaner enterprise.

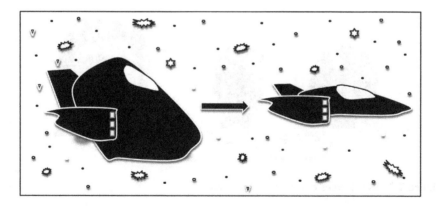

Figure 2-2. Shedding processes and non-value-added activities to be a faster and leaner enterprise

WEIGHING THE VALUE EXERCISE

Observe the behavior of management and employees, and their contribution to non-value-added work. Do you see any parts of a process or activity they are involved in that seems to have little benefit in the delivery of customer value or are sub-optimized to the needs of internal people? Each step of each organizational process should be weighed against the customer value delivered. What do you observe?

Management Closer to Customer Value

Every senior and C-level manager should be as close to customer value as the product owner, salespeople, marketing department, and development teams building products. I've been in some organizations where management and other significant company members have never seen the products their teams are building or met the customers those products are meant for. If a company has dozens of products, I'm not suggesting that leadership must be close to all of the products, but they should be very close to the top 5 or 10 products, including those where there is an investment toward innovation.

The key is narrowing the gap between the employees and customers. The two-degrees-of-separation rule can be an effective means to determine how far away an employee is from a customer. Two degrees of customer separation would be "you (as an employee) connected to an employee connected to the customer," as illustrated in Figure 2-3.

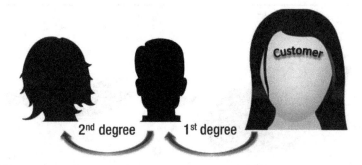

Figure 2-3. Two degrees of customer separation

The further away an employee is from the customer, the less likely that employee understands what the customer considers valuable. Worse yet is the less employees understand customer value, the less likely they will consider customer value in their work and decision making. This can further lead to sub-optimizing toward their own work.

The goal is for all senior managers and C-level professionals to have witnessed the company products their teams are building or to have met the customers those products are meant for. This can be in the form of (and not limited to) attending product demonstrations as part of a sprint review, attending a customer advisory board, and visiting customers who are using products from the company.

CLOSE TO THE CUSTOMER EXERCISE

Consider conducting research by asking these two questions. Even if you only do this as a mental exercise, what might you uncover?

- How many of our leaders have attended a demonstration of all of our top products (or some percentage of them)? This can be a telling tale. I suggest that your leadership should be equally comfortable in providing a demonstration of at least some of the company's top products.

- Ask each employee (at all levels and functions), "How connected is your work to the delivery of customer value?" The goal is to make employees aware of the degrees of separation from the customer and themselves and at what level their work is related to customer value.

Are You Optimized for a Culture of Customer Value?

Moving to a culture where customer value is paramount is an important step in achieving an enterprise that is truly Agile and the business benefits it can bring. Applying a CVD framework and its customer-value engine allows you to focus your company's horsepower primarily on delivering customer value.

Focus on the meaning of having an engine for customer value, the benefits of the discovery mindset, the risks of certainty too early, the strategies to methodically gain certainty, the task of challenging assumptions to better understand the initial perceived value, the necessity of shedding those enterprise processes and non-value added activities that are weighing down the organization. And, last but not least, focus on getting management closer to the actual customer.

It takes a smart leader to recognize the need to change and a strong leader to make the changes needed for an enterprise to optimize for the customer. This will often mean creating an enterprise where everyone is now one or two degrees closer to the customer. It will require a hard look at the current talent of managers and individual contributors.

Are people sub-optimizing for themselves? Are they bringing pretend or arrogant certainty to their work? Are they engaged with activities that focus on customer value? Are they promoting or passively allowing non-value added activities to occur at the expense of focusing on customer value? Have they actually seen or operated the top products of the company?

The answers to these questions can help you understand the enterprise you have. Once you understand this, you can adapt toward the customer-value-driven enterprise you need.

For additional material, I suggest the following:

- *The Lean Startup: How Today's Entrepreneurs Use Continuous Innovation to Create Radically Successful Businesses* by Eric Ries, Crown Business, September 12, 2011

- *The Black Swan: The Impact of the Highly Improbably,* Second Edition, by Nassim Nicolas Taleb, Random House, May 11, 2010

Achieving Better Business Outcomes

It's not about achieving Agile for Agile's sake. It's about achieving better business outcomes.

—Mario Moreira

I'm Agile, you're Agile, everyone is Agile. Or folks think they are. But are they really? If Agile is implementing a mechanical process to you, then it's not Agile. If Agile is pretending certainty without continuous feedback from customers, then it's not Agile. If Agile is commanded from above with no ownership from teams, then it's not Agile. Unfortunately, what is known as Agile in some places is certainly something, just not Agile.

■ **Agile Pit Stop** Moving to Agile is not about reaching an Agile destination. Instead, it is an enabler in achieving better business results.

© Mario E. Moreira 2017
M. E. Moreira, *The Agile Enterprise*, DOI 10.1007/978-1-4842-2391-8_3

Moving to Agile is not about achieving an Agile milestone. It is not a destination, but an enabler in achieving better business outcomes. As part of the CVD framework, the Agile culture and practices provide an adaptive mindset to discover and deliver customer value in an incremental manner. From my journey through the professional world of Agile, I have discovered three primary success factors in achieving the chemistry for positive business outcomes, as shown in Figure 3-1.

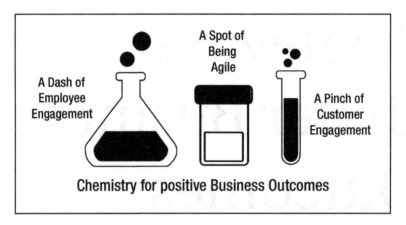

Figure 3-1. Agile plus engaged customers and employees equals better business outcomes

The first factor is applying an Agile mindset based on the Agile values and principles (both end-to-end and top-to-bottom) focused on customer value with practices that are best suited for your context and environment. The second factor is the importance of engaging customers to learn what they consider valuable. The third factor is the importance of engaging employees who create that value. I call this building an Agile customer-value-driven culture with a spot of being Agile, a dash of employee engagement, and a pinch of customer feedback—a combination that serves as the chemistry for better business outcomes.

Embracing the Agile Values and Principles

What is Agile? Most people think it is a process, a set of practices, and even tools. But it is none of those things. *Agile is nothing more and nothing less than a set of values and principles.* As it relates to success, Agile is the enabler that harnesses the power of employees and feedback from customers for successful deliveries in a frequent manner.

I purposefully include Agile values and principles in this chapter as a reminder and refresher. It is important to read and internalize the *Manifesto for Agile Software Development* if you are serious about understanding an Agile state of mind and truly want to "be Agile."

The key change within the manifesto I would encourage, both in the values and principles, is to replace the word "software" with "product" or "services," depending on your context. The reason is that the iterative and incremental nature of Agile can work well beyond software and into any creative and knowledge work, whether it be products, services, or other types of work.

As a reminder, here is the Agile manifesto[1]: It is comprised of just 73 words and was signed by 17 authors in 2001.

Manifesto for Agile Software Development

"We are uncovering better ways of developing software by doing it and helping others do it. Through this work we have come to value:

Individuals and interactions *over processes and tools*

Working software *over comprehensive documentation*

Customer collaboration *over contract negotiation*

Responding to change *over following a plan*

That is, while there is value in the items on the right, we value the items on the left more."

The last phrase helps you understand the authors' intentions. They are not saying there is no value in the items on the right, but instead that there is more value with the items on the left. It is importance to strike the right balance. As you evolve toward Agile, you will find that you will lean more toward the items on the left.

Principles behind the Agile Manifesto
We follow these principles[2]:

Our highest priority is to satisfy the customer through early and continuous delivery of valuable software.

Welcome changing requirements, even late in development. Agile processes harness change for the customer's competitive advantage.

[1]*Manifesto for Agile Software Development,* agilemanifesto.org
[2]Principles behind the Agile Manifesto, agilemanifesto.org/principles.html

Deliver working software frequently, from a couple of weeks to a couple of months, with a preference to the shorter timescale.

Business people and developers must work together daily throughout the project.

Build projects around motivated individuals. Give them the environment and support they need, and trust them to get the job done.

The most efficient and effective method of conveying information to and within a development team is face-to-face conversation.

Working software is the primary measure of progress.

Agile processes promote sustainable development. The sponsors, developers, and users should be able to maintain a constant pace indefinitely.

Continuous attention to technical excellence and good design enhances agility.

Simplicity—the art of maximizing the amount of work not done—is essential.

The best architectures, requirements, and designs emerge from self-organizing teams.

At regular intervals, the team reflects on how to become more effective, then tunes and adjusts its behavior accordingly.

AGILE PRINCIPLES ALIGNMENT EXERCISE

Take a moment to reflect on these principles. In a group, what principles do you agree with or disagree with and why? How can you promote and adapt your enterprise to better align with these principles?

Enabling Agile with Processes and Practices

The goal of an Agile process, method, practice, and technique is an attempt to absorb the Agile values and principles and put them into practice. As part of the *spot of being Agile*, an enterprise needs to embrace the Agile values and principles and apply Agile processes, practices, and techniques that support the Agile values and principles that enable it to deliver customer value in a incremental manner.

The Agile processes and methods include Scrum, eXtreme Programming (XP), Dynamic-System-Delivery Methodology (DSDM), Feature-Driven Development (FDD), Test-Driven Development (TDD), Lean Software Development, Kanban, Scaled Agile Framework (SAFe), Disciplined Agile Delivery (DAD), Lean Startup, and Value Flow Quality (VFQ). This book also introduces you to the customer-value-driven (CVD) framework that applies a discovery and incremental approach that focuses on engaging customers in each aspect of the product journey from identification and recording the idea, revealing it for priority, refining it, realizing it, releasing it, and reflecting on its value for the customer.

In addition, a further array of innovative Agile practices can be applied in various parts of your Agile galaxy in an attempt to ensure Agile is occurring at all levels of an enterprise. This expands the groundwork done by a number of Agile innovators that established many of the current Agile processes and practices. By highlighting the many processes, frameworks, and practices does not imply that any one is better than another or others not discussed here. There is no one correct process or methodology. What you will find is that what suits your working environment and your type of work is the best for your company. My goal is to harness you with a collection of Agile concepts, mindset, processes, practices, and techniques to enable you to more effectively help your enterprise discover and deliver customer value.

Engaging Your Customers and Employees

Success factors in creating a thriving business is the level of engagement from the people within and around your enterprise. In other words, do you have a culture where customers and employees are engaged? I'm not talking about the lip service that is prevalent today. In some cases, you see quite the opposite, where employees are disenfranchised and customers are rarely engaged. Instead, the goal is to have a culture and practices in place that truly gain the benefits of engaging with customers and employees. By applying a *dash of employee engagement* and a *pinch of customer feedback*, a company draws its power from an Agile culture and, I contend, becomes a thriving company.

In creating that engine of customer value introduced in Chapter 2, employees are the mechanics of the engine and customers are the drivers. If there is little customer and employee engagement, the enterprise is going nowhere or it is going in the wrong direction. The more engagement at both levels, the more positive the progress.

Agile Pit Stop Engaged customers are the drivers and empowered employees are the mechanics of the engine of customer value.

When you have a riveting focus on the customer, you have the basis for a relationship where you can truly understand what the customer wants. When you have a sharp focus on employees and provide them the ownership to make decisions and own their work, you will begin to understand the value an engaged employee base can provide. I will cover ways to engage customers and employees in Chapter 6 and Chapter 7.

Focusing on Outcomes

Becoming Agile should not be an end goal. Becoming Agile should be a means to an end. The end goal is the desired outcome of achieving better business results. The Agile mindset and practices, therefore, should be an enabler for better business results. This end goal is often lost in the enthusiasm of becoming Agile. An outcome is defined as the result of a particular action or, in Agile's case, an Agile transformation. Since moving to Agile requires a change in skills, process, and culture, it involves effort. The whole point of the effort is to achieve better outcomes for the company.

■ **Agile Pit Stop**   If the focus is delivering something the customer wants, you must move from primarily measuring outputs to primarily measuring outcomes.

To achieve better business outcomes, you must deliver products that customers like. An output is the delivery of a release or the number of releases. An outcome is how many customers either bought or used the product. Often people focus on outputs because they tend to be easier to measure or are a carryover from a more traditional mindset.

The danger of focusing on outputs is that you may have a high number of outputs with a low number of outcomes. Outcomes are what drives business success. As illustrated in Figure 3-2, it appears that the output of the fourth quarter is the best. However, if you look at the outcomes chart, the third quarter is the best quarter with revenues of $80,000 instead of only $20,000 in the fourth quarter. While the output of four releases sounds good, $20,000 is not favorable to good business results. Outcomes ask you to measure different things, with a particular focus on customer value.

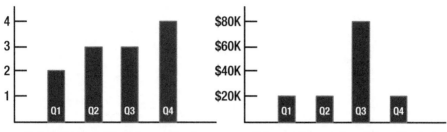

Output: Number of Releases per Quarter   **Outcome:** Revenue from Sales of Product

Figure 3-2. Output vs. outcome measures

Becoming outcome-focused has several business advantages. Outcomes focus on the impact of your work (for example, the number of customers and the number of sales). Just because you delivered a release (in other words, output) doesn't mean you had a positive impact to your sales numbers. An outcome focus also changes your perspective from an internal one to a customer or external perspective. This enables you to better understand what you are aiming for in the CVD world that you need to establish. For a deeper discussion on using outcome measures to help run your enterprise, consider visiting Chapter 20.

Do You Have the Recipe for Success?

Moving to Agile is not about achieving an Agile milestone. Instead, Agile and the CVD framework is about achieving better business outcomes. A move to Agile is a move to a culture focused on customers and what they identify as valuable as well as on engaged employees who create that value. It is a shift in mindset.

Then you add the enabler of Agile and the continuous and adaptive nature it brings. This can lead to better outcomes such as an increase in customer satisfaction and customer revenue. This can be the differentiator between the success of your organization compared to the success of other organizations. Do you have the recipe for success? This recipe consists of a spot of being Agile (culture), a dash of employee engagement, and a pinch of customer engagement for a taste of better business outcomes. The areas of Agile culture, employee engagement, and customer engagement will be expanded further in subsequent chapters.

For additional material, I suggest the following:

- *Manifesto for Agile Software Development,* www.agilemani-festo.org/

Building Your Agile Galaxy

*Being Agile and deriving the business outcomes means you need to have
a thriving top-to-bottom and end-to-end Agile landscape.*

—Mario Moreira

Agile has been in the limelight for well over a dozen years. Agile has secured
its place within the software development community and now it is spreading
into many other areas of business where the incremental nature and promise
of better business outcomes are very tantalizing. Many people are realizing that
a more iterative approach allows them the flexibility to adapt to the changing
needs of customers and the continuous churning of the marketplace. Others
would like to apply Agile because they are hearing about it from all corners of
their professional life and think maybe its time to get on the bandwagon. For
many reasons, there are real benefits that can be derived from applying Agile.

As simple as it may seem, to establish the Agile landscape and reap the positive
business outcomes requires a combination of Agile processes, roles, and the
all-important culture. For Agile to work well, all levels of the enterprise must
play their part in the Agile journey and toward the delivery of customer value.
This journey includes having Agile culture and practices applied at all levels.

■ **Agile Pit Stop**   To reap positive business outcomes requires a combination of Agile processes,
roles, and the all-important culture.

© Mario E. Moreira 2017
M. E. Moreira, *The Agile Enterprise*, DOI 10.1007/978-1-4842-2391-8_4

Finally, establishing Agile implies a strong cultural element that focuses on how individuals and organizations must behave and operate to truly focus on a customer-value-driven approach. To be specific, Agile processes, practices, and techniques and those playing the roles must operate within an Agile cultural context and that context must exist at all levels of an enterprise.

Landscape of the Agile Galaxy

As we look across your enterprise, it is important to establish a landscape to better view where Agile is being applied. I term this landscape the "Agile galaxy" (see Figure 4-1). It is the landscape where all Agile processes, roles, and culture live that have a focus on delivering customer value. It helps us understand where Agile is adopted.

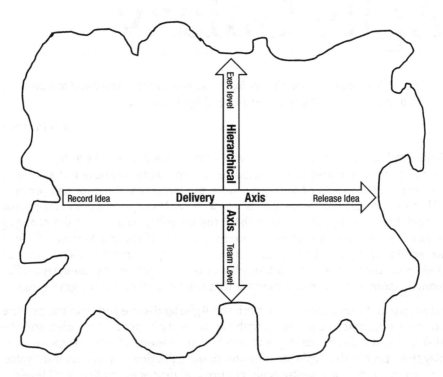

Figure 4-1. Agile galaxy: Landscape for your Agile culture and practices

The Agile galaxy has a vertical view titled the hierarchical axis, where the executives are at the top and the teams are at the bottom (although this can be reversed). It also has a horizontal view titled the delivery axis that illustrates the end-to-end flow of work from the moment an idea is recorded to the point where it is released and then reflected upon. The delivery axis is the channel by which the enterprise is focused on delivering customer value.

The purpose of establishing your own Agile-galaxy construct is for you to understand where along both the delivery and hierarchical axis you have Agile-related elements (such as concepts, mindset, practices, processes, and techniques) being applied and where in relation to this landscape they are occurring. Where is Agile primarily being implemented? What Agile practices are being applied? Where do we see an Agile culture and the behaviors being adopted?

Whether you are in the midst of your Agile transformation or you are looking to begin the journey, it is beneficial to have a living Agile galaxy related to your enterprise. This will help you understand where Agile is occurring and where you need to focus next. It is very reasonable to approach an Agile transformation in an incremental manner. For each increment, you should reflect on what practices are being applied, what roles are applying it, and the current state of the culture from an Agile perspective. You may consider it a heat map of where Agile is occurring. As you plan the next increment, you can use this as input on where you want to go next. Let's more fully explore your Agile galaxy.

Holistic Process View of an Agile Galaxy

The goal of building your Agile galaxy is having Agile applied at all levels with a focus of delivering customer value. However, what tends to be common is a propensity to initiate Agile at the team level. It is not surprising that Agile has lived through its first dozen years with a more-or-less team focus. The reasons are severalfold.

The evolution of many of the early and current Agile processes, practices, and techniques are primarily focused on the team level. There are few Agile elements focused on the beginning of the delivery axis (such as recording and refining ideas). There is less focus on the Agile culture regarding behaviors and mindset. Many Agile coaches tend to be experienced mostly at the team level with few who have substantial experience at the enterprise level. It is also much easier for management to ask the team to make the change to Agile without themselves committing to the Agile change.

■ **Agile Pit Stop**   Many organizations still have a team-centric view of Agile.

Because of these reasons, it is not uncommon to primarily see Agile practices occurring in the bottom right corner of the Agile galaxy. Because of this team-centric view of Agile, companies have Agile elements in action at the team level, and they have fewer elements as they move up along the hierarchical axis toward middle management, then senior leadership, and finally toward the beginning of the delivery axis in valuing ideas.

Using the Agile-galaxy context, Figure 4-2 illustrates what a team-centric implementation of Agile might look like. Each Agile element represents an Agile process, practice, or technique. A dot is not meant to be specific to a particular Agile element, but to illustrate where Agile elements most commonly live in team-centric Agile implementation.

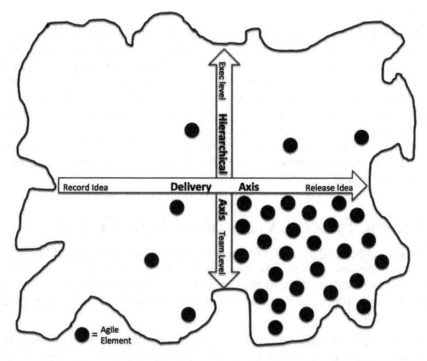

Figure 4-2. Where Agile elements live in a team-centric implementation of Agile

It will be very challenging for teams to operate in an Agile manner when the more senior level of the organization is not. If management along the hierarchical axis and recording and refining ideas along the delivery axis are applying a big-batch view of the work, it can be hard for teams to apply an incremental and adaptive view of the work. Also, if the enterprise operates with an annual budget cycle where ideas are recorded and parsed once a year, it can be very hard for a team to adapt to customer needs and marketplace when new ideas are coming in regularly.

■ **Agile Pit Stop**   Having one part of the enterprise work on an annual scale while another works on an iterative and incremental scale creates a pace difference that causes great tension within the system, inhibiting adaptability and innovation.

A more holistic and healthy Agile galaxy is where an enterprise has Agile elements occurring throughout the galaxy, both on the delivery axis and the hierarchical axis. This way the concepts, mindset, practices, processes, and techniques being applied are Agile-related, and the company does not experience the tension of the pace difference when one part of the enterprise runs as Agile and the other part runs as traditional.

A more holistic and healthy Agile galaxy has a reasonable application of Agile elements in all quadrants of the galaxy. Figure 4-3 illustrates this Agile galaxy. Compare it to Figure 4-2, which illustrates a team-centric Agile galaxy. Notice how there are more Agile elements in the upper part of the hierarchical axis and more elements in the front part of the delivery axis.

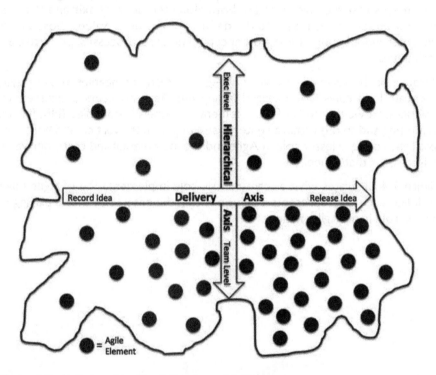

Figure 4-3. Holistic and healthy Agile galaxy of Agile elements

While newer processes and practices are being established beyond the team level, I contend that there needs to be a fundamental shift toward approaching Agile in order for companies to take the most advantage of the business outcomes it can bring.

AGILE ELEMENTS IN YOUR AGILE GALAXY EXERCISE

What Agile elements (processes, practices, tools, and techniques) do you have and at what levels are they implemented? Consider creating the process view of your current Agile galaxy using the landscape illustrated in Figure 4-1.

Holistic Roles of the Agile Galaxy

Similar to the Agile process elements, a more holistic and healthy Agile galaxy is where all members of an enterprise plays their role within an Agile context. This means that the roles that are both along the delivery axis and the hierarchical axis are contributing to the delivery of customer value. Those playing the roles would apply the Agile concepts, mindset, processes, practices, and techniques.

Because of the team-centric view of Agile in many companies, those playing the team-level roles have engaged in applying Agile concepts, processes, and practices. However, levels of management and operational roles (HR, finance, marketing, and so on) within an enterprise along both the vertical and horizontal axis tend to play a lesser role in Agile and the incremental and customer value-driven focus that is needed.

Figure 4-4 illustrates what a team-centric-role implementation of Agile might look like. Each dot represents a person within the enterprise that is playing his or her role in an Agile manner.

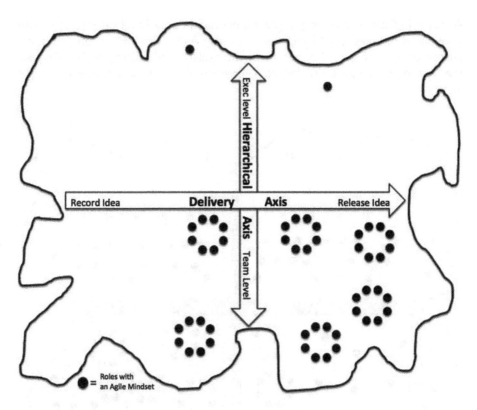

Figure 4-4. Agile roles that live in a team-centric implementation of Agile

Interestingly enough, in some enterprises, there is often a CEO or head of engineering that is pro-Agile, as illustrated in Figure 4-4 (the two dots toward the top of the hierarchy). However, in those same organizations, there is often little or no buy-in of Agile at the middle-management level. Having some roles engaged in Agile while others engaged in a more traditional or command and control manner creates tension regarding ownership and pace of work.

■ **Agile Pit Stop**   Interestingly, there is often a CEO or head of engineering as pro-Agile while there is little or no Agile buy-in at the middle-management level.

A more holistic and healthy Agile galaxy has people in all quadrants of the galaxy who have adapted their roles to apply Agile with a focus on delivering customer value. Figure 4-5 illustrates the holistic and healthy Agile galaxy so that it can be compared to Figure 4-4, which illustrates a team-centric Agile galaxy.

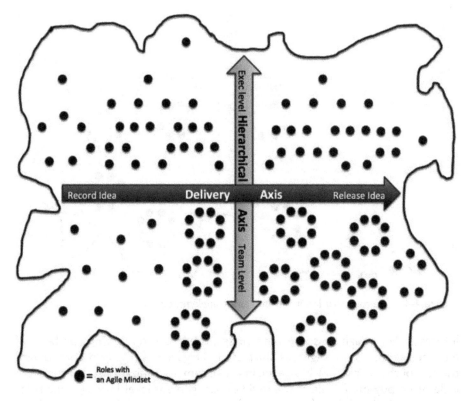

Figure 4-5. Holistic and healthy Agile galaxy where all roles are aligned with Agile

Organizational functions must all play a role in transforming to Agile. Each role or function must be structured such that they can readily adapt to the changing needs of customers and conditions of the marketplace. To understand the expectations of what roles and responsibilities would look like within an Agile landscape, please visit Chapter 8.

AGILE ROLES IN YOUR AGILE GALAXY EXERCISE

What roles do you see that are engaged in Agile and are focused on primarily delivering customer value? Consider creating the roles view of your current Agile galaxy using the landscape illustrated in Figure 4-1.

What Does Your Agile Galaxy Look Like?

When I explore the concept of the Agile galaxy with colleagues, I often witness "a-ha" moments. For so long now, Agile has been implemented at the team level that for some it is a new revelation when they look above their current Agile horizon and realize there is more territory to cover. Roles at all levels in the enterprise must play their part in the creation of customer value. The need to have Agile processes, practices, and techniques for all levels in the enterprise is becoming apparent to many.

The good news is many people are starting to make the connection that it does take an enterprise to establish an effective Agile galaxy focused on delivering value to the customer. Hopefully, this book helps you in that journey to evolve your current Agile implementation toward the enterprise level, cultural level, and the customer-driven level where it needs to be.

For additional material, I suggest the following:

- *Being Agile: Your Roadmap to Successful Adoption of Agile* by Mario Moreira, Chapter 2 and 9, Apress, October 1, 2013.

Activating an Agile Culture

Culture highlights the type of company you are. But what type of company do you really want to be?

—Mario Moreira

People are often searching for the silver bullet to transport an enterprise toward Agile and the business benefits it can bring. For some, Agile has become little more than a superficial badge without aligning to the real cultural shift that is needed to truly become Agile. Many tend to lean toward implementing a set of mechanical practices or processes. While this is part of the equation, the most important part is having a commitment to adopt the Agile mindset.

A move to Agile implies a change to the organizational culture. It is a cultural disruption that takes effort and that is never painless. Adopting Agile is more than a matter of learning skills or understanding a process; it requires adopting a set of values and principles that require change in people's behavior and the culture of an organization.

A culture change implies a behavioral change in people in response to a change in the values and assumptions of their organization. In other words, they need to assume a new way of thinking. It also asks them to measure different things, with a particular focus on customer value and the activities focused on obtaining customer value. This kind of culture change takes time. This is why I suggest that you think of your change to Agile as a *cultural journey*.

© Mario E. Moreira 2017
M. E. Moreira, *The Agile Enterprise*, DOI 10.1007/978-1-4842-2391-8_5

Agile Mindset

Agile is a disruptive innovation where the Agile values and principles require a significant change of mindset and behavior to the culture adopting it. I discuss the concept of this significant change as *crossing the Agile chasm* in my book *Being Agile.*[1] The chasm represents a leap from the old mindset and ways of thinking to a specific cultural mindset of "being Agile" in order for the enterprise to fully realize the business benefits Agile can bring.

■ **Agile Pit Stop**   Crossing the Agile chasm means that you are always operating with a mindset that is aligned with the Agile values and principles and a focus on customer value.

Crossing the Agile chasm means your mind has achieved an Agile mindset. As illustrated in Figure 5-1, in order to achieve an Agile mindset, you must embrace the Agile values and then operate in a manner that aligns with the Agile principles with a focus of delivering customer value. The result of achieving an Agile mindset means you should see different behaviors and a change in the culture. Simply aligning with Agile values and principles should lead you to behavioral changes in responsibilities, assurances to engage customers, commitment to empower employees, an obligation to bring business and development together, and more.

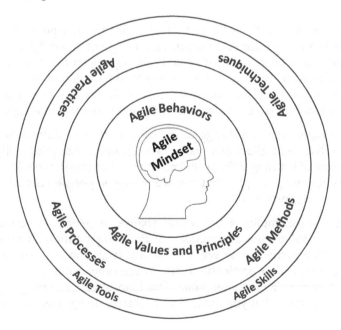

Figure 5-1. Getting to an Agile mindset

---

[1]*Being Agile,* Chapter 2, by Mario Moreira, Apress, October 1, 2013

To help an enterprise put the Agile values and principles into action, various Agile processes, methods, frameworks, practices, and techniques (in other words, mechanics) have been created. However, without a commitment to the Agile values and principles, you may find that you are going through the mechanical motions without grasping the benefit of uncovering better ways of working.

As an example, a retrospective can mechanically occur with no actions for improvement upon completion. Without embracing Agile principles, the objective of tuning and adjusting behaviors can be forgotten. Some Agile implementations have adopted the outer ring of Agile processes while not embracing Agile values and principles. Without embracing the values and principles, you cannot achieve the behaviors necessary for an Agile mindset.

Those companies that are "doing" Agile have not actually adopted the values and principles and not made the mindset shift to actually "being" Agile. Such companies continue to look at Agile as a set of skills, tools, and process changes, but they have not made the integrated behavioral and cultural changes. They have not made the significant change of mindset required to make the leap across the Agile chasm.

Three Dimensions of an Agile Culture

What a more holistic and healthy Agile galaxy should look like is where those playing the roles in all quadrants of the galaxy have embraced the Agile mindset of applying the Agile values and principles—a discovery and incremental mindset; they have embraced the various Agile elements of processes, practices, and techniques, and they are primarily focused on delivering customer value. As you may recall, the Agile galaxy illustrated in Figure 4-1 is two-dimensional. There is also a third dimension that factors in the cultural aspect, as shown in Figure 5-2. Have the people in your Agile galaxy embraced the Agile mindset and begun to exhibit Agile behaviors of the Agile values and principles?

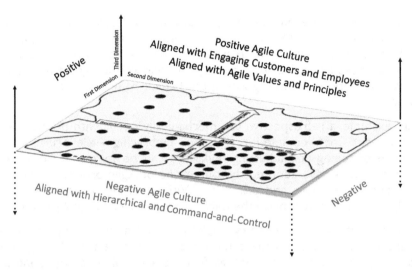

Figure 5-2. Third dimension of the Agile galaxy: The culture

Because of the team-centric view of Agile in many companies, there is a likelihood that some people playing the team-level roles have adapted an Agile mindset. However, levels of management and operational roles (HR, finance, marketing, and so on) within an organization along both the vertical and horizontal axes tend to play a lesser role in Agile and, in many cases, have not evolved their roles toward an Agile mindset, which includes an incremental and customer value-driven focus.

For every practice being implemented and for every role being played, there is a view of the cultural and behavioral alignment to the Agile values and principles. Is it positive where behaviors are aligning with an Agile mindset? Is Agile still a mechanical implementation where behaviors are neutral (in other words, neither particularly positive or negative toward an Agile mindset)? Or is the attitude toward Agile more negative where people are openly disdainful of Agile and there is still an alignment to the hierarchical, traditional, and/or command-and-control mindset?

Your three-dimensional Agile galaxy may have areas in the positive where people have embraced the Agile mindset, some areas that are neutral, and some areas in the negative. The 3-D view can help you understand the starting point of where your culture is today and help you understand the culture change that needs to occur.

CULTURE OF YOUR AGILE GALAXY EXERCISE

As you look across your current galaxy, do you see people and groups applying the Agile elements (processes, practices, and so on) in a manner that is aligned with the behaviors of Agile values and principles and a discovery and incremental mindset? Are they focused on delivering customer value? Is it positive where behaviors are aligning with an Agile mindset? Is it neutral (neither positive or negative) toward an Agile mindset or negative toward an Agile mindset? Apply a designation by individual, group, or area.

Culture of Agile Values

Everyone in the organization should understand and embrace the Agile values and principles. Chapter 3 provides us with a section on the Agile values. Although many people are aware of them or have seen them at one time or another, few remind themselves of what it means to be Agile on a regular basis, particularly when they are buried in the mechanics of doing Agile.

It is beneficial to periodically review the Agile values and discuss them at a deeper level. Here is a deeper look at the four polar pairs of agile values declared in the Agile manifesto.

*"**Individuals and interactions** over processes and tools."* This value helps us understand that the way we work may adapt over time. It also ensures that a predefined process or tool does not dictate how we interact.

*"**Working software** over comprehensive documentation."* This value helps us understand what the customer values as well as the business perspective of the product we are building. I often replace the word "software" with "product" or "service" since not everything built is software.

*"**Customer collaboration** over contract negotiation."* This value helps us understand the importance of the customer relationship and the collaboration that is needed to get to what the customer finds as value.

*"**Responding to change** over following a plan."* This value helps us respond to the changes in customer needs and market conditions, and apply an inspect-and-adapt approach with customer feedback to lead to customer value.

Ordering Agile Values Exercise: In groups of three, rank in order of importance the values and explain your ranking. Share the reasons of your rank order with other groups.

Remembering the Agile Principles

The Agile principles provide us with guidance on how to operate within an Agile galaxy. Chapter 3 provides us with the 12 Agile principles for your review. Interestingly, many involved with Agile have a hard time remembering the principles. I have hypothesized that those involved in Agile are more knowledgeable about the mechanics of "doing Agile" than they are regarding the mindset shift needed for "being Agile." I have also hypothesized that fewer people could name three of the twelve Agile principles than could name three of the five Scrum events (Sprint, Sprint Planning, Daily Scrum, Sprint Review, and Sprint Retrospective).

I tested my second hypothesis with an experiment that asks people to record the Agile principles and the Scrum events. For the Agile principles, I was willing to accept even a keyword or phrase of the principle (for example, "welcome change"). From two different Agile professional events, I asked participants to write down as many of the five Scrum events and as many of the twelve Agile Principles they knew. I accumulated 109 survey responses. The results were revealing and supported my hypothesis, as shown in Figure 5-3.

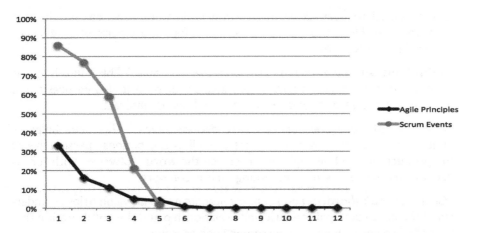

Figure 5-3. Percentage of respondents who could name a specific number of Agile principles

Of the 109 Agile participants, 59% knew three of the five Scrum events. This emphasized knowledge of the mechanics, or *doing Agile*. As illustrated in Figure 5-3, only 11% knew three of the twelve Agile principles. Could it really be true that only 11% of Agile enthusiasts could name just three Agile principles? This small percentage is particularly concerning since the Agile values and principles form the basis for what an Agile culture should look like.

■ **Agile Pit Stop**   Many people are only mechanically "doing" Agile via a process and have not yet begun to "be" Agile (that is, actually applying the values and principles of Agile).

Based on this data, I concluded with two hypotheses for such a lack of awareness of Agile principles. The first is there is very little education focused on the Agile values and principles. While many people have once visited the Agile values and principles (typically in training), they tend to not visit it again. The second is that many Agile efforts jump right into *doing Agile* by applying an Agile process (the mechanics) with little focus on the Agile values and principles (the culture). I contend that it is much easier to show progress for a mechanical change (for example, "Here is our backlog." "See the daily scrum.") than show cultural and behavioral changes, which takes longer for the changes to be felt.

AGILE PRINCIPLES REFRESHER EXERCISE

Ask each person on your team to write down the Agile principles they know. Collect their answers. Then discuss each of the Agile principles with the team, explaining each one and asking team members what they think about each principle. Once your team members have had time to think about each principle, ask each person to again write down as many Agile principles they know and collect this answers. Tally up both sets of answers (before and after) and highlight the increase in learning. Doing this test periodically is a good way to remind people why they are being Agile.

Cultural Color of Your Organization

To delve a bit deeper into understanding more about what an Agile culture might look like, it is worth exploring the book *Reinventing Organizations*.[2] In this book, Frederic Laloux discusses the past and current organizational models. He describes organization paradigms as an evolution in human consciousness. The more recent paradigms can provide insight into organization attributes that lend themselves to an Agile culture. Figure 5-4 illustrates the evolution of these paradigms.

---

[2]*Reinventing Organizations* by Frederic Laloux, Nelson Parker, February 20, 2014

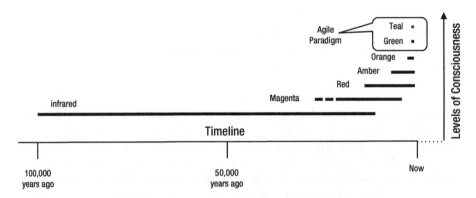

Figure 5-4. Where the Agile paradigm aligns with Laloux's organization paradigms

The early paradigm starts with the reactive-infrared paradigm and then the magic-magenta paradigm. Both of these embody the early stages of human kind which include smaller groups such as tribes of people. This is followed by the impulsive-red paradigm, which has the guiding metaphor of a wolf pack illustrated by tribal militia, mafia, and street gangs.

The conformist-amber paradigm has the guiding metaphor of an army illustrated by the hierarchy of a church, the military, and most government agencies. Next is the achievement-orange paradigm, which has the guiding metaphor of the machine illustrated by multinational companies and charter schools. A majority of the organizations today tend to reflect a red, amber, or orange paradigm.

A general alignment can be made to two of the latter paradigms that may be considered as behaviors you would hope to see in an Agile enterprise. These are the pluralistic-green and the evolutionary-teal paradigms.

While these two stages are not meant to be Agile-specific, in understanding what an Agile culture might look like, they help shed light as to where you may want to explore. Since Agile may be considered the next step in the evolution of product development, it should come as no surprise that the green and teal paradigms are the latest in organizational evolution.

Where Pluralistic-Green Supports Agile

The pluralistic-green organization strives to bring equality where all viewpoints are treated equality, irrespective of position and power. It uses the family as the guiding metaphor where all members are in it together and help each other out. This is highly reflective of the expectation of an Agile team.

One of the breakthroughs of a green organization is empowerment. Empowerment is focused on pushing a majority of decisions down to the frontline (in other words, where the work is). This is directly aligned with Agile thinking where there is a focus on pushing down decision making to the lowest possible level where the most information resides regarding the topic. This leads to decentralized authority where employees are trusted to come up with the answers and think of better ways to solve problems.

Another breakthrough of a green organization is that it is a values-driven culture. There is an understanding that culture drives how an organization will live and breathe. The green organization understands that a shared culture where leaders play by shared values is the glue that makes those in organizations feel appreciated and empowered. There is a focus on culture and empowerment to achieve extraordinary employee motivation. This values-driven culture described in the green paradigm is very much aligned with the importance of leading with Agile values and principles.

Leaders in a green organization are servant leaders. Servant leadership is common in Agile literature. Leaders need to listen to their employees, motivate them, empower them, and help them develop their own skills. When hiring for leadership within a green organization, look for the right mindset and behavior and ask if the candidates are ready to share power and lead with humility.

■ **Agile Pit Stop**   The Pluralistic-Green and the Evolutionary-Teal Paradigms include the level of human consciousness and the manifest behaviors you hope to see in an Agile enterprise.

Where Evolutionary-Teal Supports Agile

The evolutionary-teal paradigm emphasizes that the organization moves beyond providing a vehicle to achieve objectives for others. Instead, it moves to provide what is best for the organization that adapts as circumstances change. Its metaphor is one where the organization is a separate living organism.

In a teal paradigm, titles and positions are replaced with roles where one worker can fill multiple roles. This is very much like the concept of the cross-functional team within an Agile team structure. It is also emphasized by the notion of lightning-bolt-shaped teams where every team member has a primary, secondary, and tertiary skill or role so that they can adapt to the need of the organization. The emphasis is on getting the work done and not on specific titles or positions and the constraints one skill will have.

The evolutionary-teal paradigm emphasizes the capability to self-organize around the organizational purpose. The hierarchical structures are replaced with self-organization focusing on the smaller teams. This is aligned with the Agile principle of self-organizing teams. (In other words, the best architectures, requirements, and designs emerge from self-organizing teams). In fact, one of the breakthroughs of moving to the teal paradigm is self-management where an organization operates as if there are no managers.

It is in the teal paradigm where we evolve beyond and become separated from our ego in order to better understand the wisdom of others. We have to learn to see our own world from the outside. The analogy that Laloux uses is "like a fish that can see water for the first time when it jumps above the surface." Once we can separate from our ego, we begin to understand how our ego has separated us from others. To a great extent, this is where the Agile retrospective helps team members see the views of others in order to improve and evolve into a more effective team.

Much like a move to an Agile culture is a leap across a chasm to a wholly different mindset, a move to the evolutionary-team paradigm. It is akin to crossing a chasm to operate in a self-managed way where mistakes are an opportunity to learn and grow, and where we strive for a wholeness within ourselves and with others.

Readying the Culture

Most Agile transformations start with implementing the Agile mechanics of processes, practices, and techniques. These types of transformations tend to ignore the cultural aspects of Agile. Since Agile is a cultural change, consider starting your Agile transformation from a cultural perspective.

■ **Agile Pit Stop**   Readiness activities are akin to conditioning the soil prior to planting the seeds. Understanding Agile values and principles improves the ability to adopt Agile.

Readying the mind is akin to conditioning the soil prior to growing the seeds. It is worth taking a long hard look at the conditions of the fields, equipment, and people—an analogy for your Agile galaxy. Strengthening the soil helps improve its physical qualities. This is similar to educating people about Agile values and principles and a customer-value-driven enterprise prior to any mechanical implementation. It provides employees with a cultural understanding of what they are trying to achieve.

What are some readiness activities you can do to begin activating the Agile culture? Begin by readying the minds or your employees with education on Agile values and principles and customer value. Ask employees what an enterprise would look like that puts the values and principles into action. Highlight what more advanced organizations can look like by discussing the pluralistic-green and evolutionary-teal paradigms. Ask what an engaged employee looks like in an Agile culture. Ask what an engaged customer looks like in an Agile culture. Also, start to examine levels of willingness and capability among the employee base so you understand the current level of commitment. You can learn more about readiness activities in the book *Being Agile*.[3]

Assessing the Culture You Have

As you begin your readiness activities, consider understanding the culture that you have. There is a saying in the culture change circles that you should "*meet them where they are.*" By understanding your Agile culture, you gain the benefit of having a baseline by understanding the pros and the cons of the culture, which helps you prioritize your Agile readiness activities ahead. It can be used in the future to see where you've made progress.

Below is an Agile cultural assessment survey based on desired Agile behaviors. It helps you understand where you are from a customer-value-driven, employee-engagement, customer-engagement, Agile-values-and-principles, and pluralistic-green-paradigm, and evolutionary-teal-paradigm perspective. For each statement, the participants choose an option that best aligns with their view. They may also rate how they think their leaders view the statement. Or they can answer for both themselves and their leaders to recognize differences. Consider applying using a Likert-scale framework as seen in Figure 5-5.

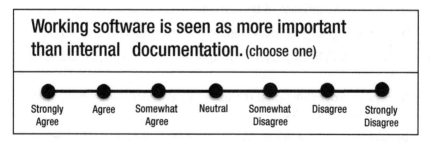

Figure 5-5. Likert scale

You may also adapt the statements into questions that can be used in a discussion setting if this works better for your audience.

---

[3]*Being Agile, Chapters 8 and 9,* by Mario Moreira, Apress, October 1, 2013

Agile Cultural Assessment Survey

We believe having flexibility to collaborate and communicate with each other helps us be more productive.

We believe working product is seen as more important than internal documentation.

We believe customer collaboration should be promoted along the way.

We are allowed to move beyond the plan and toward the direction of value.

We are focused more on satisfying (external) customers than on satisfying (internal) management.

We welcome change to requirements throughout the product development life cycle.

We believe in frequent delivery in smaller increments.

We believe in business and development working together along the way.

We believe in trusting individuals and valuing employees' opinions.

We believe in face-to-face communication and keeping teams collocated.

We believe that working product is the primary measure of progress.

We believe in allowing teams to establish their own sustainable pace.

We believe in promoting attention to technical and business excellence on teams.

We believe in maximizing the amount of work not done.

We believe in the importance of self-organizing teams who have ownership and decision-making rights of their work.

We believe in regularly reflecting and committing to improvements.

We believe in simplified project management (lean plans, backlogs, no status reports).

We believe in cross-functional teams with lightning-bolt-shaped skills able to perform most of their work.

We believe in moving work to the team instead of teams to the work.

We believe that team members should interview future team colleagues.

We believe performance appraisals are done at the team level by team colleagues.

We believe organizational space should primarily be designed to make the team more productive, including quiet spaces.

This is not meant to be an exhaustive statement list and you may adapt it to fit your needs. You may find additional questions that can help you gauge whether you are aligning with an Agile culture in the books *Being Agile* (Chapters 8 and 9) and *Reinventing Organizations* (Appendix 4).

"What Culture Do You Have?" Exercise: Arrange to have a group of leaders together. Share the statements with them and ask them to choose their level of belief for each statement (from strongly agree to strongly disagree). Tally up the results and find the average score. Also capture the range of scores (3 at Strongly Agree, 2 at Agree, 4 at Somewhat Agree, and so on). Identify an area of improvement.

What Culture Do You Have?

There is a recognition that it is time to get serious about adapting to an Agile mindset and the behaviors and culture change it brings instead of a having a mechanical approach. A strong Agile culture must focus on how individuals and organizations behave and operate at all levels of an enterprise.

Consider understanding the culture that you have by establishing the 3-D version of your Agile galaxy. Also consider completing the Agile cultural assessment survey initially with some of your trusted colleagues and then branching out to other teams.

For additional material, I suggest the following:

- *Reinventing Organizations* by Frederic Laloux, Chapter 1 and Appendix 4, Nelson Parker, February 20, 2014

- *Being Agile: Your Roadmap to Successful Adoption of Agile* by Mario Moreira, Chapters 8 and 9, Apress, October 1, 2013

Embracing Customers

If you are not optimizing for customer value, why are you in business?

—Mario Moreira

What is a customer? A customer is someone who has a choice of what to buy and a choice of where to buy it. As it relates to your company, a customer pays you with money to help you stay in business by purchasing your product. Because of these simple facts, engaging the customer is of utmost importance. Customers are external to the company and it is their feedback that matters most. While you can find value in what an internal person says, it is an opinion and that person cannot provide your company with money.

■ **Agile Pit Stop**   Customers are a very specifically defined. (1) They have a choice to buy your product, and (2) they pay money to your company. This definition represents an important mindset shift.

In working with a number of companies, two challenges have become clear. The first challenge is that some companies do not really engage their customers to get their feedback. As mentioned in Chapter 2, instead there may be the certainty mindset occurring, either pretend or arrogant. This prevents the opportunity of gaining the valuable customer feedback.

© Mario E. Moreira 2017
M. E. Moreira, *The Agile Enterprise*, DOI 10.1007/978-1-4842-2391-8_6

The second challenge is that the term "customer" is being applied to a number of people "in" the company who are "not customers." For further clarification, a customer is someone external to the company and meets the conditions previously stated (has a choice and pays). When you incorrectly title someone a customer when they are not, your company will not really be customer-value-driven as you are not using actual customer feedback to drive toward customer value.

Driver of Customer Feedback

Customer engagement focuses on establishing meaningful and honest customer relationships with the goal of gaining continuous customer feedback to truly identify what is valuable to the customer.

The key to engaging customers is to gain their precious customer input and feedback. The input and feedback should be the basis for driving a majority of your decisions and setting the direction of a product. As you look to build a customer-value-driven engine within your enterprise, the customer, or more specifically customer feedback, is the "driver" that steers the engine of customer value, as illustrated in Figure 6-1.

Figure 6-1. Customer feedback is the driver that steers the customer-value-driven engine

If you start driving with certainty, either pretend or arrogant, you can be led to the wrong planet, moon, or satellite because you are flying blind and missing the signs that steer you toward value. The question is, "Who do you want steering your spaceship?" Do you want someone internal to your company that embraces certainty but is wearing blinders, or do you want someone who embraces customer feedback and continually adapts (that is, steers) their way toward customer value?

Customer Feedback Bull's-eye

The customer provides the most effective feedback to help shape product direction toward customer value. The customer provides both input for ideas of value and feedback for validating the product in its process of getting created. It is critical to engage customers. Look around you at your teams. Are you and your teams directly applying customer input and feedback toward customer value? If not, then you are probably guessing, and this means that it is time to methodically engage with customers.

■ **Agile Pit Stop**   Customer input and feedback are the two primary guides toward customer value.

Within an Agile context, the customer is the most important voice in shaping the direction of the product. Your goal is to identify and engage customers, which can help you shape the product journey. Not all customers are created equal. Some customers are committed to your product, while others may have mild interest. Some customers use the product one way, while others use the product another way.

This is where the importance of customer personas comes into play. If one user uses a computer to program and another uses a computer to work on spreadsheets, you have two different customer personas who use a computer. The primary message is to understand that there are various types of customers in your customer journey. You can learn more about the importance of personas and how to establish and use personas to get closer to customer value in Chapter 14.

Since you may have multiple customers, you need someone to engage with the various types of customers. Within an Agile context, the product owner is meant to be the voice of the customer and should be educated on how to engage, solicit, converge, and prioritize feedback from customers. You can learn more about the product owner and other roles in an Agile context in Chapter 8.

■ **Agile Pit Stop**   To learn more about the product owner role, go to Chapter 8. To learn how to create customer Personas, go to Chapter 14.

As you look beyond customers and product owners, you must recognize that there are people within the company that are engaged in bringing a successful product to market. I term these people the stakeholders. They contribute to the success of the product by providing a healthy environment to work, crafting a strategy or vision, identifying product and services ideas, understanding the marketplace, engaging with customers at some level, or building the product. Now that you are familiar with customers, product owners, and stakeholders, the next step is to establish your customer feedback bull's-eye.

Figure 6-2 illustrates the concept of a customer feedback bull's-eye where the customer is in the middle followed in the next ring of the circle by the product owner. They are surrounded by stakeholders. Those stakeholders closer to the customer that bring customer feedback into the process would be the next circle within the target. This would be followed by those less customer-focused.

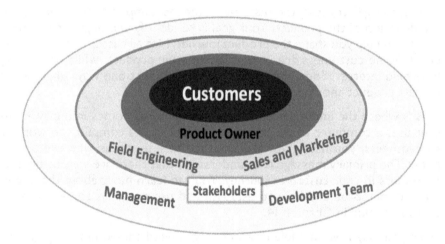

Figure 6-2. Customer feedback bull's-eye

CUSTOMER BULL'S-EYE EXERCISE

Create your customer feedback bull's-eye diagram. Do you have engaged customers in the middle? Do you have committed product owners in the next ring? What other stakeholders within your enterprise play a role in contributing to customer value? Consider the ratio of feedback coming from the customers vs. stakeholders. Do you think your company can benefit from more direct customer feedback?

Customer Universe Surrounding the Agile Galaxy

Chapter 4 discusses the Agile galaxy and how it represents the Agile land-scape within your company. Where do customers live in relation to your galaxy? From a business context, your Agile galaxy is within a sea of the cus-tomer universe. As illustrated in Figure 6-3, customers live all around your Agile galaxy (or at least you hope they do!). What you hope is to tap into those customers and find out what they need and then build it.

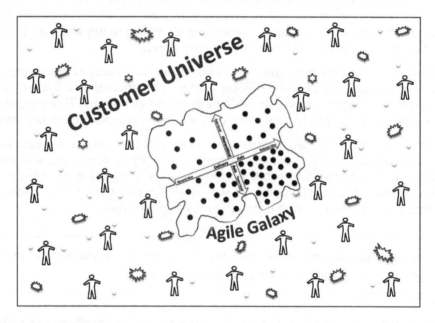

Figure 6-3. The Agile galaxy surrounded by the customer universe

On the left side of the delivery axis of the Agile galaxy is where you capture ideas of customer value. The ideas can come from various places—from people within the company and from customers external to the company. Engaging customers can start by soliciting their ideas for customer value or getting their feedback on whether an idea is perceived to be of value.

There are many places to gain the valuable customer input and feedback all along the delivery axis. Customer feedback is an important component of the CVD framework. This includes customer input and feedback when cap-turing, valuating, refining, developing, and releasing an idea to reflecting on the results of an idea.

Customers form the basis for a value-driven enterprise. A well-run startup painfully understands the value of customer feedback since it can make a difference whether it goes under or grows. Ensure customers are an integral part of your value-driven engine. To put customer feedback into action, consider reading Chapter 14, where you learn how to establish a customer feedback vision.

Customers in a Value-Driven Enterprise

How are customers and a value-driven enterprise related? The definition of a CVD enterprise is a company that optimizes for what the customers find as valuable and more specifically what they are willing to buy and use. This is why it is so important to think like the customers.

What the customers see as progress is not the standard project documents, a project plan that indicates the task completion, or status reports. Rather, customers see progress as tangible working product functionality. They purchase working product, not the plans, status reports, and other administrative items.

Customers delight in seeing working product in action and the inspect-and-adapt approach allows customers to consider and adjust their needs until they are transformed into a valuable working product. Progress is not advanced until a piece of functionality is built with quality, meets the customer acceptance criteria, and is available for review by the customer.

■ **Agile Pit Stop**   What the customer sees as progress is not a project plan or status reports. Rather, customers see progress as a tangible working product.

Functionality equates to value for the customer and ultimately means delivering business value. This implies that you have to continuously engage with the customer to get there. Engaging with customers only while gathering requirements and approaching product release is not enough. You need to *continuously* engage with customers as you are actively building the product throughout its life cycle.

Learning Your Way to Customer Value

The concept of learning what the customer finds as valuable is an important mindset in the journey of customer value. It allows us to shed the dangerous attitude of pretend or arrogant certainty and allows us to really explore what the customer needs. When you fix customer requirements up front and plan the path to delivery without continuously engaging with the customer, you might stick to the plan with success, but you will incrementally veer away from what the customer finds valuable. Figure 6-4 illustrates this challenge.

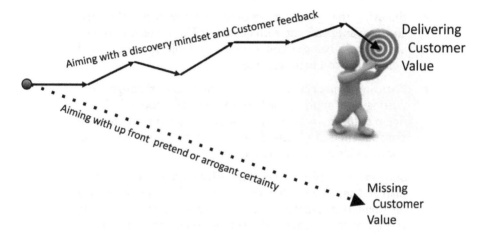

Figure 6-4. Aiming for customer value

The question is, "Is it better to stick to the plan or adapt toward customer value?" How many people have seen companies decide to stick to the path of pretend or arrogant certainty, inevitably creating a product that few customers want, ergo missing customer value? While this may sound obvious, have you ever encountered companies where the plan rules?

The moment you engage with customers on a continual basis, the plan will not survive. Is it better to deal with a changing plan and deliver something the customer actually wants, or is it better to stick to the plan and end up delivering functionality the customer does not want? Keep in mind that if you are not listening to your customers, your competitors will be.

The better approach is to incorporate the concept of learning what is customer value. This is a discovery method of gaining incremental information through various methods associated with getting customer feedback and taking what you learned to continuously adapt toward customer value. Continuous learning of customer needs is important to get closer to certainty. As illustrated in Figure 6-4, the incremental nature of adapting to what is learned leads us toward the customer value target. Learn more about the discovery mindset and how it can help you adapt your way to delivering customer value in Chapter 10.

Enterprise Anti-patterns of Attaining Customer Value

Value is in the eye of the beholder. Smart people will say that the beholder is the customer. While in most companies, there will be a saying similar to "the customer is king," some have lost their way and have somehow forgotten the importance of customers and their feedback. The result is enterprise anti-patterns that impede customer value. There are a number of anti-patterns on why this occurs and the following are four:

- Believing that you can pretend to know what the customer wants upfront with certainty. This *Pretend Certainty* anti-pattern has the consequence of limiting options and being blind to customer needs.

- Focusing primarily on driving efficiencies through cost cutting and applying high utilization of people. This *No Room at the Innovation Inn* anti-pattern has the unintended consequence of a lesser focus on the customer with little room to innovate and adapt.

- Sub-optimizing for the comfort of having a well-established plan and set of well-defined processes. This *Sub-optimizing for Comfort* anti-pattern has the consequence of limiting change at the expense of adapting to customer needs.

- Engaging few customers to represent the customer pool. The *Few and the Missing* anti-pattern has the consequence of missing customer needs.

When you are a startup, you realize the importance of being customer-value-driven because if customers don't buy the product, the startup goes under. That doesn't mean that a startup has the right product, culture, or processes to become successful; it is that they know that without understanding customers' needs, their hopes for a successful product or service are slim. Because of this and their small size, most startups will stay very close to the customer or potential customer.

When companies become larger, there is a greater chance the anti-patterns that impact customer value will exist. There is a likelihood of adding more processes, which results in more steps away from employee to the customer. As companies grow, there are tendencies to put more controls in place to manage cost and, unfortunately, this leads to restricting change. A company begins to optimize for its own processes and plans. This distances itself from customers. As a company grows, there needs an explicit action to remain close to the customer. The question for you is, "Do you see these anti-patterns effecting customer value in your enterprise?"

▓ **Agile Pit Stop**   As companies grow, controls are put in place to manage cost and more processes and plans are used. Both can restrict change and increase distance from customers.

One of the Agile values is responding to change over following a plan. While there may be a high-level benefit to a plan, responding to changes from customers is where there is more value. More information on the Agile manifesto and its values and principles can be found in Chapters 3 and 5.

Customer Challenges of Understanding Value

Another primary reason why it can be challenging to get to customer value is that many times the customers don't really know what they want. They think they know what they want and they will attempt to provide their best guess on what they are looking for.

There are number of reasons for this. First, customers cannot always articulate their needs at the moment you ask. Instead, they may provide an idea that may solve their most current issue, which may not really lead to their biggest need. Second, customers are not aware of the options or possibilities so they tend to gravitate toward what they know. A rumored quote by Henry Ford highlights this mindset, "If I'd asked customers what they wanted, they would have said 'a faster horse'." Third, the landscape of customer needs changes regularly. Customer value can be an elusive target and changes constantly. If customers have to wait six months or a year for what they want, they may have moved on and now want something different.

▓ **Agile Pit Stop**   Often customers don't know what they want until they see it, ergo the importance of the sprint review or demonstration.

This is where the advantage of a discovery and incremental mindset comes in handy. This way, you can learn what the customer wants. A corollary to this is that the customers don't know what they want until they see it. By initiating demonstrations, customers can see what they said they wanted and can respond toward what they really want. Inversely, when building something that is considered innovative, showing the customers something that is incrementally being built offers them the opportunity to respond toward customer value.

Is Customer Feedback an Integral Part of Your Customer-Value Engine?

This chapter walks us through many aspects in understanding customers and the importance of their feedback. A customer is very specifically defined. Customers have a choice and they pay money to your company. Some organizations apply the term "customer" too liberally to those internal to the company. While such people are stakeholders, they are not the customer. This is an important mindset shift, and this message needs to be shared with all of those within the enterprise.

Customer feedback provides the direction that steers the customer-value engine toward the direction of customer value. Customers see progress as working product and delight in seeing working product in action. The discovery and incremental approach allows customers to reflect on and adjust their needs until they are transformed into a valuable working product. Believing that progress is best realized in the form of working product is an important mindset shift to embrace.

Identifying what the customer finds as valuable is a learning opportunity and an important mindset in the journey toward customer value. It allows us to shed the dangerous attitude of pretend or arrogant certainty and really explore what customers need. At the end of the day, it is important to make the customer king. You just need to ensure the customers are guiding you by gaining their valuable feedback along the way.

Embracing Employees

Treat employees as if they are your partners because they are the voice of your company.

—Mario Moreira

One of the Agile values and two of the Agile principles specifically focus on the importance of employees. The Agile value states, "Individuals and interactions over processes and tools." The Agile principles state: "Business people and developers must work together daily throughout the project" and "Build projects around motivated individuals. Give them the environment and support they need, and trust them to get the job done."

Extracted from these values and principles are collaboration, motivation, and trust. These are key values of an Agile culture where employees matter. When employees are engaged, they become instrumental to the success of the company. They are empowered to make decisions, they are motivated themselves and they motivate each other, they willingly contribute innovative ideas, and they are willing to go the "extra mile" to get the work done. When employees have ownership, they have more passion for their work. The question is, "Are you investing in the cultural change where you embrace employees and ensure they know they matter?"

© Mario E. Moreira 2017
M. E. Moreira, *The Agile Enterprise*, DOI 10.1007/978-1-4842-2391-8_7

Mechanics That Tune the Engine of Customer Value

Applying the analogy that a company is the engine of customer value, we realize that an engine needs mechanics. As illustrated in Figure 7-1, employees are the mechanics that make your customer-value-driven engine purr. A mechanic that feels ownership of the engine is motivated to work on the engine, enjoys collaborating with others on the engine, is empowered to improve the engine, and is trusted to make the changes in a safe environment. As a result of this ownership, you will find that you have an engaged and happy employee.

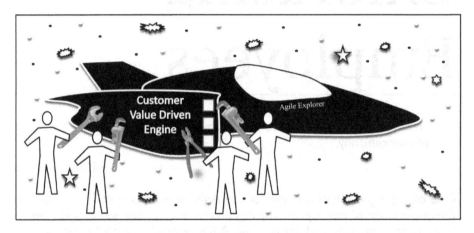

Figure 7-1. Employees are the mechanics that make the engine of customer value purr

An unhappy employee will be disengaged and allow the engine to sputter. When employees are disengaged, they take long lunch hours and will not stay in the office a moment longer than they have to. More importantly, they will not engage their minds to solve problems effectively. They may not contribute to and may even impede their company's success.

Happy employees continuously look for ways to improve the engine. Frederic Laloux[1] writes that pluralistic-green organizations, which focus on culture and empowerment, achieve extraordinary employee motivation. The study "The Impact of Empowered Employees on Corporate Value"[2] reveals that employee empowerment within the corporate culture is a "potential source for sustained superior financial performance." Employees can be a company's greatest assets. They can be the mechanics that keep the CVD engine purring to move the company forward.

---

[1]*Reinventing Organizations* by Frederic Laloux, Nelson Parker, February 20, 2014
[2]"The Impact of Empowered Employees on Corporate Value" by Darrol J. Stanley, *Graziadio Business Review*, 2005 Volume 8, Issue 1

▧ **Agile Pit Stop** A culture where employees matter can achieve extraordinary employee motivation and is the potential source for sustained superior financial performance.

Just saying, "Our employees are our most valuable assets," is not enough and has become a standard cliché. Can you back it up? Here are areas that you can explore to gauge if your enterprise believes that employees matter.

The COMETS within Your Agile Galaxy

COMETS stands for *Collaboration, Ownership, Motivation, Empowerment, Enthusiasm, Trust,* and *Safety*—the values that an organization must embrace if they believe employees matter. These values should be nurtured and become part of an Agile culture that values its employees and understands their importance for the success of building customer value. (See Figure 7-2.)

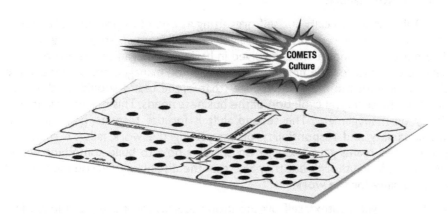

Figure 7-2. Employee culture of COMETS builds texture to your Agile galaxy

It is important to understand that when the term *employee* is used, it applies to all employees, from team members to executives. As illustrated in Figure 7-2, the COMETS culture should be pervasive across your enterprise. All levels should be exhibiting collaboration, ownership, motivation, empowerment, trust, and safety (just in different ways). For example, ownership implies a bounded authority where executives have ownership of work at their level (for example, strategy) and teams have ownership at their level (for example, user stories in backlog). (See Chapter 8 for more on bounded authority.)

As you explore each value, what actions and behaviors would you expect to see? The following is a quick definition of each of the attributes of COMETS. *Collaboration* is the ability to work with someone to build something. *Ownership* is feeling that you have the right to control and enjoy an area of work or work item. *Motivation* is a willingness or desire to do your work. *Empowerment* is the belief that you have the right to set the direction of something. *Trust* is confidence regarding an expectation. *Safety* is having the belief that it is safe to learn and take risks.

Self-Organizing Teams

COMETS form the building blocks to self-organization. Key to having an Agile environment where employees are engaged and believe they matter is establishing a culture where employees have the ability to self-organize around the work. Self-organizing teams are defined as a group of people who have autonomy and a common purpose for deciding how to build something in a collaborative manner.

The Agile manifesto calls out self-organizing as one of its principles, "The best architectures, requirements, and designs emerge from self-organizing teams." There are two mindset shifts involved in having self-organizing teams become part of the culture. The first mindset shift is for management to understand that those with the most knowledge (that is, the team) should be the ones deciding the technical evolution of the business needs. This means less dependency on management. The second shift is for the team to be aware that accountability and responsibility of completing the work falls on them. As you can see, teams gain flexibility on deciding how to build something within their bounded authority, but they also gain the discipline of accountability and responsibility for the work.

Within an Agile context, self-organization requires several key elements. The first is that there is a common purpose for the work to help guide the team (such as release goals and sprint goals). The second is that there is a bounded authority on the work the team owns and they are empowered to determine how to build the product. The third is that the team uses a build-inspect-adapt type model (applying one of the Agile processes). Inspecting requires both verification (testing) and validation (customer feedback) to help build in the direction of customer value.

Agile Pit Stop   Within an Agile context, self-organizing teams require a common purpose, bounded authority, and a build-inspect-adapt type model (an Agile process).

The primary benefit of self-organizing teams is that when employees feel they own the work, they tend to have more passion. Consequently, they are likely to invest more of their time and energy. The implication is that the company may gain the benefit of stronger employee commitment and performance, leading to potentially superior financial results. Now let's explore the building blocks of self-organization (that is, COMETS) in more detail.

Collaboration

Collaboration from an Agile and business perspective is defined as two or more people creatively working together with a common purpose to produce a positive business outcome. Within the context of self-organizing teams, it is important for team members to collaborate. Notice I used the terms "creatively" and "positive" in my definition. Collaboration is meant to produce an outcome. It is meant to bring people and their knowledge together to create something new or different. If two people are not being creative, then it is just two people doing something operational.

Collaboration in my definition is meant to be positive. There is such a thing as "bad" collaboration when not everyone has the same common purpose. "Good" collaboration relies on an environment where people honestly align with the common purpose and willingly accept new knowledge in an open and trusting manner to create something new.

▓ Agile Pit Stop   Collaboration is defined as two or more people creatively working together with a common purpose to produce a positive business outcome.

From the employees' perspective, collaboration provides them with the opportunity to team up with people pursuing a common purpose and to learn from each other along the way. Effective collaboration requires employees to connect with people and with their inner selves. It teaches them to work more effectively and can lead to a high-performing team.

It is important not to confuse collaboration with communication and coordination. Collaboration is a two-way action where two or more people work together to produce a positive outcome. Communication is a one-way action of sharing information in writing, speaking, or other medium. Coordination is often a one-way action of bringing together various elements to enable an activity.

Coordination can promote a more effective collaboration outcome, and communication can be used to share the results of the collaboration. Combined with ownership and empowerment, collaboration allows employees to own and change the direction of the work. This leads to happier employees who feel their abilities are being put to good use.

Ownership

Ownership is probably the most important factor in gauging whether employees matter. Ownership is defined as having the authority and the resources necessary to do work effectively. When employees feel ownership of their work, they typically take more pride, put more effort, and bring more quality to their work. Within the context of self-organizing teams, each team understands what work it owns within its bounded authority.

■ **Agile Pit Stop**   When you own a home, you will likely take better care of it. You will likely invest time and money to improve it because you feel the pride of ownership.

In which scenario will a person put more effort? Is it to maintain a rented apartment or maintain an owned home? If you don't own something, you are likely to invest less effort. When you own a home, you will likely take better care of it and be more likely to invest time and money to improve it because you feel the pride of ownership. In fact, you are more likely to protect and defend it. If employees feel ownership of their work, they will much more likely be willing to invest extra time and bring high-quality labor to the work.

As illustrated in Figure 7-3, a change in ownership will involve a cultural shift to move the level of decisions to the lowest possible level. This may include reducing the need for numerous approvals. This can be a big change for most organizations, but it has the benefit of speeding up the flow of work. Make sure you remember that management still has a role to play. Managers need to establish an environment where employees can be most productive and provide them with a vision of where the enterprise is headed.

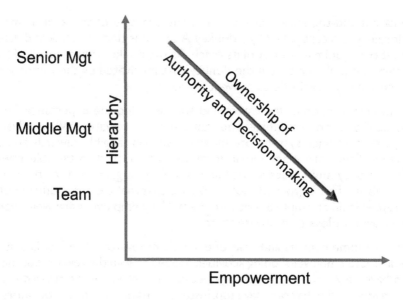

Figure 7-3. Empowerment model: Moving authority to the lowest level where knowledge exists

Motivation

There is a strong link between successful companies and those companies whose employees describe themselves as motivated. Motivation is a construct of internal and external factors that drive how people behave. A motivated employee may put in more effort with a greater focus on quality. Employee motivation methods have been explored for years due to the possibility of increased company success. In the context of self-organizing teams, the goal is to provide employees with reasons to be motivated.

What are the drivers of employee motivation and what does it mean to an employee? Early notions of motivation tended to focus on the extrinsic motivation methods to engage employees, while more recent research recommends exploring the intrinsic motivation methods that are better suited to engage employees.

Extrinsic Motivation

The extrinsic motivational methods focus on motivators that come from outside the employee. In the early twentieth century, extrinsic motivation techniques were characterized by the use of both rewards and punishments.

The carrot-and-the-stick method is an early example of an extrinsic motivator. It refers to a cart pulled by a donkey. A carrot is tied to a stick and dangled in front of the animal just out of its reach. As the donkey moves forward to get the carrot, it pulls the cart. If the donkey isn't motivated by the carrot, a stick hits the donkey's backside to move it forward.

The modern version of the carrot and stick is called the Expectancy Theory (that is, if you do something, you can expect a reward). While advanced, today's performance systems are mostly based on tangible rewards and punishments. There are many extrinsic motivators related to tangible rewards such as money and grades as well as psychological gains such as recognition and celebrity. These types of motivation are external elements outside of the employees in an attempt to motivate them. Many employees are well aware of these obvious ploys to motivate them.

There are some benefits and risks of extrinsic motivators. The first is that they may promote employees' doing activities needed to gain the reward, but this will often have only a short-term change because the moment the reward is gone, the activities and behaviors may stop. Instead, consider intrinsic motivators.

Intrinsic Motivators

The intrinsic motivational methods focus on those motivators that come from inside the employee. These are driven by an interest that exists within the individual. In this case, the motivation to engage in an activity or behavior arises from within the employee because it is intrinsically rewarding and not because of an external prize.

■ **Agile Pit Stop**   Intrinsic motivators come from within the employee. Extrinsic motivators come from outside the employee. Intrinsic motivators are more effective.

There are intrinsic motivators related to a sense of value, meaning, progress, and competence. These types of motivation may be driven by enjoyment, curiosity, ownership, autonomy, and pride. What are specific examples of intrinsic motivators? They may involve contributing to a team (for example, building a product), to a cause (such as increasing the number of women in leadership), or to a movement (for instance, being Agile). They may involve gaining mastery in a domain (for example, Agile and Java programming).

Intrinsic motivators are best applied when identifying an employee's consequential purpose. The more consequential the purpose, the more self-motivated an employee becomes. In relation to an Agile culture, it may mean that you have a feeling of ownership of the work. It may mean that you have autonomy in your work, such as deciding what work you do, how you do the work, and what the pace of the work will be.

There are major benefits for intrinsic motivators. Employees are often more creative when they are intrinsically motivated. This can lead to more innovation of products. If the intrinsic motivation has to do with competence, there can be higher quality in the products being built. Intrinsic motivators lead to long-term change of mindset since the motivator is from within and doesn't rely on an external reward, which can disappear.

Avoid mixing external motivators with internal motivators. It can be tempting to identify the intrinsic motivator and add an extrinsic reward to it. For example, when you offer a reward to something that an employee already finds fun, it often transforms the "fun" into work or obligation.

WHICH MOTIVATORS EXERCISE

Within your own organization, what extrinsic and intrinsic motivators do you see occurring? Are there any extrinsic motivators that are getting in the way of progress? Are there intrinsic motivators that could be promoted?

Empowerment

Everybody has heard the term *empowerment* in organizations—typically to hype up a new initiative so that employees will feel empowered. However, it should be a core value of an organization's strategy and not a trend that comes and goes. Unfortunately, this is not the case for many organizations. Empowerment is defined as having the autonomy and accountability to organize and make changes to one's own work and his or her surroundings. Within the context of self-organizing teams, team members are empowered to decide how to build their product (architecture, design, UX, development, testing, and more).

▧ **Agile Pit Stop**   Employee empowerment isn't just a warm and fuzzy benefit for the workers, and it can lead to tangible performance and financial gain for an organization.

What exactly is employee empowerment? In Figure 7-4, Jane Smith presents an employee empowerment model that includes three degrees of empowerment.[3] The first level encourages employees to play a more active role in their work. The second level asks employees to become more involved with improving the way things are done. The third level enables employees to make bigger and better decisions without having to engage upper management. The third level is key for an Agile culture.

---

[3]*Empowering People* by Jane Smith, Kogan Page, 2000

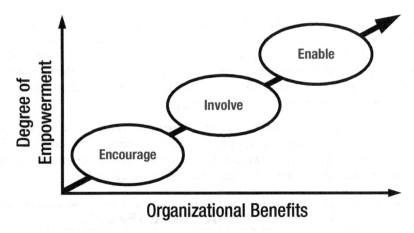

Figure 7-4. Employee empowerment model

If management is earnest about applying a model like this, managers may see improvements in the quality of their product delivery, more innovation, increased productivity, and a gain in competitive edge. Empowerment is enhanced when an adaptive framework like Agile is applied, which advocates a team-based model. If the team feels truly empowered and can self-organize, they will naturally increase their productivity because they are empowered to make decisions to guide their work lives.

Trust

One of the Agile principles states, "Build projects around motivated individuals. Give them the environment and support they need, and trust them to get the job done." Trust is defined as having confidence in another person that something will get done. Within a self-organizing team, trust is developed among team members when they can rely on each other that work will get done or that help will be asked for.

Some people say trust is earned. I suggest that trust should be given. This is often seen as a change in mindset. Much of what you learn about trust is through negative experiences. This can teach some of us to start with a guarded view, which makes us believe that trust should be earn. It can feel safer, but this can be a less productive way of approaching trust.

You hire people who you trust can do the job. At the same time, either by your negative experiences or by the multiple levels of approvals, you build an environment where there is insufficient trust given. Have checks and safeguards been added to replace trust? If you don't trust, the safeguards are only a process layer that bandages the problem of trust and are often impeding the speed of delivery.

A better way is to start from a trust position. In the COMETS culture surrounding your Agile galaxy, is it better to start with a positive and approachable worldview or from a negative and adverse worldview of those around you? Give your colleagues the trust and support to get the job done. Trust is a critical element for healthy relationships, teams, organizations, and communities. Employees are your partners. Giving them the right environment, tools, and culture will help them thrive and, in turn, it will help the business thrive.

■ **Agile Pit Stop**   Instead of saying trust must be earned, a better way is to start from a positive position of trust. You hired people who can trust, didn't you?

Accept the fact that everyone is indeed human and subject to faults. Also, before assuming that anyone is at fault, verify that you provided team members with the support, impediment removal, and lean processes that would enable them to succeed. Often the reason trust is broken is because the system, processes, or cultures around a team are broken. Always look to see what you can fix for a team or employees.

Trust Relationships

Trust is developed through relationships with those around us. These relationships are at various levels and need to be developed and continually maintained. As illustrated in Figure 7-5, relationships tend to be horizontal (peer-to-peer at roughly similar levels) or hierarchical (employee-to-manager or seasoned employee to junior employee).

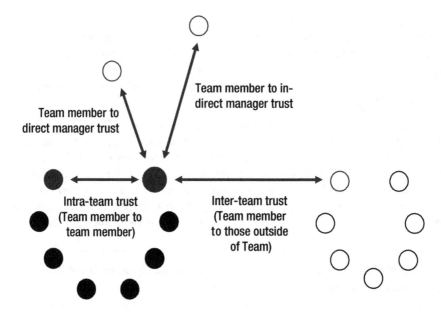

Figure 7-5. Trust relationships

In most work places, there is more complexity to building a trusting environ-ment beyond your peers and manager. Relationships can include intra-team trust from team member to team member and inter-team trust from team member to a member of another team, team member to direct manager, and team member to indirect manager.

In any of these scenarios, start from a trust position. Attempt to make con-nections with anyone you work with beyond work tasks. This helps employ-ees gain familiarity and empathy with each other. When it comes time to work together, emphasize listening skills to reduce misunderstanding. Building healthy relationships among employees and between employees and managers will be discussed further in Chapter 8.

Safety

There are two types of safety that factor into a healthy and productive enter-prise environment. The first is physical safety. A physically safe environment is where employees are free from physical hazards and can focus on the work at hand. This type of safety should be part of the standard workplace promoted by company and government regulations.

The second safety type is psychological safety, which is core to enterprise effectiveness. According to Google research, high-performing teams always display psychological safety. This phenomenon has two aspects. The first is where there is a shared belief that the team members are safe to take interpersonal risks and be vulnerable in front of each other. The second is how this type of safety, along with increased accountability, leads to increased employee productivity and, hence, high-performing teams.

■ **Agile Pit Stop**   Psychological safety is a shared belief that the team members are safe to take risks and be vulnerable to each other. With accountability, this leads to high-performing teams.

Psychological safety helps establish an Agile environment that promotes a safe space for employees to share ideas, discuss options, take methodical risks, and become productive. An Agile mindset promotes self-organizing teams around the work, taking ownership and accountability, and creating an environment for learning what is customer value through the discovery mindset, divergent thinking, and feedback loops. Agile with psychological safety can be a powerful pairing toward high-performing teams.

However, accountability without psychological safety leads to great anxiety. This is why there is a need to move away from a negative mindset when results aren't positive or new ideas are seen as different. If employees do not feel safe psychologically, they are less willing to share ideas and take risks. Instead, consider ways to build psychological safety paired with team ownership and accountability of the work.

Everyone has a role to play in establishing a psychologically safe enterprise. ScrumMasters and Agile coaches can educate and coach teams to apply psychological safety and accountability. Leadership can provide awareness of the importance of a safe environment, give education on this topic, and build positive patterns in the way employees respond to the results of risks taken by team members and others. Employees at all levels must be aware of the attitudes and mindsets they bring.

Understanding Employee Engagement

How do you know you have engaged employees? Organizations have used Gallup, Inc., for years to help understand their employees' level of engagement. Gallup spent decades developing the Q12 instrument, which provides 12 well-honed questions measuring the extent to which employees are "engaged" in their work. While some will say correctly that a manager or supervisor has the greatest impact on the level of a satisfied or engaged employee, Gallup indicates that it is realistic to assume that numerous people in the workplace can influence an employee's engagement level.

Since a number of people may influence an employee's engagement level, you need to address the culture in which the employee works. In relation to Agile, one way to gauge employee engagement is to discuss it in relation to the Agile values and principles, which provide strong guidance at both the individual level and the organizational levels.

SUPPORT FOR AGILE PRINCIPLES EXERCISE

Ask employees at what level (strongly agree to strongly disagree) of support they feel that the organization around them gives the 12 Agile principles. For those with lower support (disagree) responses, ask what better support for a principle would look like. Consider sharing results with senior management.

Another way to gauge the employee engagement level is to ask employees the Gallup's 12 questions and gather their responses (strongly agree to strongly disagree). To gain triangulated feedback, it may be beneficial to ask them from both from the Gallup view and from the Agile view.

■ **Agile Pit Stop**　What are some ways to gauge employee engagement and find out if employees understand that they are important to the company? Just ask them. Asking them directly gets to the point.

Of course, there is the direct way. You simply ask them. Ask the employees if they feel they matter to the enterprise. Ask them if they feel they can collaborate. Ask them if they feel ownership of their work. Ask them if they are motivated. Ask them if they feel empowered to make changes to their work environment. Ask them if they trust their teammates and their managers. As them if they believe they are allowed to self-organize around their work. This approach will require someone who is trusted to lead the people through the questions or it can be done in a self-organizing way where employees lead themselves through the questions.

What Is Your Employee Culture?

When you look across your enterprise, what employee culture exists? Is the culture focused on self-organizing teams and aligned with the values of COMETS and the Agile values and principles? Do the employees feel ownership of maintaining the engine of customer value? Are they free to collaborate? Are they motivated to do their best? Are they empowered and self-organized to determine how to improve the engine and build the customer value? Are they trusted to make the decisions and do what is best? Do they feel safe to take risks? If they are, congratulations! If not, you have an opportunity to embrace a culture where employees matter.

For additional material, I suggest the following:

- *Drive: The Surprising Truth about What Motivates Us* by Dan Pink, Riverhead Books, April 5, 2011

- *Overview of the Gallup Organization's Q-12 Survey* by Louis R. Forbringer, Ph.D., O.E. Solutions, 2002

- *VFQ Motivation*, Emergn Limited, Emergn Limited Publishing, 2014

- *VFQ Communication, Collaboration, and Coordination*, Emergn Limited, Emergn Limited Publishing, 2014

Evolving Roles in Your Agile Enterprise

If your role has not adapted, you may not be part of the Agile transformation.

—Mario Moreira

An Agile and customer-value-driven enterprise is an organization that optimizes its roles in a manner that focuses on the Agile values and principles and customer value. This focus may necessitate shifts within an enterprise. The first shift is that employee roles should evolve toward aligning as closely to the customer and the creation of customer value. The second shift is that enterprises should add Agile activities that support customer value and remove activities that do not directly link to customer value.

In both shifts, the implication is that roles may evolve or become obsolete, or new roles may emerge. A litmus test to gauge whether your enterprise is Agile is to determine if any of the roles have changed. If you don't see a change in roles when the enterprise evolves to become more Agile, then it probably isn't Agile.

© Mario E. Moreira 2017
M. E. Moreira, *The Agile Enterprise*, DOI 10.1007/978-1-4842-2391-8_8

Optimizing Enterprise Roles for Agile

Organizational roles and their functions are part of transforming to Agile. What this means is that each function must operate such that it can readily adapt to the needs of customers and market conditions. Are current roles and their functions constraining or embracing the need to adapt toward customer value? Embracing the need should be the goal.

What roles and functional areas should be optimized to the changing needs of customers and marketplace in order to have better business outcomes? The short answer is all roles and job functions should contribute. Figure 8-1 illustrates many of the key roles that are new or should adapt toward an Agile mindset and align with the delivery of customer value.

Figure 8-1. Roles in an Agile enterprise

What you are really looking for is what roles directly contribute to customer value. As discussed in Chapter 2, the two-degrees-of-customer-separation rule can be an effective means to determine how far away any one employee is from the customer. Two degrees of customer separation would be "you (as an employee) connected to an employee connected to the customer." The farther away employees are from the customer, the less likely they understand what is considered valuable to the customer. Aligning the roles in your Agile galaxy to customer value will often require a shift in how the organization is run and may entail adapting roles and responsibilities.

Obvious Agile Roles

If you look across an Agile galaxy, there are obvious roles and less obvious roles that should be adapted toward an Agile mindset and aligned with the delivery of customer value. As illustrated in Figure 8-2, the obvious roles tend to primarily focus on the team level. However, in an Agile enterprise, the norm is that all roles adapt toward an Agile mindset and align with the delivery of customer value. If they do not, there may be an opportunity to streamline toward alignment to customer value.

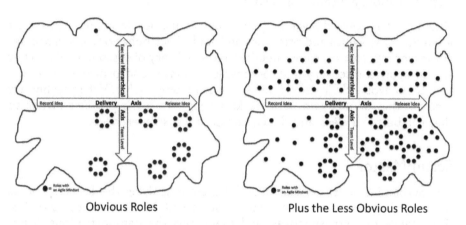

Obvious Roles   Plus the Less Obvious Roles

Figure 8-2. Obvious plus less obvious equals an Agile enterprise

Roles in the "obvious" group tend to be the first to apply Agile for several reasons. Development teams are more receptive to apply Agile. Management departments, on the other hand, find it easier to ask teams to change to Agile without themselves committing to the change. Also, team-level Agile processes are more prevalent and have a mechanical feel, making it easier to apply the culture changes.

■ **Agile Pit Stop**   It should be obvious that all roles should adapt toward an Agile mindset and align with customer value. Today some are obvious and some are less obvious.

In both the obvious and less obvious sections, there is advice on how to adapt each role. However, all roles should start by gaining the knowledge of the information in Chapters 2–7. These chapters highlight what it means to be a customer-value-driven enterprise, the importance of the customer and employee, what an Agile galaxy looks like, and what it means to embrace the Agile mindset. All roles should have this level of understanding. The role or functional areas that tend to fall into the "obvious" grouping are:

Development Teams

A development team consists of a group of people focused on building the product or service. It is comprised of cross-functional roles such as development, quality assurance (QA), database, user experience (UX), documentation, education, and so on.

When moving toward Agile and customer focus, development teams must learn the Agile values and principles and apply Agile behaviors and processes as they incorporate customer needs into the delivery of customer value. They should apply a discovery and incremental mindset and processes that will help them evolve their deliverable toward customer value. While technically focused, they should gain business knowledge from the product owner so they can better understand the customer and customer value.

ScrumMaster

The ScrumMaster is the facilitator for a team applying the Scrum process when building customer value. ScrumMasters lead the team through planning, daily stand-ups, retrospectives, and supporting the demonstrations. If not using Scrum, the role may be called the Agile facilitator or coach.

When moving toward Agile and customer focus, this new role focuses the team on the Agile mindset, Agile processes and practices, and the delivery of customer value. This new role in Agile often replaces project managers; ScrumMasters act more as facilitators of the Agile process and servant leaders to the team. This may be a significant shift for some companies where functional managers or project managers have always played a more directive role.

Product Owner

The product owner (PO) role is responsible for identifying and prioritizing the work according to customer value and for incorporating customer input and feedback to better align with customer value as the product evolves.

When moving toward Agile and customer focus, the PO is the champion and owner of customer value. This may be a shift for some companies where others play this role. The PO works with the team to ensure the team members realize customer needs and the business perspective of the work. The PO is the customer advocate and captures customer feedback to move the product in the direction of what the customer actually needs. The PO contributes to sprint planning and invites customers to attend the demonstrations.

■ **Agile Pit Stop**   The PO is the champion of customer value and the customer advocate. The PO captures customer feedback to move the product in the direction of what the customer actually needs.

This new role may be played by an existing role engaged with the customer, such as product manager or business analyst. It requires the person performing the role to engage regularly with the team. The PO must have decision-making rights to steer the product toward the direction of customer value. For more information on PO responsibilities, see Chapter 14.

Product Owner Constellation

A PO works within a sea of ideas that come from many places. Many ideas come directly from customers and others come from those within the company. To bring customer value ideas together, a PO should form a product owner (PO) constellation, consisting of employees who help the PO focus on customer value. Figure 8-3 is an example of a PO constellation.

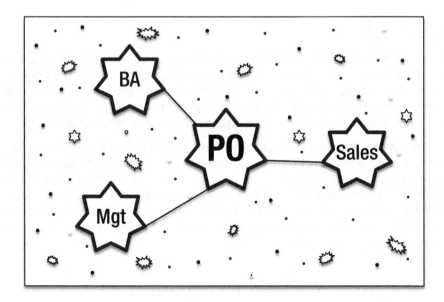

Figure 8-3. Product owner (PO) constellation

While the PO is the person ultimately responsible for prioritizing and owning customer value, it is good to have a PO constellation that includes other roles and functions that provide input to decision making for determining customer value. Other roles that can provide input are business analysts, management, salespeople, marketing experts, and field engineers.

Less Obvious Agile Roles

There are role and functional areas that are often missing from the Agile galaxy. These roles and areas need to be more engaged and adapt to an Agile mindset and practices to make for a more thriving Agile customer-value-driven enterprise. Given that early Agile processes tended to focus on the team level, this is not surprising. However, in order to have an end-to-end and top-to-bottom enterprise focused on the engine of customer value, all those within an enterprise need to adapt and play their role.

For those in this group, I often start by offering an Agile 101 session, which includes an emphasis on the Agile values and principles and a view of the Agile galaxy highlighting both axes. I focus on what it means to be customer-value-driven. Next, in the spirit of self-organizing, I ask the participants how they think they can adapt their role to align with the Agile mindset and the incremental nature it brings and how they can contribute to delivering customer value. Consider reading Chapter 9 for addition education options and guidance. The roles or functional areas that tend to fall into the "less obvious" grouping include:

Customers

A customer is someone who has a choice on what to buy and where to buy it. By purchasing your product, a customer pays you with money to help your company stay in business. Because of these facts, engaging the customer is of utmost importance. Customers are external to the company and may provide the initial ideas and feedback to validate the ideas into working products.

While not always obvious, the customer role should be front and center when working in an Agile context. Your customers are your business partners and your goal is to build strong customer relationships. While customers should be invited to product demonstrations and provide feedback, they should really be asked for their opinions all along the idea journey from identification to delivery to the reflection of customer value. For more information on customers, see Chapter 6.

Executives and Senior Management

Executives and senior management establish company goals, strategies, and objectives, and they provide leadership and guidance.

When moving toward Agile and customer focus, senior leaders must initiate a strategic shift in how the enterprise works. The senior leader should become the sponsor of the Agile initiative, encouraging buy-in to Agile. They must play a continuous role in advocating for Agile via e-mails, company meetings, and celebrations. Executives learn the language of Agile and customer value and become more conversant with those they lead.

■ **Agile Pit Stop**   Senior management may only have one person on its team who has sponsored the Agile change; others may not yet be on the Agile bandwagon.

Executives should support the concept of customer-value-driven enterprise, advocating for a discovery mindset where customer feedback loops are used to incrementally gain an understanding of what is valuable to the customer. They should also advocate for metrics that gain insight into learning what the customer value is and the fastest possible speed for delivering that customer value.

Senior leaders should adapt the enterprise from hierarchical to self-organizing. When employees feel they have more ownership and decision-making accountability, they apply more brainpower and bring passion to their work. This should include hiring direct reports who have a discovery mindset while retraining current directs who have a certainty mindset.

Business Leaders (Including Marketing and Sales)

The business department, including marketing and sales, focuses on developing products and services that meet customer needs. They focus on customer value by understanding current demand, marketplace trends, competition, brand value, and overall customer needs. The best product owners come from the business side and its employees can be an effective part of a PO constellation.

When moving toward Agile and customer focus, the business side (specifically the product owners) becomes the driver for capturing customer value. All those on the business side should learn Agile, embrace the discovery mindset, and begin to operate in more of an incremental manner. Roles in this space should be no more than two degrees of separation from the customer. All business personnel associated with a product should attend demonstrations as products evolve.

Middle Management

Traditionally, middle managers carry out the strategic vision of executives, create effective work environments, coordinate and control the work, and supervise groups of people who do the work. They may have functional and technical ownership of products. They also provide performance management and career development to their people.

When moving toward Agile and customer focus, middle managers must build a healthy Agile culture by encouraging their teams to align with Agile values and principles and focus on being customer-value-driven. They must adapt and act as a coach and servant leader toward their teams and become less directive. They must trust their teams to make good decisions, establish bounded authority, create safe work environments, and remove employee and team roadblocks. They should focus on the optimal location of people that reduces impediments and enables the flow of work. They should promote career and personal development through continuous education and apply Agile-minded performance excellence.

Agile Pit Stop   Middle managers must adapt their role by backing away from their functional leadership since the PO now owns much of that work.

If middle managers have strong product knowledge, some functional management members shift their roles and become a PO since the PO now owns the product direction. Because of less functional responsibility of their teams, some managers may evolve from a functional manager to a resource or career manager.

Middle managers are often the lynchpin that allows the executive's vision for Agile to thrive in the team setting. If they embrace Agile, then the change may succeed. Otherwise, they can block the change toward an Agile culture if they feel the need for control and won't allow a team to self-organize.

Human Resources

Human resource (HR) departments focus on managing company processes, policies, and standards, while carrying out management programs that focus on employees. More specifically, HR engages in recruitment, employee relationships, performance management, corporate communications, employee benefits, and pay structures.

When moving toward Agile and customer focus, HR can help build a healthy Agile culture that optimizes for engaged and happy employees. HR should be knowledgeable in Agile and what it means to be a customer-value-driven enterprise. HR should promote the values of collaboration, ownership, motivation, empowerment, trust, and safety (COMETS) for employees.

HR should recruit those candidates with an Agile mindset and align performance management from individuals to teams. HR works to adapt all roles toward an Agile mindset as described in this chapter and, in particular, to move management toward a coaching and servant leader role. For more on evolving HR to be more Agile, see Chapter 21.

Finance

Finance employees are primarily responsible for the fiscal health of an organization. They are focused on the financial side of funding decisions, facilities support, and staffing and, as a result, they manage the supply-and-demand system of the organization. A specific activity undertaken by finance is managing the annual budget process and periodically reporting and monitoring the financial health of the enterprise.

When moving toward Agile and customer focus, budgeting departments should adapt to a continuous Agile budgeting or at least a quarterly budgeting cycle. Finance needs to understand the importance of customer feedback and how it can change the direction of customer value to better know where to invest the enterprise's money. Since the demand for certain products and services can change quickly, finance needs to establish a system that can adapt supply according to the demands of the customer and market conditions.

■ **Agile Pit Stop**   Business (including marketing and sales) and finance become stewards of capturing customer value, embracing the discovery mindset, operating in an incremental manner, and applying customer feedback, all of which lead to better business outcomes.

For healthier decision making, finance should participate in two activities related to the value of ideas. The first is to challenge the assumptions and certainty thinking being demonstrated when people say an idea is of high value. The second is to advocate for Agile budgeting where the company funds only increments of an idea to place smaller bets and ensure that feedback is collected before any further funding. In addition, finance should adapt reporting toward a more incremental and outcome-driven manner. Finally, finance should learn Agile and what it means to be a customer-value-driven enterprise. For more on finance and their role in Agile budgeting, see Chapter 19.

Portfolio Management

Portfolio management (PM) teams focus on identifying what work is deemed valuable to an organization. These teams are found near the early part of the delivery axis of the Agile galaxy. In a more general sense, PM is a group within an organization that defines the standards of how the portfolio or work is managed. Traditionally, these employees are often involved in having authority and making decisions on what work gets done. PM often supplies metrics and reporting on the progress of the work.

When moving toward Agile and customer focus, PM should move toward a servant leader role. These employees adapt from being a key decision maker to enabling effective decision making by the business side. They set up an enterprise pipeline of ideas being considered or those that are already underway, focusing on the value of the work instead of the status. Information on the enterprise idea pipeline should be publically available.

PM can be instrumental in supporting a customer-value-driven organization by providing transparency on how the work has gotten prioritized, what prioritization methods have been used, what assumptions have been made, what customer feedback loops have been applied to validate customer value, and what team(s) have or may be involved in the work.

PM should also encourage a discovery and incremental mindset that, instead of moving a large idea into development, promotes the activity of decomposing an increment of the idea to validate its value. It should also adapt reporting toward recognizing value delivered, rate of delivery, quality of delivery, and business outcomes of revenue generated. Of course, PM should learn Agile and what it means to be customer-value-driven.

Project Management Office (PMO)

The project management office (PMO) focuses on defining project standards and supporting projects in the latter part of the delivery axis of the Agile galaxy. Traditionally, the PMO is directly involved in managing projects and often supply project managers to lead them. PMOs supply output metrics and report on the status of projects. They may initiate project status meetings to determine how projects are doing.

When moving toward Agile and customer focus, there may be a significant shift in how the PMO operates. Since most work in Agile is facilitated by a ScrumMaster with the Product Owner deciding the value and priority of the work, there is less work for a project manager to do. It is not uncommon for some project managers to become ScrumMasters, depending on their ability to adapt to an Agile mindset and act as a coach and facilitator.

■ **Agile Pit Stop**   If you have a portfolio and/or project management office, the focus should be less on decision making and more on servant leadership for enabling customer value.

It is not uncommon for a PMO to adapt to a leaner AMO (Agile management office). In an Agile environment, the focus is not the project, but the incremental delivery of value. Establishing a project implies you can know customer value upfront. In Agile, the team creates increments of value and the PO collects customer feedback used to adapt the product toward customer value. While the PMO may be leaner due to the ScrumMaster and PO, the PMO may focus on managing bigger releases where multiple teams are required to build the product.

As the PMO adapts to an Agile culture and processes, it should also adapt reporting toward understanding value delivered, speed of delivery, quality of delivery, and business outcomes of revenue generated. Of course, the PMO should learn Agile and what it means to be customer-value-driven.

The Importance of an Agile Coach

The Agile coach plays a big role in getting Agile off the ground. It can be beneficial to have a coach with enterprise Agile experience because he or she can help you navigate toward an Agile culture and the deep Agile implementation knowledge that ensures teams are implementing Agile effectively. While education will provide initial knowledge, a coach can keep you on the Agile path and prevent you from reverting back to old, traditional habits. The coach also understands the short-term and long-term pitfalls of adopting Agile and that Agile is a culture shift and will take time. The coach can help the team move to Agile in a more effective and efficient manner.

With that being said, it is important to gauge whether the Agile coach really understands Agile and what levels he or she has operated in (for example, team, management, and enterprise). As a tip, ask perspective coaches if they can articulate and discuss the Agile values and principles (without referring to a book or the Internet). Ask them what level(s) they have coached. For each level, ask them what challenges they have encountered and how they overcame them.

Bounded Authority

As you move to an enterprise where employees are engaged and teams self-organize around work, there is a benefit to providing guidance on the boundaries of the various roles and their activities. Instead of approaching this by trial and error where teams bump into the boundaries with often negative consequences, consider applying the concept of bounded authority.

Bounded authority is defined by the sphere of responsibility determined by who has the most knowledge and experience over a particular aspect of work. Those people should have the authority and decision-making rights over that work. For example, the group having the most knowledge about enterprise strategy is senior management. The group having the most knowledge about designing and building a product is the team.

Within a hierarchical structure of a company, bounded authority can help at multiple levels. For simplicity, Figure 8-4 illustrates team-level, middle-management-level, and senior-management-level boundaries. You may also add functional areas such as HR and finance.

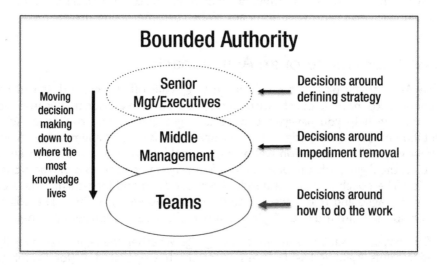

Figure 8-4. Bounded authority to help with self-organization

Within an Agile context, the goal is to push ownership and the authority and decision making it brings to the lowest possible level where the most information and experience dwells. For an Agile team, the members self-organize around the work in the product backlog that has been prioritized by the PO. Once that work is available at the team level, the team has authority to make architecture, design coding, and test decisions, and it can self-organize around how to build the product.

The key to bounded authority is that each level knows what work it should self-organize, what it is empowered to change, and the areas in which it can make decisions. Another key is that each level knows the authority of another level. Equally important is that this implies what authority a level does not have.

■ **Agile Pit Stop**   Within an Agile context, the goal is to push authority and decision making of the work to the lowest possible level where the most information and experience dwells.

If the team's work is prioritized by the product owner, what does middle management do? Can they assign work to the team? The short answer is no since the team gets their work from the PO via the product backlog. While the team self-organizes around the work, middle management helps optimize flow for their teams by removing impediments and enabling the teams to be its most effective.

Senior management should be focusing on the work where they have the most knowledge and experience. Their bounded authority of work may be to provide a strategy for the enterprise. This means they must help teams understand strategy and help them align strategy with their work.

Another option is the concept of seven levels of delegation where the bounded authority guidance is at the activity level instead of the role level. Established by Jurgen Appelo, this concept expands the binary view of authority of a decision (for example, you have authority or I have authority) into seven levels of delegation. They are the following: tell, sell, consult, agree, advise, inquire, and delegate.

As you may guess, on one end of the spectrum "tell" means that the manager fully owns the decision, and on the other end "delegate" means the decision is fully owned by the team while not even telling the manager the outcome. The value of this model is that some managers are not ready to give total authority of the decision away, so they may incrementally move to a less authoritative position (for instance, from tell to consult) where the manager now asks for input before making a discussion. You can learn more about the seven levels of delegation in *Managing for Happiness*.[1]

BOUNDED AUTHORITY EXERCISE

Create a bounded authority map similar to Figure 8-4. Include executive, middle management, product owner, and team. Create two columns below each role (for example, the current and traditional context and what an Agile context might look like). For each context, determine what activities along the delivery axis (such as identify value, prioritize value, develop value, and deliver value) each role owns. Compare each context. What differences do you see?

---

[1]*Managing for Happiness* by Jurgen Appello, Chapter 3, Wiley, 2016

Healthy Employee Relationships

A big part of building an Agile enterprise is evolving roles to better connect people together. Promote activities where employees can interact, build empathy, and collaborate. Sharing each other's delights and concerns is a meaningful way to build understanding and trust. In Agile, there are many related practices that promote people working together (for instance, pair programming, story mapping, and grooming). Informal activities, such as eating and socializing together, can further the connection.

■ **Agile Pit Stop**   Sharing each other's delights and concerns is a good way to build trust and understanding.

Strong connections occur when two people bond in a face-to-face manner. Since nonverbal communication makes up a major portion of all communication, face-to-face communication helps people better understand each other and how they are feeling about a discussion. While physical face-to-face contact is preferred, there are online applications that bring you face-to-face. Consider using a virtual alternative when physical face-to-face is not an option.

It is not uncommon in a distributed organization to have members at the remote site visit and bond with team members at the local site. This is a way to get team members to know each other, which promotes collaboration and builds trust. When members return to their designated site, the trust that has been built will promote stronger relationships.

Healthy Manager-to-Employee Relationships

As you look at the various trust relationships, an important connection is between an employee and his or her direct manager. Managers are responsible for maintaining a healthy and happy workplace. Managers need to make extra efforts to build trust with their employees and promote an open and honest workplace. As a manager, consider ways you can get to know team members and they can get to know you. Key ingredients in building trust are transparency, listening, integrity, and growth.

■ **Agile Pit Stop**   To build healthy relationships between managers and their employees, apply transparency, listening, integrity, and growth to the relationship.

Transparency is about sharing information regarding the company, division, and group so employees know what is going on. This may include sharing the latest changes, strategy, group goals, and anything else that has an impact on employees. When trust is established, transparency becomes a two-way street. As a manager shares more, employees will share more with the manager about what is really going on around them.

Listening is allowing employees to lead the agenda in a one-to-one encounter. By being an active listener, you have the opportunity to learn about the employees and what they care about. Another example of listening is walking the gemba (in other words, the real place where work gets done) where employees are sitting. Stop by and say hello. Ask them if there is anything they need.

Integrity is about being fair and honest with the way you treat employees and avoiding favoritism. Deliver on commitments to employees and only promise something when you mean to do it. If you ask employees to take risks, provide them a safe environment to do so. If you respond negatively to an employee failure, this will be a sure way to lose trust. Instead, address what was learned (focus on the positive) and how that learning can be incorporated for better results in the future.

Growth is about showing employees that you care about their personal goals and career growth. This goes well beyond the notion of promotions by providing them learning opportunities both within the workplace and outside. Periodically check in to discuss their goals to see how they are doing.

Holocracy

When considering how to evolve roles to align for the changing needs of customers, you may look at the holocracy model. *Holocracy* can be defined as a different way of operating an enterprise that moves power from a hierarchy management structure and distributes it across autonomous teams, as illustrated in Figure 8-5. Holocracy has clear rules and definitions for what teams and individuals can do.

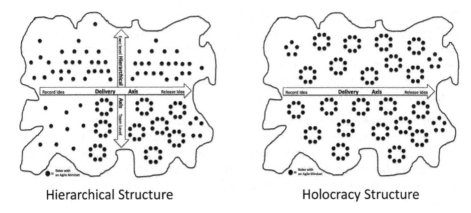

Hierarchical Structure   Holocracy Structure

Figure 8-5. Hierarchical and holocracy structures

In holocracy, teams are the basic components and building blocks of an enterprise. Teams are given a consequential purpose and then self-organize around the work and determine how to best achieve the need. Teams are not part of a business unit. This allows for dynamic movement of teams and individuals toward the work of perceived high customer value.

From a customer-value perspective, teams have customer value as their driving consequential purpose. As customers' needs change, so do the teams. Because team members have a number of skills and experience, they may move from team to team to where the highest value work is occurring.

Holocracy leverages a number of concepts. Transparency is applied where strategy, policies, and decisions are made public so you don't need to rely on the politics of who you know to get information. Self-organizing teams are responsible for their work, decide how to do their work, and determine who will do the work without any managerial input.

Lightning-bolt-shaped teams ensure team members have a primary, secondary, and tertiary skill set, experience, or ability to work on different types of work to make it easier to move from team to team. Bounded authority is applied where ownership and decision making is moved to where the most knowledge lives, which is often at the team level. Also, the concepts of open source, Agile processes, and lean enterprise are often seen as part of holocratic organizations.

Enterprises that move to a holocracy model will see their organizations' structure adapt to allow for more teams working on customer value and more employees who are closer to the customer. The two-degrees-of-customer-separation rule (where every employee is no more than two degrees of separation from the customer) almost becomes automatic.

It may be challenging for some employees, including those in management, to move to an holocracy model. I suggest first experiencing self-organizing and applying lightning-bolt-shaped teams before considering holocracy. For more insight, consider exploring *Holocracy* by Brian J. Robertson, *The Evolutionary-Teal Paradigm* by Frederic Laloux, and the Agile mindset on how an organization may evolve to be better align with customer value.

Have You Evolved Your Roles Yet?

It does take an enterprise and the whole Agile galaxy to move to Agile and the focus on customer value. Every role should evolve to become closer to customer value. If you are an Agile enterprise, you should see new roles, adaptation to existing roles, and the minimization of other roles. Avoid optimizing on the title of the role and instead optimize on what is needed to more effectively deliver customer value.

For additional material, I suggest the following:

- *Managing for Happiness: Games, Tools, and Practices to Motivate Any Team* by Jurgen Appelo, Wiley, 2016

- *Being Agile: Your Roadmap to Successful Adoption of Agile* by Mario Moreira, Chapter 12, Apress, 2013

- *Holocracy: The New Management System for a Rapidly Changing World* by Brian J. Robertson, Henry Holt and Co., 2015

Building a Learning Enterprise

Education is more than training. It includes coaching, mentoring, experiencing, experimenting, and giving back.

—Mario Moreira

In today's fast-paced life where everything is changing around us and advancing toward new technology, processes, and cultures, it is important that you give yourself the opportunity to learn. Learning allows you to stay current with the latest trends and directions of your industry and allows you to incorporate new concepts, technologies, and practices to your work.

Enter the continuous learning Agile enterprise. This is an enterprise that understands that it is the people (both employees and customers) that will make them more successful. The Agile manifesto reminds us of this by emphasizing "individuals and interactions over processes and tools." Educate the individuals and they can help adapt the enterprise. It is important to remember that employees are the mechanics of the customer-value-driven engine. Educate them in the ways of Agile and customer value and they will help the enterprise succeed.

© Mario E. Moreira 2017
M. E. Moreira, *The Agile Enterprise*, DOI 10.1007/978-1-4842-2391-8_9

A continuous learning enterprise also understands that you can learn from a variety of difference sources in a variety of different ways. This enterprise believes that there is no end state for being Agile just as there is no end state to learning what is valuable to the customer. Just as teams should have a consequential purpose to help them focus on their work, an enterprise should have a consequential purpose to help it realize the variety of education that can help with that purpose.

■ **Agile Pit Stop**   There is no final destination for being Agile just as there is no end state to learning what is valuable to the customer. Both are adapted over time.

As illustrated in Figure 9-1, the consequential purpose of achieving customer value helps an enterprise focus its culture, process, skills, and roles education. Since Agile is an enabler to delivering customer value, Agile topics form the core of the education needed to deliver customer value.

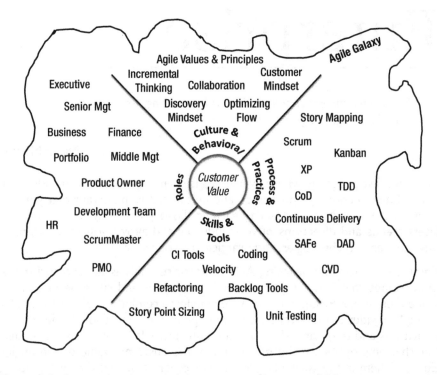

Figure 9-1. Focusing learning around the consequential purpose of delivering customer value

Because Agile requires a cultural shift in the way you think about work, you need to first ready your mind by learning the Agile values and principles and the importance of focusing on positive business outcomes. You also need to understand the cultural shifts necessary for the Agile journey. Then you must learn the various Agile processes, practices, and skills needed to make the journey. Finally, you need to be joined by a guide (that is, a coach) who can help you transform to an Agile mindset as you experience and learn what Agile feels like. Of course, as you work through continuous learning, you need to gain feedback and adapt to people's educational needs.

Education Is More than Training

Does your Agile education begin and end with a touch of training? A number of colleagues have told me that their Agile training was completed in one hour, one day, or two days, and then they were expected to apply and master the topics. Agile isn't simply a process or skill that can be memorized and applied. Will such limited training time suffice for a transformation to Agile? Probably not, as insufficient training time limits the success of effectively implementing Agile.

Education is an investment in your people. A shift in culture requires an incremental learning approach that spans across time. What works in one company doesn't work in another. Education should be an intrinsic part of your Agile transformation that includes skills, roles, process, culture, and behavior education with room to experience and experiment.

■ **Agile Pit Stop**   Continuous learning is more than event-driven training. It is reading, coaching, mentoring, experiencing, experimenting, and giving back on a continuous basis.

When you want to adapt your enterprise culture, you need education that includes more than just skill building. Culture change is a transformation that involves the most change and requires the most time for an organization to adapt. To support that change, there are educational elements that are suited for achieving the Agile skills, roles, processes, and culture as illustrated in Figure 9-2. These elements include training, mentoring, coaching, experiencing, experimenting, reflecting, and giving back. These education elements should be included in your culture change.

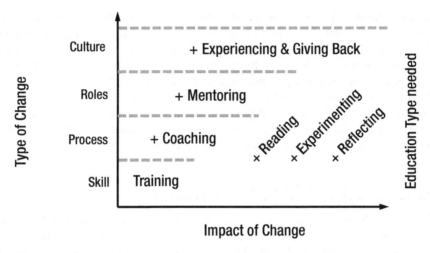

Figure 9-2. Educational elements for different levels of change

Training is applied when an enterprise wants to build employee skills, educate employees in their roles, or roll out a process. It is often event-driven and a one-way transfer of knowledge. What was learned can be undone when you move back into your existing culture, and it can be forgotten if not applied quickly. Coaching can reaffirm the training. Also, training can occur in an instructor-led manner where it is scheduled or in a web-based manner where the material is pre-recorded and can be used on demand.

Reading allows individuals to focus on topics of their own interest and at their own pace, but it does require self-motivation. Readers can use a physical book or e-book. The reading often includes articles, journals, podcasts, and blogs. Reading offers the advantage of going back to the source of the article, chapter, or section. Reading can also be done in with the aid of book clubs where teams or groups read and then discuss a topic.

Coaching helps a team put the knowledge of process and roles into action and lays the groundwork for transforming the culture. Coaching provides a two-way communication process so that questions can be asked along the way. If you do not have a coach, it is very easy to apply a process incorrectly or give up and revert to the old process. A coach has been on this journey before and can help you until you are enacting the process or practice correctly with the right behaviors for the culture you want.

Mentoring focuses on relationships and building confidence and self-perception. The person being mentored (*mentee*) invests time by proposing topics to be discussed in the relationship. In this two-way communication, deep learning can occur because the mentee is asking questions and seeking answers without being prompted. Mentoring allows individuals within an enterprise to better understand their place in the culture.

Experiencing focuses on living in the new process, applying the skills, and experiencing the new roles. This provides individuals with first-hand knowledge of what they've learned, allowing them to better understand the behavior changes needed. It allows for deeper questions, further exploration, and experimentation.

Experimenting focuses on trying something new for a short period of time in order to test a proposed change. The change often begins with a hypothesis on what might work better and then is crafted into a short test to see if the new idea had the effect or improvement set out by the hypothesis. Experimenting is a way to try concepts and practices before fully committing to a change.

Reflecting focuses on taking the time to consider what you learned—whether it is a skill, process, role, or culture—and determine what you can do better and what else you need on your learning journey. In effect, it is similar to an Agile retrospective that can occur at the employee, team, or enterprise level. It is a feedback loop to consider where you've been and what you need to achieve an Agile culture and a customer-value-driven enterprise.

■ **Agile Pit Stop**   When you get employees willing to give back to their community, it indicates a movement where employees are committed to the Agile transformation.

Giving back occurs when the employees have gained enough knowledge, skills, and experience to start giving back to their community. It is a commitment to start helping others. This provides a feeling of ownership in a transformation of the culture. Giving back can be to the company, local community, or greater community.

It takes a repertoire of educational elements to achieve an Agile culture. These elements help a team develop skills, learn its roles, navigate a process, and grasp behavioral changes toward achieving an Agile mindset. Ensure you apply a repertoire to your learning.

Agile Education Universe

There is a wealth of topics that can be covered in achieving an Agile mindset and customer value as illustrated in Figure 9-1. In an Agile galaxy context, you can learn about the early part of the delivery life cycle where ideas get articulated and prioritized, processes are applied, and motivation and trust become a priority. What you can learn is limitless.

Since learning is a journey, you may apply different education elements, depending on the topic. For some Agile topics, looking at a topic from several different angles enables learners to fully digest and understand it. Also there are certain core topics that can be building blocks in achieving an Agile culture. This is why I strongly recommend avoiding process and role topics up front and instead focus on topics that can ready the mind for an Agile culture.

Agile Education to Ready the Mind

Since Agile requires a cultural change, consider starting your Agile transformation by focusing on the current culture of the company. Begin readying the mind by educating employees on Agile values and principles and the behavioral changes needed. When you start with Agile mechanics of processes or roles, people may think Agile is first about mechanics and then the achievement of an Agile mindset.

■ **Agile Pit Stop**   Focus early Agile education on topics that begin the cultural changes such as Agile values and principles, discovery mindset, and self-organizing teams.

I often start an Agile transformation by offering an Agile 101 session that emphasizes the Agile values and principles. I ask employees to rank order the Agile values to initiate discussion and thinking. Then I'll walk through each Agile principle and ask them if they agree, are neutral, or disagree with it. If people are neutral or disagree, discussion and debate will ensue. I'll only spend five minutes on each principle as the purpose isn't to persuade employees, but to have a discussion. Sometimes a mindset shift takes time, so don't rush it.

After Agile 101, I continue with a session that focuses on the Agile galaxy with an emphasis of both axes, and what a customer-value-driven enterprise means. I'll ask where on the galaxy most people are applying Agile today so the participants better understand the state of their Agile galaxy. Next, I'll discuss the discovery mindset and behaviors that may be expected. This will include a focus on self-organizing and bounded authority.

You may notice in the early Agile education, I have not once mentioned education on an Agile process or Agile role. Instead, focus early on readying the mind for Agile with Agile mindset education.

Topics in the Agile Education Universe

There is a wealth of Agile education on the market. Much of it focuses on Agile processes and roles. While this is an important part of your Agile journey, ensure your education includes a strong focus on the Agile culture and the behaviors necessary to achieve an Agile mindset. Also focus on education that provides knowledge regarding the delivery of customer value.

In searching for education topics, I've been impressed with the Value, Flow, Quality (VFQ)[1] curriculum. While VFQ includes a focus on Agile processes and roles, it primarily covers many of the concepts that get to the heart of effectively running an Agile enterprise. VFQ focuses on topics to help you increase value through delivering early and often, optimizing the end-to-end flow for faster delivery, and enhancing feedback through fast feedback loops. Here are some of the topics that VFQ covers:

Why Change?	Delivering (Value) Early and Often	Optimizing Flow	Feedback
Teams	Motivation	Collaboration	Communication
Understanding Your Customer	Requirements	Prioritization	Estimating and Forecasting
Trade-Offs	Batch Size Matters	Work in Progress	Attacking Your Queues

In addition, there are a number of topics that go well beyond Agile processes and roles and should be considered when building an Agile culture and focusing on delivering customer value. They include the following:

---

[1] Emergn Limited, Emergn Limited Publishing, 2014

Agile Values and Principles	Servant Leadership	Self-Organizing Teams	Bounded Authority
Pluralistic-Green and Evolutionary-Teal Paradigms	Holocracy	Culture of Learning	Coaching and Mentoring
Customer-Value-Driven Enterprise	High-Performing Teams	Lightning-Bolt and T-Shaped Teams	Teamocide
Personas	Customer Feedback Vision	Feedback Loops	User Stories
Trust	Shu Ha Ri	Story Mapping	Tuckman's Model
Discovery Mindset	Hypothesis Thinking	Divergent Thinking	Incremental Thinking
Certainty Thinking and Epistemic Arrogance	Challenging Assumption	Cost of Delay (CoD)	Cost of Delay/ Duration (CD3)
Lagging to Leading Metric Path	Requirements Hierarchy	Velocity	Lean Canvas
Work Decomposition (Idea to Task)	Definition of Done	Agile Budgeting	Supply and Demand in Agile
Psychological Safety	Self-Management	Agile Governance	5R Idea Management
Gamification	Value Stream Mapping	Agile UX	Agile Design

These two tables provide over 50 topics beyond Agile roles and processes, and there are certainly hundreds more. Getting educated on these topics helps you gain a more thorough understanding of how to apply Agile for your team or for the Agile galaxy that represents your enterprise. The topics shared in this book may get you farther along in your Agile journey, knowing there is more to learn.

Finally, irrespective of the education you receive on Agile topics, I strongly recommend that you periodically revisit the Agile values and principles. As people gain more experience in Agile, they may grasp the Agile values and principles more fully over time. The one change I make for advanced learners in the Agile values and principles education is that instead of the instructor explaining the Agile principles, I ask the advanced students to explain them to the class. Then I ask the class if the explanations were accurate and clear. Let the discussion begin!

Importance of Work-Based Learning

Work-based learning is an approach to education where for every topic that you learn, you must apply the knowledge. This supports the discovery mindset and provides a deeper level of learning for students. The first-hand experience gained by students provides a deeper learning environment.

Within the Value, Flow, Quality (VFQ) education, Alex Adamopoulos includes the work-based approach to education, which helps organizations learn Agile and business topics and then gain immediate business benefits from applying them. Students learn a topic, exercise the topic in class, and then apply the topic with their team members in their actual working environment.

■ **Agile Pit Stop**   Work-based learning moves beyond theory and asks you to apply what you learned into your real working environment.

A similar approach is the learn-apply-share model, which includes learning a topic in the classroom, applying it in exercises, using it in a real work setting, and finally sharing and explaining the topic to others. When you have to explain a topic to others, you more fully understand the topic, which deepens your learning opportunity.

When you expand the notion of continuous learning, not only do you learn Agile topics, you also "learn your way to customer value." A learning enterprise goes beyond learning processes and tools. The type of enterprise that uses this approach recognizes that you learn from each other and you learn from your customers. Just as it takes a discovery mindset with multiple customer feedback loops to zero in on customer value, it takes multiple types of Agile topics to operate in an Agile manner to achieve customer value.

Agile Education Vision

Agile is a cultural shift that is often larger than most people realize. As you look to change your culture and gain the business benefits, you have learned in this chapter that there are hundreds of Agile and customer value related topics. You have also learned there are many ways to become educated. So, how do you organize Agile education in a manageable way?

Enter the Agile Education Vision. This vision is an adaptive education roadmap where you can iteratively plan and apply the repertoire of topics and educational elements to support your transformation toward an Agile culture. The vision can be applied to an employee, a team, and/or an enterprise.

Agile Pit Stop   An Agile education vision is your backlog of educational topics that you can iteratively plan and apply to support your transformation toward an Agile culture.

You may consider an Agile education vision as a prioritized product backlog of education topics based on needs. In each iteration, some form of education is provided that builds Agile knowledge, skills, and capabilities toward achieving an Agile mindset. At the beginning of each iteration, topics may be added and reprioritized for what is most important at that time.

- When applied at an individual *employee* level, ask what education may help a person develop the skills, process, and experience to better grasp Agile and understand how to achieve customer value. An employee may have personal learning goals such as gaining more knowledge on story point sizing and gaining new experiences by meeting actual customers.

- When applied at a *team* level, ask what education may help employees improve Agile teamwork and the flow of their work? A team may have goals focused on collaboration or learning to decompose work from user story to task. In the spirit of self-organizing teams, the Agile education vision is meant to be self-organized by the teams and their education needs.

- When applied at the *enterprise* level, ask what education can help the organization shift toward an Agile mindset and be more customer-value-driven by aligning roles more closely to the customer. This may start with basic Agile education that all employees should have such as Agile values and principles. An enterprise may then focus on applying self-organizing teams and applying the discovery mindset to meet customer needs.

As an added tip, any time an education item is time-consuming (one-day training, reading a book, and so), consider including it as a story with a story point value. As the owner works on this item, the story card can get moved across the board to indicate progress of the education. This highlights that education is considered valuable and illustrates the progress made in completing the education work item.

How will your teams be educated? An accumulation of education elements at different points in time will provide the comprehensive focus to help you, your team, and your organization. Consider applying a self-organized education vision that best serves your goal toward being Agile. You want to create a self-organizing education culture where employees are eager to learn, act, and give back to their community.

AGILE EDUCATION VISION EXERCISE

As you consider your individual education needs, document what Agile education you have had to date. Now review the two tables of topics in "Topics in the Agile Education Universe" section. Identify at least three topics you would like to learn more about. If you are sufficiently motivated, consider working with your team to do the same (for example, document what education the team has had and identify at least three topics that the team would like to learn more about). Now act on getting education on one of the topics within the next two weeks.

Building an Agile Community

Another form of education involves engaging the broader Agile community. Building an Agile community creates a continuous online and physical presence of Agile support. It provides a platform where employees collaborate with and educate each other. The platform encourages sharing progress and success stories. It provides employees the opportunity to share knowledge and give back to their community. Some building blocks for a healthy Agile community may include the following:

- *A website to share practices with the community.* When an Agile culture has been established, information such as culture, processes, glossary, pointers to education, and more are placed on the company Agile website so that teams have ready access to this information moving forward.

- *A venue for online social collaboration among the community.* This provides an online space for those on the Agile journey to pose questions to those outside of their teams to hear their thoughts, ideas, and lessons learned as well as to provide answers to others who are posing questions. This space provides an opportunity to discuss and collaborate on a variety of topics. It is also a place to share internal blog articles.

- *A venue for live forums for the community.* This is a place to host the latest advances in Agile by Agile coaches or where Agile champions can give back to the local community. These venues may include seminars and webinars as platforms to share the latest progress or support for Agile by leaders.

Is It Time to Learn?

Do you work in a continuous learning enterprise? Injecting a continuous learning mindset can help people understand that there is a lot to learn and that the knowledge gained can only help your enterprise succeed. It takes a repertoire of educational elements to achieve an Agile culture. An accumulation of education elements at different points in time will provide the comprehensive focus to help you, your team, and your enterprise.

Consider establishing an iterative and adaptable Agile education vision for yourself, your team, and your enterprise that best serves your goal for an Agile transformation and the delivery of customer value. Ultimately, you want to create a self-organizing learning culture where employees are willing and eager to learn new topics and make themselves and their enterprise more successful.

Applying a Discovery Mindset

The best way to recognize customer value is to be open to discovery.

—Mario Moreira

Bold moves in space exploration occurred because we dared to discover what lies beyond our world. Prior to our journeys into space, there were discoveries of unknown places on earth made by Portuguese, Italian, English, Spanish, Norse, Dutch, and Chinese explorers, among others. In our desire to discover the unknown and manage risks, a discovery mindset was applied.

The Portuguese didn't get to India on their first sailing trip, but, instead, each expedition ventured just a bit farther than the previous one. This allowed what was learned to travel back to Portugal. There, cartographers updated maps with the new information the explorers provided about the landscape, sea hazards, tides, details of the local flora and fauna, and sailing lanes for the next expedition.

People involved in space exploration had similar experiences. The moon wasn't reached the first time humans broke through the earth's atmosphere.

© Mario E. Moreira 2017
M. E. Moreira, *The Agile Enterprise*, DOI 10.1007/978-1-4842-2391-8_10

Instead, attempts where made to go a little farther into the universe with each rocket launch, testing the capability of the technology along the way. During the exploration of both the earth and space, a variety of innovations occurred, making it possible to get to the next leg of the journey.

A discovery mindset is a belief that acknowledges uncertainty and applies a variety of thinking approaches to continuously learn through incrementally gathering knowledge of what lies beyond. This includes a combination of a curiosity to learn and a drive to innovate. A discovery mindset isn't one where you voyage haphazardly about, but, instead, apply methodical concepts that lead to a more informed journey.

■ **Agile Pit Stop**   A discovery mindset is a belief that acknowledges uncertainty and applies a variety of thinking approaches to continuously learn what lies beyond.

A discovery mindset leads with establishing behaviors of learning as we go, focusing on what we don't know, and using various thinking approaches to gain knowledge toward the direction of customer value. A discovery mindset avoids certainty thinking as well as upfront and big-batch approaches.

Discovery Mindset for Business

From a business perspective, the discovery mindset ensures that you are not using your funding and investment toward a path of false certainty, but rather heading toward a path where you learn the direction. You course-correct when you discover that you are headed in the wrong direction.

Using a discovery mindset has four primary benefits. The first benefit is that it helps you adapt toward the direction of customer value and (hopefully) product success. The second is that it helps with innovative work because less is known at the beginning so discovery of customer value becomes more important. The third is that, in relation to a transformation (since discovery involves working in increments), it can be much easier for people to commit to a short-term experiment than to commit to a long-term, often unknown, future. The fourth benefit is that it helps move an enterprise toward an empirical and disciplined approach to work.

Enhancing the Culture with Discovery

In Chapter 5, I discussed the importance of activating an Agile culture within your Agile galaxy. This means all roles from team to management and operational roles (HR, finance, and so on) in all quadrants of the galaxy should embrace the Agile and discovery mindset. This enhances the third dimension of your Agile galaxy as illustrated in Figure 10-1.

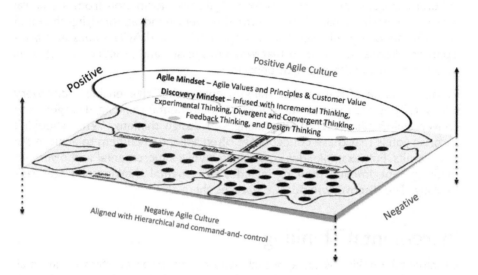

Figure 10-1. Third dimension of the Agile galaxy where the discovery mindset lives

It is within this third dimension of your Agile galaxy that the discovery mindset and thinking approaches belong. The discovery mindset complements the Agile cultural attributes of COMETS (Collaboration, Ownership, Motivation, Empowerment, Trust, and Safety) discussed in Chapter 7. While COMETS are attributes you want to see in the people within an Agile galaxy, the discovery mindset contains the approaches people can use to methodically learn what is valuable to the customer. The goal of both is to cultivate positive behaviors. The three-dimensional view can help you understand your starting point, where the discovery mindset is occurring, and where you need to focus.

Leading with a Discovery Mindset

Imagine that you started your Agile transformation with a discovery mindset and thinking approaches instead of mechanical practices. The advantage of leading with a focus on mindset is that it sets the tone for the behaviors that you are looking for in people. Additionally, it avoids the trap of people thinking that Agile is about mechanically applying Agile processes or practices.

■ **Agile Pit Stop**   Leading with a discovery mindset and thinking approaches sets the tone for the behaviors needed for an Agile culture and how to adapt toward customer value.

As discussed in Chapter 5, a mechanical implementation of Agile processes and practices tends to ignore the cultural aspects of Agile. Since Agile is a cultural change, consider starting your Agile transformation from a cultural perspective with a strong focus on the discovery mindset. Readying the mind with the discovery mindset, thinking approaches, and Agile values and principles conditions the mind so that when processes and practices are applied, they are done so with the right behaviors.

What are some of the various thinking approaches that enable a discovery mindset? They are incremental thinking, experimental thinking, divergent and convergent thinking, feedback thinking, and design thinking. What shouldn't surprise you is that these concepts are often applied in tandem to achieve the best results. For example, design thinking involves incremental and divergent thinking. Experimental thinking includes incremental thinking and feedback thinking. The discovery mindset embraces them all.

Incremental Thinking

Incremental thinking is an approach where you embrace thinking in small pieces and in short timeframes. Instead of making big bets with limited knowledge, you take smaller bets and use what was learned in the current increment to course-correct your direction for the next increment. This reduces risk and prevents investment from going down the wrong path for too long.

In Agile, there are the concepts of iteration and increment. These two concepts are confusing for some in that they are often used interchangeably while they are in fact different. An iteration is the period of time a team works to build something. In Scrum, the concept of a sprint is used to provide a team with a period of time (for instance, one to four weeks) to produce a deliverable. The deliverable from an iteration is termed an increment.

An increment is the outcome of an iteration and, if aligned with the Agile values and principles, should produce working software or product. As it relates to incremental thinking, the goal is to move away from big-batch delivery and instead think in smaller batches aligning with the Agile principle of "deliver working software frequently, from a couple of weeks to a couple of months, with a preference to the shorter timescale." Figure 10-2 illustrates the incremental thinking approach toward customer value.

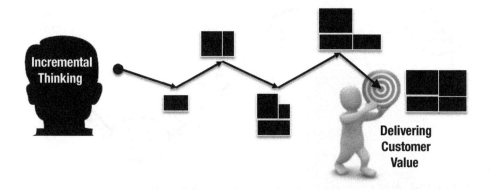

Figure 10-2. Applying incremental thinking toward delivering customer value

Incremental thinking supports the concept of learning what the customer finds as valuable. Incremental thinking allows us to shed the dangerous attitude of pretend or arrogant certainty and instead explore what the customer needs. Instead of fixing customer needs up front, you iteratively learn your way to what the customer finds valuable by building increments of product that the customer can inspect and provide feedback for.

Experimental Thinking

Experimental thinking is an approach where you embrace a more systematic way of navigating toward certainty. Instead of guessing, this type of thinking uses a scientific approach where you hypothesize your next move. It is meant to provide more rigorous methods toward identifying customer value.

As you consider customer needs at the beginning of a project, you are at the time where you have the least information or evidence of the need. Instead of guessing, you establish a hypothesis for the next increment of work based on the information currently available and what may be the right direction.

As illustrated in Figure 10-3, you conduct your experiment and apply measurable data and feedback loops (that is, validating with customer demonstrations and more) to identify what you have learned. The results provide you knowledge and help you determine where to go next by either affirming or rejecting the hypothesis. Then you take what was learned into the next incremental experiment where adaptation occurs.

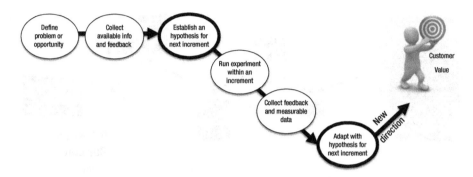

Figure 10-3. Applying experimental thinking toward customer value

In the context of a business or new product idea, a discovery mindset helps you systematically learn whether an idea has value to your customers. Each change—whether a new feature, a change to an existing feature, or removal of a feature—should start with a hypothesis.

Power of the Hypothesis

A hypothesis is an idea or supposition based on current evidence as your starting point. The ingredients of this hypothesis are a hypothesis statement related to a customer need, time-boxed iteration, and customer feedback to prove or disprove a direction. In other words, it should no longer be good enough to guess which direction you should move.

Any affirmation or rejection of a hypothesis is not meant to be a judgment. Instead, it should be looked at as a course-correction toward customer value. If you have hypothesized correctly, you may invest further effort into continuing with the hypothesis. If you have not, create a new hypothesis based on the feedback received.

■ **Agile Pit Stop**   The best way to learn what the customer wants is by establishing a hypothesis and then running an experiment to determine if it is valid or not.

Drilling down, the elements of the hypothesis statement should include the change you are trying, the impact you expect from the change, and who should be impacted. The "change" should include the name of the change (feature, app, and so on). The "impact" should be quantifiable and data-driven involving an increase or decrease in a current measure. The "who" should include a persona or market segment that is being targeted. You may also add a time-frame for how long the test will run. Here are three examples:

- The new feature will be liked by 60% of our current user base in the next demonstration event.

- The new checkout design will decrease drop rates by 30% for shoppers who have goods in shopping carts over the next 30 days.

- The new app will increase revenue by 10% for mobile app users over the next four weeks.

You should consider certainty-building activities as an experiment. It is important to have a discovery mindset in all of the work you do, particularly when it comes to moving toward the direction of customer value.

Divergent and Convergent Thinking

Divergent thinking embraces an approach that promotes collaboration to generate ideas and numerous solutions with no censoring of ideas. Once an allocated time box to share and discuss ideas and options is concluded, divergent thinking is paired with convergent thinking to more quickly come to consensus. This is illustrated in Figure 10-4.

A traditional divergent technique is brainstorming, which focuses on generating ideas in an unstructured manner. But due to the fast pace of most companies, we are quick to shut down brainstorming by criticizing the opinions of others (including our own). Because of this, I recommend ten minutes of silence for all brainstorming activities to ensure all ideas get a chance to be revealed prior to any discussion.

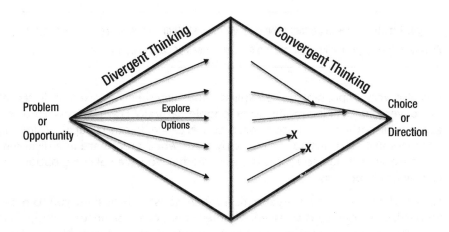

Figure 10-4. Divergent and convergent thinking

People generate their ideas with no discussion so no one's ideas are dismissed by people who are more assertive. As you may guess, often the quiet team members (that is, introverts) have great ideas and a divergent "quiet" period allows the talented introverts to get their ideas on the table. The key to divergent thinking is that there is absolutely no censorship of ideas or solutions coming forth. All ideas are valuable.

Once the divergent time box is concluded, it is time to commence with convergent thinking. Convergent thinking is an approach to systematically limit your options and focus on one direction. From divergent thinking, there are often more ideas and possible solutions than can be handled.

In convergence, various techniques can be applied to bring together ideas. This may include looking for affinities where common themes may arise from some of the ideas. It can also include red-dot voting, a non-confrontational prioritization technique where people quietly place their dots on what they think are the top ideas for solving the problem. Ideas with the largest number of dots are discussed until a top option is selected.

The value of divergent thinking cannot be underscored. Spending as little as a few hours of collaborative brainstorming coming up with ideas is a drop in the bucket compared to the thousands of hours spent in building a solution. The tiny investment is worth ensuring that many options are made available.

Also, the divergent and convergent pairing can occur in a continuous manner. For every customer need expressed in a user story in the beginning of an iteration or sprint, divergent thinking can be used in sprint planning to consider options prior to jumping into the sprint where you build the customer need. When the next iteration or sprint begins, you move back to divergent thinking to consider options for the next set of user stories prior to embarking on the sprint.

■ **Agile Pit Stop** It is important to be explicit about whether you are in a divergent or convergent thinking mode so people know if you are soliciting ideas or closing down options.

It is also very important to be explicit about whether you are in a divergent or convergent thinking mode. Some people naturally gravitate toward divergence while others gravitate toward convergence. It can reduce tensions in interpersonal relationships to explicitly state whether you are in a divergent or convergent mode so that it is clear whether you are soliciting options or closing down options.

Finally, when you have an organization that is constantly pushing you to move forward, convergence is stressed, whether consciously or unconsciously. This is a detriment to innovation and being open to numerous possible solutions.

It may take an organization to explicitly initiate divergent thinking to achieve more innovation and ideas.

DIVERGENT/CONVERGENT EXERCISE

Identify two people for a three-minute discussion on the topic of re-organizing desks in the department. Before starting, secretly instruct one person in the pair to think in a divergent mode where he or she attempts to brainstorm ideas and options of how the desks can be reorganized. Secretly instruct the other person in the pair to think in a convergent mode where he or she attempts to come up with one choice. Upon conclusion, ask the participants how the conversation went. Was it frustrating for them? Have they encountered this frustration before?

Feedback Thinking

Feedback thinking is the belief where you embrace feedback, realizing how it provides you with information that can guide you toward what is valuable. Collecting feedback can shatter the certainty mindset since feedback will often highlight differences in what is stated upfront as customer value and what a customer actually finds valuable. Key to feedback thinking is not just capturing customer feedback, but using it to adapt toward customer value.

Applying feedback thinking can be a big shift for some organizations that embrace a certainty mindset, don't currently collect and apply customer feedback, or don't intuitively understand the value it will provide in building products of customer value. Feedback thinking means that there is a pervasive need to collect customer feedback via feedback loops in as many areas across the delivery axis as possible, as illustrated in Figure 10-5.

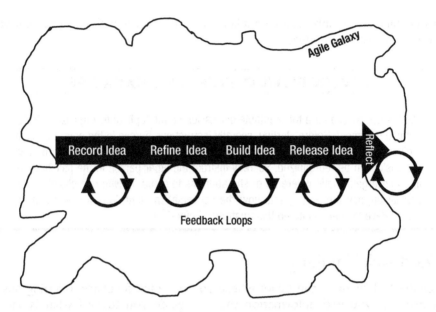

Figure 10-5. Applying feedback loops to support feedback thinking

Feedback thinking brings in many voices to validate the direction through multiple feedback loops and is crucial to help course-correct toward customer value. The primary feedback collected should be from the actual customer. The customer is the most important voice in shaping the direction of the product. Customer feedback should be the basis for driving a majority of your decisions and setting the direction of customer value.

A benefit of feedback thinking is you gain real-time information on what the customer finds valuable since what customers find valuable changes over time. Incremental thinking along with feedback thinking to build customer value allows you not only to learn what the customer wants but also to gauge if there is a shift in the marketplace. This real-time data (in other words, feedback) allows you to adapt to the ever-changing customer landscape.

Feedback thinking is an integral part of the discovery mindset. Feedback works well when paired with incremental thinking, experimental thinking, divergent and convergent thinking, and design thinking. To learn more about how to apply feedback thinking and put customer feedback into action, consider reading Chapter 14.

FEEDBACK ON YOUR SPACESHIP EXERCISE

On a piece of paper, draw the best-looking spaceship you can draw in 30 seconds. Then on five separate pieces of paper, draw five more spaceships (each in 30 seconds). Then ask 10 people which spaceship they like best. Do you think they will like the first spaceship you drew? The odds are that your first drawing (that is, your first idea) is rarely your best, and people have varying ideas of which is the best-drawn spaceship; hence, feedback is important.

Design Thinking

Design thinking is an approach where teams have the space to consider the best options for solving a problem. It empowers those with the most knowledge to work through a solution. It also involves applying iterative and validated customer learning. It combines some of the incremental and divergent thinking in its approach.

Illustrated in Figure 10-6, design thinking starts by understanding the problem or opportunity by empathizing with the customer. To initially align with customers, observe them dealing with the problem or talk to those who may benefit from the opportunity. Then, based on what you learned, define (or redefine) what you think is the problem or opportunity. (See Figure 10-6.)

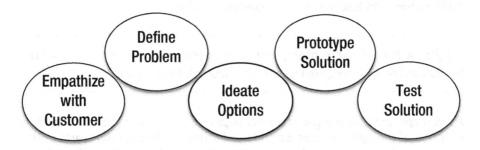

Figure 10-6. Design thinking approach

Design thinking applies divergent approaches to come up with options on how to solve the problem. This may include research and bringing people together to brainstorm ideas. From the top ideas, collaboratively converge by having the team self-organize around an option that the team thinks will solve the problem or address the opportunity. Convergent approaches such as affinity and red-dot voting may be used to select an option.

As you approach prototyping the chosen solution, apply a hypothesis to prove or disprove the option chosen for a more systematic way of navigating toward certainty and customer value. Test the option by using an iterative and incremental framework to validate if the hypothesis (that is, option) moves you toward the direction of customer value. The iterative framework may be one of the Agile processes that exist today.

Once an experiment is concluded, examine the results. Based on the results, either move forward with the original option or adapt toward another option. This requires customer involvement to continuously provide feedback to validate that you are moving in the right direction.

Designing thinking is a good way to bring together the employee and customer. As employees are collaboratively engaged and empowered to decide how to build customer value, customers are brought in via feedback loops to validate whether it meets customer needs.

Is It Time to Lead with the Discovery Mindset?

The discovery mindset and the thinking approaches are meant to create the behaviors for the Agile mindset to move the culture toward agility. They are great to ready-the-mind and set the tone for the behaviors that focus on customer value. Leading with mindset activities avoids the trap of believing that mechanically applying an Agile process makes you Agile. Instead, it is a great way to achieve the Agile behaviors that can help your enterprise shift to an Agile culture and lead you toward customer value.

■ **Agile Pit Stop** Consider infusing incremental, experimental, divergent and convergent, feedback, and design thinking into the early part of your Agile transformation.

As you approach your Agile transformation or you realize that you need an injection of the Agile mindset, consider educating leadership and teams with a discovery mindset and the thinking approaches it embraces. Consider infusing incremental thinking, experimental thinking, divergent and convergent thinking, feedback thinking, and design thinking into your Agile environment in the early part of your transformation.

For additional material, I suggest the following:

- *The Innovative Mindset: Five Behaviors for Accelerating Breakthroughs* by John Sweeney and Elena Imaretska, Wiley, 2015

- *Design Thinking: Four Steps to Better Software* by Jeff Patton, Stickyminds, 2000

Visualizing the Enterprise Idea Pipeline

An enterprise idea pipeline provides transparency of your options and allows you to quickly be aware of and respond to high-value work.

—Mario Moreira

Much of Agile implementations focus on the work within a product backlog. This is a good start and helps a team and product owner focus on the development work ahead. When an enterprise is small or focused on just a few products, the initial ideas can go directly into the product backlog. What happens when the organization is medium to large? How do you view the incoming ideas in a timely manner and how do you make investment decisions on where to focus? The answer is via enterprise idea pipeline.

© Mario E. Moreira 2017
M. E. Moreira, *The Agile Enterprise*, DOI 10.1007/978-1-4842-2391-8_11

Pipeline of Ideas

The enterprise idea pipeline provides three primary benefits to an enterprise. First, it is a channel that provides an end-to-end flow of ideas from the moment they are recorded to when they are released and reflected upon. Second, it is the enterprise-level portfolio backlog of ideas. Third, it is meant to highlight high-value ideas the moment they come in so that the enterprise does not miss the idea's window of opportunity.

The culture needed for the enterprise idea pipeline is one where the enterprise immediately considers ideas as they come in because they are based on a current problem or opportunity. You don't wait for the next budget cycle to consider the idea. The pipeline is a more adaptable way of managing the portfolio of work across your enterprise since ideas can be admitted anytime and feedback may change its priority or reshape the idea. Also, the pipeline brings enterprise-wide visibility and transparency to the work occurring within an organization.

■ **Agile Pit Stop**   For an enterprise idea pipeline to operate effectively, it must be in a culture where ideas are immediately considered without waiting for the next budget cycle.

Before moving on, what is an idea? An idea is something that is deemed as valuable but has not yet been created. At the moment it is recorded, it may be small or large. Depending on its level of customer value, it may become work that is worthy of evolving into a product or service.

As part of the Agile galaxy, the enterprise idea pipeline is a working example of the delivery axis focused on delivering customer value, as illustrated in Figure 11-1. As the delivery axis represents the end-to-end flow of customer value from the recording of the idea to the point where it is released and then reflected upon, so is the enterprise idea pipeline.

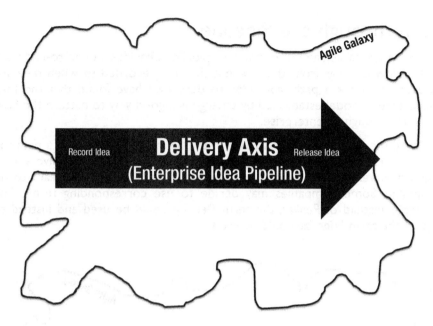

Figure 11-1. The enterprise idea pipeline is a working example of the delivery axis.

The enterprise idea pipeline is known by different names such as a portfolio backlog, enterprise kanban board, and idea pipeline. What makes all the terms similar is that they imply that the big ideas may eventually (or immediately) be worked on by teams. The enterprise idea pipeline acts as the parent and feeder to all of the product backlogs and helps you connect strategy and ideas to user stories (and even tasks) and vice versa.

An enterprise idea pipeline is primarily used in medium to large companies, when visibility is needed to make investment decisions across portfolios to better understand where the highest-value work lives. It also helps when there are dependencies across multiple products, or when ideas do not have an obvious resting place in a product backlog. When an enterprise is small and made up of a singular product, the product backlog acts as the enterprise idea pipeline as it contains the ideas that may be included in the future of that product. Even at the backlog level, new ideas need to be valued to ensure that the highest-value idea gets worked first. The moment there are multiple products, there may be a need for a portfolio-level backlog that becomes the pipeline for upcoming work.

Path through the Pipeline

As discussed earlier, an enterprise idea pipeline provides an end-to-end view of the flow of ideas from the moment they are recorded to when they are released. It offers a path from idea to delivery. I have found that the Idea Management model established by Emergn is a good way to pattern the flow of work through an enterprise.

Utilizing the first five patterns to form the 5R model, you create a path for your work. As illustrated in Figure 11-2, the five Rs consist of five stages: Record, Reveal, Refine, Realize, and Release. The 5R model is meant to be adaptable. Some companies may decide to use corresponding terms. For example, instead of *Realize*, the term *Develop* could be used and instead of *Reveal*, the term *Prioritize* could be used.

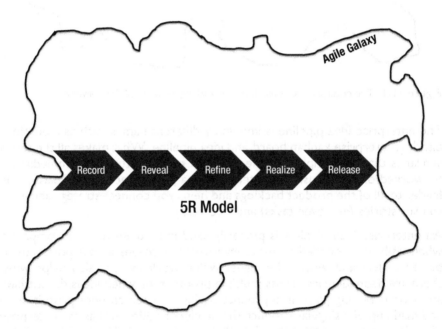

Figure 11-2. The 5R model as a path to deliverying customer value

Each stage represents a progression of the idea. It is important to note that the path isn't linear. Some ideas may get to the Reveal stage and are too low in value to move farther. Some ideas may get an increment cut in the Refine stage and then, once in the Realize stage, feedback is received from customers in a demo that find it more valuable, which requires updating the value in the Record stage.

YOUR 5R MODEL EXERCISE

Review the stages of the 5R model (Record, Reveal, Refine, Realize, and Release). What terms could be used in your enterprise that represent each of the stages in the 5R model? Draw out your example.

Recording the Idea

The *Record* stage is a place to begin documenting what is known about the new idea. The documentation should be visible and transparent to everyone in the enterprise. Who typically submits or records ideas? Effectively anyone can record an idea, but more commonly it is a product owner, a portfolio leader, a business or marketing leader, or a manager who is in touch with customers. Recording the idea should include a description, persona or market segment, the value, the risks of doing the idea or not doing the idea, and the assumptions being made. Figure 11-3 illustrates a simple example of recording an idea.

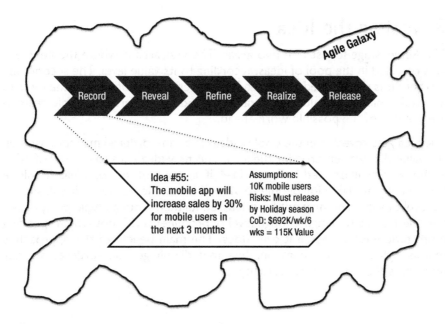

Figure 11-3. Simple example of recording an idea

Within an Agile context, limit the amount of time spent on documenting the idea's details since the idea has not yet been committed for work. The documentation should provide enough information to gain a general understanding of the idea, but not so much that it is a waste of time if the idea is not selected to work on. For example, avoid writing a bulky business case for the idea since this takes a lot of effort this early in the stage of the idea.

There are several ways that an idea can be recorded. It can be in a *freestyle* format with the necessary information. It can be in a *hypothesis* format, as discussed in Chapter 10, along with any additional information. Alternatively, it can be written using a *Lean Canvas* format. You can learn more about how to capture ideas using a Lean Canvas in Chapter 13.

A key detail for the Record stage is the proposed value of the idea. I recommend using cost of delay (CoD) and CoD divided by duration (CD3) since this provides data on how much money you lose weekly or monthly by delaying the value delivered. You can learn more about CoD and CD3 in Chapter 12. However, other value techniques may be used. Once the idea, including description, persona, value, risks, and assumptions, is recorded, the idea is added to the enterprise idea pipeline, where it gets revealed.

Revealing the Idea

The *Reveal* stage focuses on two areas. The first area is where the new idea gets revealed in the pool of ideas, according to its value level. The second one is where it is determined if the idea has high enough value so that the owners and stakeholders of value (for example, product owners) and Agile team(s) are notified of the possible work ahead.

The idea gets revealed in the pool of ideas in a rank-ordered manner based on the value that was entered for the idea. This new idea rises to its level of value in the pool, as illustrated in Figure 11-4. If it is one of the top ideas, it will be prominently available for people to view. If it has a lower value, it will sink to its level of value and may not be discussed further. From an Agile perspective, if it doesn't rise to a high-enough level of prominence, it's not worth spending more time until it does, if it ever does. The main benefit of this approach is that as high-value ideas come in, they immediately get rank-ordered so they don't miss their market opportunity.

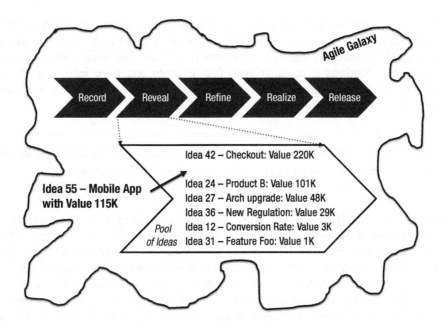

Figure 11-4. The idea moves into the pool of ideas, where it gets revealed

Who typically reviews and evaluates the recorded idea? Owners or stakeholders of value (such as product owners and chief product owners) and those that help drive investment decisions (for example, business leaders, marketing, and senior management) should be the ones who do this work. They should all have a stake in the success of the work and operate with a discovery mindset.

If the idea floats toward the top of the pool in your enterprise idea pipeline based on its value, several things occur. First, there should be a healthy discussion surrounding the idea. The owner or contributor of the idea should share the details, the risk of doing or not doing the work, how the value was calculated, and the assumptions being made in calculating the value. It is important for the owners of value to periodically check the pool of ideas so that high-value ideas are promptly discussed.

In an effort to continue to validate the value of the idea, stakeholders should challenge the assumptions made that determined the value. Toward the beginning of the idea journey is when the least amount of information is known about the idea. Challenging the assumptions of value is beneficial to the health of the enterprise as it will determine where investments in people and resources are being made. Challenging assumptions of value also reduces gamesmanship of the data's value.

Let's consider a hypothetical situation: The owner of the idea assumed that the potential market for the idea included a hundred million customers. However, current data indicates that it is only twenty million. The importance of challenging assumptions is to start with fair assumptions, ergo fair value. More information on challenging assumptions can be found in Chapter 2 (more general) and 12 (specific to value).

■ **Agile Pit Stop** Challenging the assumptions of value is beneficial to the health of the enterprise as it will determine where investments in people and resources are being made.

Once discussion is concluded, changes are made to the idea, which may include updating details about the idea and adapting the value. The idea floats to the level of its adapted value. If it continues to appear that the idea is of high value, it is time to consider the team (or teams) that will work on it and the dependencies the team may have on other teams and resources. Once identified, the team is notified of the idea coming its way. The purpose is to gauge how much work that team already has on its plate. From here, people and prioritization decisions can be made.

When making people decisions, if it is clear that this team is the target for a lot of high-value work, then it behooves the enterprise to add people to the team or adapt another team's skills to that type of work. When making prioritization decisions, if it is clear that this new idea has a higher value than current work in the team backlog, then a re-ordering of work should occur.

If a high-value idea requires the help of two or more teams, a chief product owner or portfolio leader can gauge how much work each team has on its plates and when it can pull the work into its backlog based on its current velocity during the Reveal stage. The goal by the end of the *Reveal* stage is for teams to provide a pull signal for the high-value work at the earliest possible moment so the idea misses as little of its market window as possible.

In order for a new high-value idea to get pulled in a reasonable timeframe by the teams, a discussion on slack time should occur. If teams' backlogs are so full that it is makes it hard for them to pull work in the foreseeable future, then you may not be allowing enough slack in the system. The benefit of slack is twofold. First, slack helps a team consistently deliver on their commitments with quality work since important design and refactoring emerges. Second, slack allows time to respond to emergencies, time to explore high value work, and time for innovation. Without slack, a lot of high-value ideas could easily sit in a wait state for some time.

Refining the Idea

The *Refine* stage consists of a combination of the team(s)' beginning to understand the idea, the team(s)' beginning to decompose the idea into an increment and user stories, and their continuing to validate the value of the idea. When the high-value idea sitting in the reveal pool gets pulled by the team(s), it is ready to get refined. The intent is to move away from the big upfront mindset where months are spent attempting to document all of the requirements. Instead, collaboratively focus on a slice of the idea where feedback is use to gain a better understanding of the value of the idea.

■ **Agile Pit Stop** The intent of the Refine stage is to move away from big upfront requirements and instead focus on a slice of the idea in a collaborative and evolving manner.

Who should be involved in refining and decomposing ideas into smaller pieces? Those that have ownership over products (product owners) and those that self-organize on how to build those products (teams) should be involved. In this case, everyone on the team should be involved including developers, testers, architects, database, and UX. They should all have a stake in the success of the work and be educated and operate with a discovery mindset. Also, you want the whole team involved so that when it is time to build the idea increment in the Realize stage, the full team has first-hand knowledge of the work involved in the Refine stage.

While you may have learned that more than one team is involved in the idea during the Reveal stage, it is in the Refine stage where you learn the details of the dependencies. An idea may cross team and division boundaries. During the Refine stage is when the beginning of cross-team coordination should occur.

It can be challenging to take an idea and decompose it into epics and user stories. One recommendation is user story mapping. The short-form story mapping is both a visual practice that provides you with a view of how a user might use an idea (in other words, the product or service) and a decomposition practice that helps you consider how you may incrementally decompose the idea. Established by Jeff Patton, the visual portion helps the team understand the customer experience by imagining what the customer process might look like. This encourages the team to think through what the customer finds as valuable.

The decomposition portion of story mapping allows the team to think through a number of options of the customer experience, cut a slice of the idea as illustrated in Figure 11-5, and get feedback from the customer. The options within the slice become epics and user stories that represent the user experience. This helps both validate the value of the idea and ensures the idea is being built in a way to provide the best customer experience.

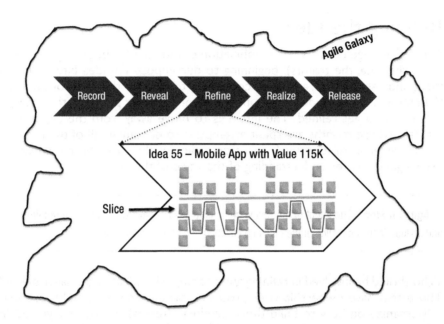

Figure 11-5. Decomposing the idea into options and cutting a slice using story mapping

A benefit of story mapping is that as you work incrementally, one slice at a time, you validate the value that has been ascribed to the idea. Instead of building the whole idea over months, you build a slice and then get actual customer feedback as to the value of the idea. The feedback is used to adapt toward customer value as well as to update the idea record and the value score.

You should *only* cut one slice at a time. You may learn that the first slice either provided the value or that the customer didn't find the idea valuable enough to move further. You can learn more about the details of story mapping and how to implement a story-mapping session in Chapter 16.

■ **Agile Pit Stop** Cutting increments of work via story mapping or use cases can help determine the value of an idea prior to the whole idea being built.

There are other ways to decompose ideas into increments. Use cases can be used to map interactions between actors (which can be personas) and a system within a particular environment to achieve a goal. Much like story mapping, the goal is to cut a slice or increment of work that represents one of those interactions and then show it to customers or users to get feedback on the value of the idea and the customer interface.

Another activity that helps decompose and, more importantly, better understand the business and technical detail of the work is the act of grooming (also known as Scrum refining). The end goal of the Refine stage is that you have a slice of work from the idea that should be in the form of epics and user stories that can be placed into your product backlog. Another goal is that you are aware of the dependencies and risks that can impact the work ahead and begin mitigating them.

Realizing the Idea

The *Realize* stage is the art and practice of building the idea into a working product. Commonly known as product or software development, it is the art of developing a product in a methodical manner. All team members who engage in building a product are involved in the Realize stage. Those involved should include all cross-functional team members such as development, quality assurance (QA), database, UX, documentation, education, and configuration management—effectively anyone who has the ability to turn the idea into a piece of customer value.

Agile Pit Stop   The PO prioritizes the work in the backlog, shares business context with the team, and incorporates customer feedback to better align with customer value.

In the Realize stage, the product owner has a strong role to prioritize the work in the backlog according to customer value, to share business context with the team, and to incorporate customer input and feedback as the idea evolves to better align with customer value.

In the Reveal stage, you may have learned that there is more than one team involved in building the increment of an idea. In the Refine stage, the teams should work together to cut the first increment. Now in the Reveal stage, the teams should establish communication touch points such as Scrum of Scrums to coordinate and collaborate as they build their pieces of the increment.

Within the Agile galaxy, it is in the Realize stage where you typically see Scrum and Kanban occurring. Irrespective of what Agile process used, an iterative process should be applied so that you can iteratively plan, build, inspect, and adapt the deliverable toward customer value.

The primary activity involved in the Realize stage is to develop an idea. From the Refine stage, the epics and user stories from the slice or increment make their way into the product or team backlog(s), as illustrated in Figure 11-6. The team(s) should further groom the epics into user stories and gain more detail about the user stories. From there, an iterative approach should be used to develop and test the product.

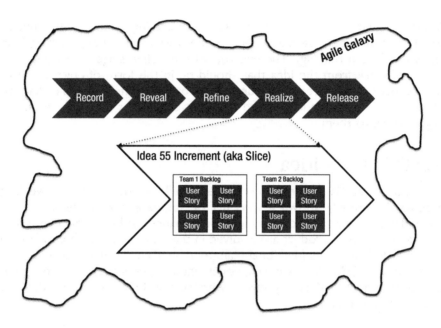

Figure 11-6. Work flows from the Refine stage into the backlogs

Iterative and incremental Agile engineering practices should be applied in the Realize stage. This may include eXtreme Programming (XP) practices such as pair programming, continuous integration, test-driven development, collective code ownership, refactoring, and more. Also, integration testing should occur for those instances where two or more teams are working on an idea. This should include system, performance, load, and any other tests that may be needed. The goal of Agile is that when the product is completed at the end of an iteration, it should be potentially shippable.

Because the Realize stage results in a potentially shippable product (that is, something to actually see), customer feedback loops should be used to validate if the idea is valuable to customers. There should be a concerted effort to invite customers based on personas to the demonstrations to gain valuable feedback to ensure the idea is being developed in the direction of customer value. Also, sales and marketing may initiate a launch plan for making current and potential customers aware of the new or updated product.

Releasing the Idea

The *Release* stage is the activity that converts the in-house built idea and launches it into the public, as illustrated in Figure 11-7. The goal of Agile is that by the end of an iteration, it should include activities to make the idea potentially shippable. Then there may be final integration testing, code preparation, packaging, and launch activities in release.

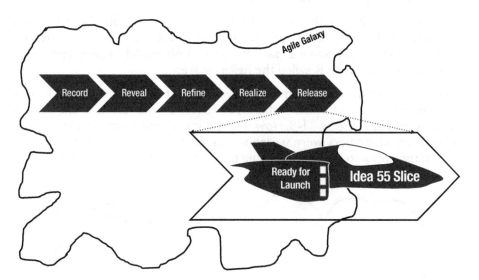

Figure 11-7. Launching the idea into the market

In some cases, there may be final integration activities, particularly when there are two or more teams working on an increment of an idea to ensure both pieces execute together. Final integration testing provides an opportunity to perform final testing to include system, integration, performance, load, and any other tests that may be needed. This should be limited since such testing or a significant portion should occur in the Realize stage.

Code preparation and packaging begins with version controlling the code used for the release. From there, activities vary by production platform. For a web site, identifying executable code and updating the website with the new code may be all that is needed. For mobile applications, packaging the new release onto an app store for people to download and providing any terms and conditions may be enough. For on-premise products where they are installed onto desktops and servers, setting up a downloadable web location for code or burning the code onto disks, packaging user guides, and crafting terms and conditions are part of the process.

Another aspect of the Release stage may be to execute the launch plan drafted by marketing and sales. This activity communicates to the current and potential customers a bit about the new increment that is now on the market. Once a release occurs, you should update the enterprise idea pipeline showing that the first increment has been released.

Reflecting on the Idea

The five stages of the 5R model have been explored: Record, Reveal, Refine, Realize, and Release. Some collapse the 5R model to 4Rs (Reveal, Refine, Realize, and Release). Some expand the 5R to a 6R model. I have found it prudent to include a sixth R called the *Reflect* stage.

While most product development life cycles end at the Release stage, I believe it is important to add a phase where you reflect on the results of the deliverable, as shown in Figure 11-8. How well did it do once it was on the market? How many customers were willing to pay for the product? Was the deliverable satisfactory to customers? Is the product being used as advertised?

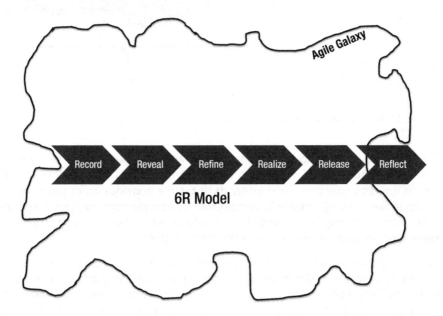

Figure 11-8. 6R model includes the Reflect stage

There are many types of feedback loops that can be used to gain an understanding of the product. This is why reflecting is very important in understanding the real value of the product. The feedback helps you determine how to adapt the idea for the future.

Most importantly, the Reflect stage ensures that you revisit the value placed on the idea in the Record and Reveal stages. Did you make the money you thought per what was written into the value or cost of delay of the idea? It is critical to the integrity of the R model that those involved understand that, once released, you will reflect on the idea and gauge its real value. While challenging the assumptions of value for an idea in the Reveal stage reduces gaming the value score, having to reflect on the actual value data once released can help further reduce any gamesmanship of the value data at the beginning.

REFLECTION OF VALUE EXERCISE

Consider the last release you were a part of. Attempt to find the value data that was used to promote the idea. This may be in the form of return on investment (ROI), cost of delay (CoD) or potential revenue data. Then look for the actual revenue made from the release. What was the difference? Has anyone actually compared the initial value data with the actual?

Are Your Enterprise Ideas Visible?

The enterprise idea pipeline provides you with an end-to-end view of the flow of ideas from the moment they are recorded to when they are released. As an enterprise-level portfolio backlog of ideas, it is meant for the enterprise to respond to high-value ideas the moment they come so the enterprise does not miss the idea's window of opportunity.

It is a more adaptable way of managing the portfolio of work across your enterprise and responding to feedback. Specifically, it is meant to highlight high-value ideas the moment they come into an enterprise so that they can be worked on almost immediately and the enterprise can take full advantage of the window of opportunity. Whatever you chose to call the enterprise idea pipeline, it holds the big ideas that will eventually (or immediately) be worked on by the teams. The enterprise idea pipeline is the parent to all of the product backlogs and helps you connect ideas to user stories.

The operation of the enterprise idea pipeline feeds right into your enterprise Agile budgeting and investment process. It can help you see where your high-value work is. You can learn more about effective Agile and continuous budgeting in Chapter 19.

For additional material, I suggest the following:

- *Lifecycles Are Good, an Idea Management Model is Best* by Andrew Husak, Emergn Limited, 2016

- *User Story Mapping: Discover the Whole Story, Build the Right Product* by Jeff Patton, O'Reilly Media, 2014

Prioritizing with Cost of Delay

Throwing a bunch of products against a wall to see what sticks is a recipe for disaster.

—Chapter co-author David Grabel

At the height of Microsoft's market domination and valuation, Bill Gates and Rich Balmer were interviewed by a major news magazine. They said that Microsoft had too much to do and not enough resources. If it was true for Microsoft, it is probably true for every single company in the world. Organizations have too many good ideas. Trying to do all of them clogs the system and little gets done. In order to deliver the most customer value in the shortest possible time, you must prioritize. There are many ways to prioritize. Which one is best for you?

What happens when a company does not prioritize? When teams have a history of being late, some leaders respond by asking for everything on the wish list. They assume that if they ask for everything, they will at least get something. Paradoxically, the reverse is true.

© Mario E. Moreira 2017
M. E. Moreira, *The Agile Enterprise*, DOI 10.1007/978-1-4842-2391-8_12

Focusing on Customer Value

When an organization works on too many ideas at once, the overhead and context switching slow teams down. The more things you start, the fewer things you finish. Even when you limit the work in progress (WIP) to the capacity of the development teams, you often overload related organizations—manufacturing, sales and marketing, training, or customer support. In her book, *Manage Your Project Portfolio*, Johanna Rothman[1] states that it is the responsibility of portfolio managers to reduce WIP.

When organizations ignore customer value, the portfolio of work can get filled with low-value items. Capacity limits force companies to ignore better opportunities. To maximize business outcomes, you need an objective way of selecting the programs that will deliver the highest customer value. In Chapter 11, the Record stage was referenced in the enterprise idea pipeline. In Record, a value is used to rank order ideas to help the enterprise focus on the highest-value work. Prioritization methods help you come up with an optimal rank order. The best ones will provide an objective value or score.

Highlighting Prioritization Methods

When working with teams and projects, you may have used some of the simpler, qualitative methods for prioritizing the product backlog. Some teams just follow the product owner's (hopefully well-informed) opinion. Some other methods include MoSCoW (Must Have, Should Have, Could Have, Won't Have), "Buy a Feature," or HiPPO (Highest Paid Person's Opinion).

At the sprint level, it is the right and responsibility of the product owner (PO) to have unilateral responsibility of priorities in the product backlog. Good POs regularly meet with their stakeholders (customers, chief product owners, sales managers, architects, technical managers, and so on) to get input for prioritization. Some POs add structure to the process using one or more of the following prioritization methods:

- MoSCoW: This method helps frame the PO's thinking to define the smallest possible solution that could possibly work. This approach places a level of importance on each requirement including a wish-list container that helps bucket features or stories that should be recognized as having been considered and explicitly deferred or rejected. This approach succinctly explains the decisions that have been made and allows the team to focus on the "must haves."

---

[1]*Manage Your Project Portfolio* by Johanna Rothman, Pragmatic Bookshelf, 2016.

- Buy a Feature: This is an online "game" developed by Innovation Games (now Conteneo) to help POs choose the features to include in an upcoming release that would be most valuable to their customers or stakeholders. Each feature being considered is listed along with a "price." The price might be related to the estimated development cost or anticipated customer value. The players (customers) are each given a fixed amount of play money to spend on features. Expensive features may require customers to negotiate and pool their money. This is encouraged. Playing this game multiple times with different sets of customers can give the PO useful data on what is more likely to satisfy customers.

- HiPPO: Senior leaders typically have many years of experience in the industry. Even when they want their teams to own decisions, they feel that it's their duty to share their knowledge and offer opinions, particularly on priorities. If they are expressing an opinion, treat it as one of many inputs from the stakeholders. If they believe their opinion is the correct one, you might have to accept their opinion as the decision. This is known as HiPPO. If you sense a trace of epistemic arrogance, as discussed in Chapter 2, attempt to discourage this certainty thinking as this removes the opportunity of options and allows the enterprise to apply a discovery mindset toward customer value.

These are all qualitative prioritization methods. They are based on opinions and individual preferences. While qualitative methods are sufficient for product backlog and sprint-level planning, enterprise-level prioritization deserves economic justification. At this level, the stakes are too high to leave prioritization to subjective methods. When you have many good ideas, you need an economic rationale to help sort the high-value ideas from the lower-value ones that clutter your portfolio and distract people and investments.

■ **Agile Pit Stop**   Qualitative methods are sufficient for product backlog and sprint level planning. Enterprise-level prioritization deserves and requires economic justification.

Many organizations make portfolio-level decisions based on HiPPO. There are rare instances where companies have completely disrupted industries and dominated their markets by implementing the vision of a single leader. There are vey few visionaries like Steve Jobs who can provide that kind of vision. Even Steve Jobs could be wrong. Remember the Newton?

Some of the common economically based prioritization methods include Return on Investment (ROI) and Weighted Shortest Job First (WSJF). ROI is (Value/Effort)*Confidence, where value is typically measured in incremental revenue. WSJF is a ranking based on a subjective, linear, and relative business value. It factors in a relative-time criticality and risk reduction. Since all three of these factors are estimated on a linear scale of 1–10, any one of these factors can be over weighted and distort this subjective view of cost of delay. While these have been used in traditional organizations, they overlook some important elements that Agile enterprises need to consider.

Exploring Cost of Delay (CoD)

Since the goal of most companies is to make profits, it is important to understand the economic consequences of prioritization trade-offs. The best way to measure the value generated by an idea is the life-cycle profit impact, which is the incremental gross margin generated by that product over its useful life cycle. CoD measures the life-cycle profit impact over time and, therefore, is an excellent way to clarify both the value and urgency for new ideas in the pipeline. It is an economic-based method that allows companies to prioritize those ideas that will create the highest value by putting a price tag on time. As Don Reinertsen has said, "If you only quantify one thing, quantify the cost of delay."

CoD is the net change in forecasted gross margin per week. CoD is typically stated per week to support the granularity of the impact of priority trade-offs. If you have an annual forecast, divide by 52.

■ **Agile Pit Stop**　Cost of Delay (CoD) is an economic method that allows companies to prioritize those ideas that will create the highest customer value by putting a price tag on time.

By focusing on life-cycle profits, CoD makes it clear that prioritization decisions can be based on more than incremental revenue. Revenue is important, but it is only one of the four major ways in which an idea can impact profits. The contributors to life-cycle profitability are as follows:

1.　Increase revenue - Grow sales to new or existing customers with ideas that delight customers and increase market share. Disruptors increase market size and make the pie bigger.

2.　Protect revenue - When competitors or market conditions threaten the revenue stream. Ideas or innovations that improve current products can sustain current market share and revenue.

3. Reduce costs - Look for ways to increase efficiency that will reduce costs that are currently being incurred. This will improve the gross margin or profit contribution.

4. Avoid costs - Make improvements to keep the current costs constant. This eliminates costs that are not currently being incurred, but may be in the future. An example is conforming to new regulations to avoid fines.

Calculating Cost of Delay

A simple way to calculate the CoD is to determine the profit via all four contributors to profitability in a given year. It can also be done for a three-year period, and then divided by three. This CoD example will use a weekly figure to drive home the impact of priority trade-offs, so you divide the annual gain by 52. Here is the working calculation with examples:

CoD = (Contributors to Profitability including Increase Revenue + Protect Revenue + Decrease Costs + Avoid Costs)/52

- Example #1: Increasing conversion rate. You have an idea in the pipeline that would improve the customer experience on your website, projected to increase the conversion rate from 5.5% to 6.0% (or a 0.5% increase). If you have approximately ten million visits to your site per year, your average sales order is $32, and your average gross margin is 30%. The increased contribution to profitability from the additional revenue in one year is (10,000,000*$32*0.005*.30) or $480,000. The weekly CoD is $480,000/52 or $9,230. This is an example of CoD to increase revenue.

- Example #2: New regulations. The Consumer Protection Agency has issued a new regulation requiring increases in information security to counter the latest threats from hackers. The company ignored this regulation when it was issued. Now the security measures must be in place or the company will face fines of $100,000 per calendar day. Since we know the cost per day, the weekly CoD is $700,000. This is an example of CoD to avoid costs.

- Example #3: New mobile application. Customers have been asking for a mobile app to access financial products. Having this application available could retain about 240,000 current customers and add another 360,000 new customers in the next year. It is estimated that the company can make \$36,000,000 in a year. The weekly CoD is \$36,000,000/52 or \$692,308. This is an example of CoD to protect revenue and increase revenue.

As a word of caution, do not use the CoD as a forecast. It is only a prioritization tool. When the CoD is used as a forecast, it becomes the target on the back of the product owner. This can drive fear into the organization and impact the value of the CoD.

As we will see later, assumptions can greatly impact the CoD. By challenging assumptions and applying a uniform set of standards about assumptions, the CoD of different opportunities can be compared. Therefore, protect the value of assumptions driving these important conversations and prioritization.

COD EXERCISE

Pick two ideas from your current enterprise idea pipeline (or list of ideas). Working with your team, look at the relevant factors for life-cycle profitability and calculate the CoD. Make all of the details of your work visible. Does the CoD that you calculated change the ranking for either of these ideas?

Enterprise Value Curve

By using the CoD, you can understand where you can have a significant impact on profitability. Consider the value curve distribution of the value of ideas that companies typically work on. As shown in Figure 12-1, all too often, companies fund or initiate few of the really high-value ideas (whose CoD can be enormous) because they are so consumed by the low-value work.

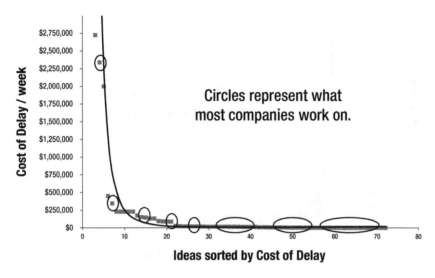

Figure 12-1. Typical company value curve distribution of ideas by CoD

Why do companies fund so many ideas with little or no value and do not fund ideas that are high value? It would seem logical that they would want to invest in primarily the ideas with the highest CoD. The problem is that companies tend to use subjective prioritization methods and trust their gut. They do not use economically based methods like CoD to make investment decisions.

When you use the CoD to select ideas from your pipeline, your value curve is more likely to resemble the one in Figure 12-2 than the typical value curve shown in Figure 12-1. You will be investing in the high-value ideas instead of the long tail of low-value ideas. Cutting the tail will increase profitability by allowing your company to focus on the highest-value work.

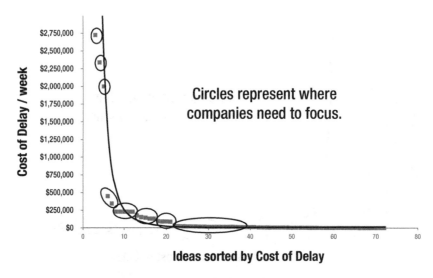

Figure 12-2. Ideal value curve distribution of ideas by CoD

Not all CoD profiles are equal. Some products have a very long lifetime and, once you hit the peak profitability, the ongoing profits are stable, as illustrated in Figure 12-3. In this case, the CoD is linear and constant. This analysis looks at the urgency profile associated with the product in its market. Other urgency profiles include short life cycle, peak affected by delay; long life cycle, peak affected by delay; and short life cycle, seasonal or date-driven.

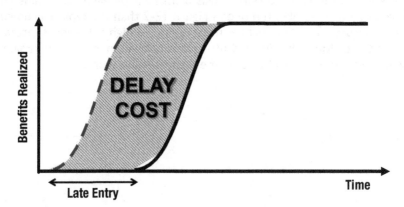

Figure 12-3. For ideas with a very long life with peak unaffected by delay

The "late entry" line highlights the cost of delaying customer value, which means delaying the opportunity to increase profitability. The longer the late entry line, the more you miss. If you wait too long, a competitor can be first to market. This changes your urgency profile to "peak affected by delay, long life cycle" and can leave you with a smaller piece of the overall pie.

Calculating CD3 for a Value Score

In order to make optimal investment decisions, you have to include one more factor—duration. Some organizations would rather fund three medium-value projects that can be delivered quickly rather than one high-value project that could take years. To complete the analysis, you get an estimate of the duration for the project.

The estimate of duration should be consistently applied to ideas. You may use "dream" or "standard" duration. Dream duration is the shortest possible duration if you have all of the people and resources able to work on the idea, while standard duration is the typical duration when including all dependencies and wait states. I recommend dream duration, but either is fine when getting started.

Agile Pit Stop   CD3 value scores provide a rough rank order and highlight when ideas are orders of magnitude in value from other ideas. When CD3 value scores are in the same order, further investigation of the assumptions and alignment to strategy should be factored.

You can calculate a value score called CD3 (CoD divided by duration). CD3 asks for the CoD amount and then you divide by your duration method (dream or standard) = (for example, Cost of Delay/Duration).

- In Example #1 above, the CoD per week is $9,230. If the dream duration is three weeks, the CD3 value score is ($9,230/3) or 3,077 or 3K.

- In Example #2, the CoD per week is $700,000. If the dream duration is 24 weeks, the CD3 value score is ($700,000/24) or 29,167 or 29K.

- In Example #3, the CoD per week is $692,308. If the dream duration is six weeks, the CD3 value score is ($692,308/6) or 115,384 or 115K.

In these examples, you will notice that Example #3 is an order of magnitude larger than Example #2, and Example #2 has a CD3 score that is an order of magnitude larger then the CD3 in Example #1.

The intent of CD3 is to provide a rough rank order. With CD3 scores of 3K, 29K, and 115K, respectively, it is clear that Example #3 should be considered as the idea with the highest value. However, if you have a CD3 score of 3K and 4K, then further investigation of the assumptions and alignment to strategy should be factored into the decision on which one to work on next.

By calculating a CD3 score for every idea in your pipeline, you can rank order them during the Reveal stage to maximize your return, as illustrated in Figure 12-4. This can help you predict which idea will yield the biggest positive impact on profitability for the time invested. Since there is much to learn about CoD and CD3, consider reading *The Principles of Product Development Flow* by Donald Reinertsen[2] and the Black Swan Farming's website.[3]

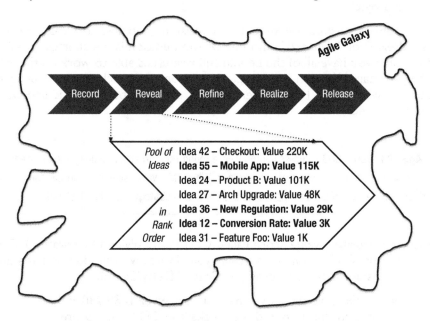

Figure 12-4. Rough rank order of Ideas by CD3 value score

Challenging Assumptions about CoD

CoD is calculated early in the idea life-cycle. As a result, in order to calculate the CoD, many assumptions have to be made. As part of transforming toward an Agile culture, it is important to apply a discovery mindset that includes positively challenging assumptions so that you can better understand the idea and you can better ensure that the idea is of the value it states or adapts accordingly for the betterment of the enterprise.

For Example #1, which is focused on increasing conversion rate, by challenging the assumptions, you learn some readily available facts such as the number of small businesses in North America. As you challenge the 0.5% increase from 5.5% to 6.0%, you learn that this conversion rate is based on a history of similar products. Some data has a high degree of confidence based on the data warehouse and some are a guess. It is important to know which is which.

[2]*The Principles of Product Development Flow* by Donald Reinertsen, Celeritas Publishing, 2009
[3]Black Swan Farming: http://blackswanfarming.com/cost-of-delay/, Black Swan Farming Limited

---

Agile Pit Stop   When moving to an Agile culture, positively challenge CoD assumptions in order to better understand the idea and provide a more objective rank order for the enterprise.

The PO might argue that the conversion rate would actually increase to 7% while the experience designers might defend the original 6% estimate. You could design a quick prototype to validate with customers to see which increase is more realistic. While different assumptions can result in widely varying initial calculations for the CoD and CD3, this process allows you to make those assumptions more visible.

When you do challenge assumptions, make sure you use open-ended questions. For example, use questions such as the following: What led you to that conclusion? What do you think the level of uncertainty is? What is your riskiest assumption? What information do you need to validate this?

When people have widely different calculations, you can challenge the assumptions behind those calculations beginning in the Reveal stage. By having reasoned conversations about those assumptions and ironing out those differences, you can get a consensus on the likely CoD and value score by applying CD3. When the value scores or rankings are based on subjective, gut feelings, those discussions can turn negative.

CHALLENGING ASSUMPTIONS EXERCISE

Have two separate teams calculate the CoD for the same idea in your pipeline. Each team should clearly document all of their assumptions. Was the CoD the same, close, or far apart? If there is a wide discrepancy, examine the assumptions and see if you can identify the differences of opinion. If so, have a conversation about why different teams made different assumptions and see if you can close that gap. These discussions can be very revealing and lead to a quick consensus on the prioritization.

Are You Cutting the Tail?

Prioritization can take many forms, from gut feelings to qualitative research to quantitative research. Since selecting the right enterprise ideas to invest in will have a major impact on the company's profitability, it makes sense to evaluate these ideas using an economic approach. CoD and CD3 are good economic methods for prioritizing ideas in the enterprise idea pipeline.

By working on the highest value ideas, it exposes the tail of low-value work that is left. The question is, will you cut the tail? It may be more challenging than you think because people will come up with many reasons why that work is important. If you apply a value-based model for identifying low-value work, you can begin making better investment decisions.

If you are not already doing so, try using CoD and CD3 for prioritizing your current list of on-deck ideas. Plot them in a value curve showing the highest CoD as your first idea and the lowest as your last. This plot is likely to look similar to Figure 12-1. Are you ignoring high-value ideas? Are you investing too much in the long tail of low-value ideas? How can you cut the tail?

For additional material, I suggest the following:

- *Manage Your Project Portfolio: Increase your Capacity and Finish More Projects* by Johanna Rothman, Pragmatic Bookshelf, 2016

- *The Principles of Product Development Flow: Second Generation Lean Product Development* by Donald Reinertsen, Celeritas Publishing, 2009

- `http://blackswanfarming.com/cost-of-delay/`, Black Swan Farming, Limited

- *VFQ Prioritization* by Emergn Limited, Emergn Limited Publishing, 2014

Capturing Ideas with Lean Canvas

Paint a robust yet lean picture of an idea on a canvas to help those seeking to understand the idea and the value of the idea.

—Mario Moreira

When an idea flows into a company, there needs to be ways to express the idea in a meaningful yet concise way without bulk and extensive time commitment. Within an Agile context, limiting the amount of time spent on documenting the idea upfront is recommend since the idea has not yet been committed for work. In other words, why invest a lot of time into something that may not be worked on?

When you include too much information about the idea, it can be overwhelming and appear too certain. On the other hand, including too little information can make the idea feel ambiguous. The challenge is the uncertainty is what you have the most of upfront. Therefore, spending a lot of time attempting to prove an idea is valuable right upfront is a fool's errand. Instead, you should look for leaner ways to document the idea in a meaningful way, knowing that discovery and learning are needed to prove its value to the customer.

© Mario E. Moreira 2017
M. E. Moreira, *The Agile Enterprise*, DOI 10.1007/978-1-4842-2391-8_13

Canvas Approach to Documenting Ideas

The traditional way to document an idea is write a business plan. There are some elements that can be gleaned from the business plan including the summary or pitch of the idea, financial highlights, and assumptions. Business plans are particularly useful when looking for money to finance an idea. Unfortunately, business plans have a reputation of being laborious because their intent is to prove upfront that the idea has value.

What are the alternatives? There are a number of vision and canvas approaches that are more appropriate for an Agile galaxy where you acknowledge you know less upfront, so the record of the idea should be equally trim. Within this chapter, I will share the Business Model Canvas, the Lean Canvas, and the Customer Value Canvas, designed specifically to support your focus on identifying and capturing customer value.

Before I introduce the canvases, it is important to know the context of where to apply a canvas. Following the enterprise idea pipeline, the Record stage is where to document the new idea in the canvas, as illustrated in Figure 13-1. In Chapter 11, I wrote that an idea can be written freestyle, as a hypothesis, or alternatively using a canvas. The key is to keep it meaningful, yet lean.

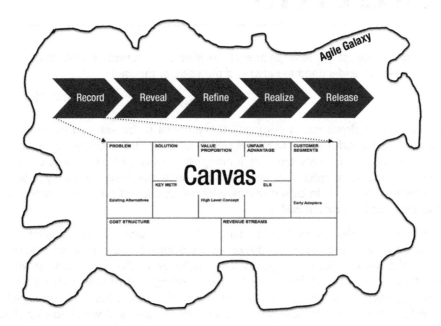

Figure 13-1. Canvas for recording an idea

Once the canvas is drafted, it should be visible and transparent to everyone in the enterprise. Just as each idea should include a description, persona or market segment, the value, the risks of doing the idea or not doing the idea, and assumptions being made, so should the canvas.

Business Model Canvas

In order to provide context to the Lean Canvas, you need to recognize the Business Model Canvas. The Business Model Canvas was one of the initial leaner ways of representing information that was typically found in a business plan. The Business Model Canvas was originated by Alexander Osterwalder based on his earlier work in business model ontology.

This canvas uses the premise that a simple business model can describe how an organization creates, delivers, and captures value. This canvas approach was created to provide a one-page, straightforward way to map business elements to a proposed business idea or strategic plan to help guide the direction of an enterprise.

Here is a quick walkthrough of the Business Model Canvas using the illustration provided in Figure 13-2. The *value propositions* are the ideas of what you are offering the customers. The *customer segment* consists of the customers or users you want to serve. The *customer channels* are ways to reach customers. The *customer relationships* are the ways you want to build relationships with customers within each segment.

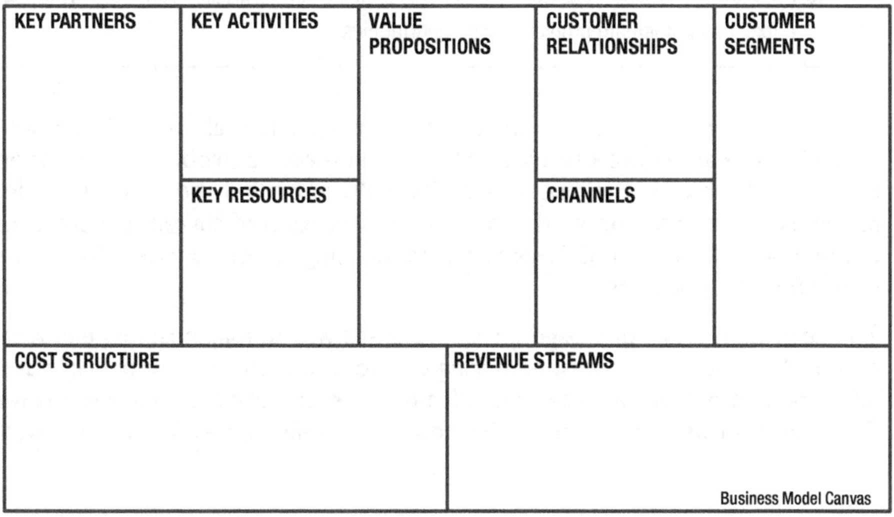

KEY PARTNERS	KEY ACTIVITIES	VALUE PROPOSITIONS	CUSTOMER RELATIONSHIPS	CUSTOMER SEGMENTS
	KEY RESOURCES		CHANNELS	
COST STRUCTURE		REVENUE STREAMS		
				Business Model Canvas

Figure 13-2. Business Model Canvas

The *revenue stream* is a calculation of revenue of how much money you can make based on what the customer will pay. *Key resources* are those people and equipment needed to turn the idea into reality. *Key activities* are those activities that turn the idea into reality. *Key partners* are those people outside your team or enterprise that you rely on. *Cost structure* includes the expected costs of building the proposition.

Within a Business Model Canvas context, you can start anywhere. I recommend you start with the proposition and work from there. However, if you are targeting a specific customer segment, then this could be a good place to start. In any case, the point of having all of the business blocks in front of you is that you can organically consider any or all of the areas in the same work period without specifically focusing on a particular area.

Lean Canvas

The Lean Canvas came about as an experiment by Ash Maurya. He felt the Business Model Canvas was effective for an existing business that focused on existing key partners, customer relationships, and business direction. However, Maurya was looking for something that helped better capture hypothesis thinking associated with a new problem or solution in a startup environment. He investigated Rob Fitzpatrick's four steps to epiphany and adapted the Business Model Canvas to form the Lean Canvas.

■ **Agile Pit Stop**   The Lean Canvas is a more actionable and entrepreneurial business plan adapted to focus on immediate problems and opportunities.

The Lean Canvas is a more actionable and entrepreneurial-focused lean business plan. It was adapted to focus on more immediate problems and opportunities and look for their solutions. The culture behind the enterprise idea pipeline is meant to support the immediate evaluation of current problems or opportunities. The Lean Canvas provides meaningful, yet concise information suited for an Agile culture.

The Lean Canvas is a one-page, straightforward way to map business elements to a problem. It gets established during the Record stage. It is particularly useful in the context of the enterprise idea pipeline as ideas are meant to evolve. The Lean Canvas is meant to evolve and pivot as new information is learned.

Here is a walkthrough of the blocks in the Lean Canvas, illustrated in Figure 13-3 as guidance. The *Problem* block is where you identify what you are trying to solve. Include the top three problems related to an area. This block also asks you to consider existing alternatives in case an existing solution is currently available in-house or on the market. The *Customer Segments* block shows the target customers or users and asks you to consider early adopters. The *Solution* block defines how to address the problem for the customer segment being targeted.

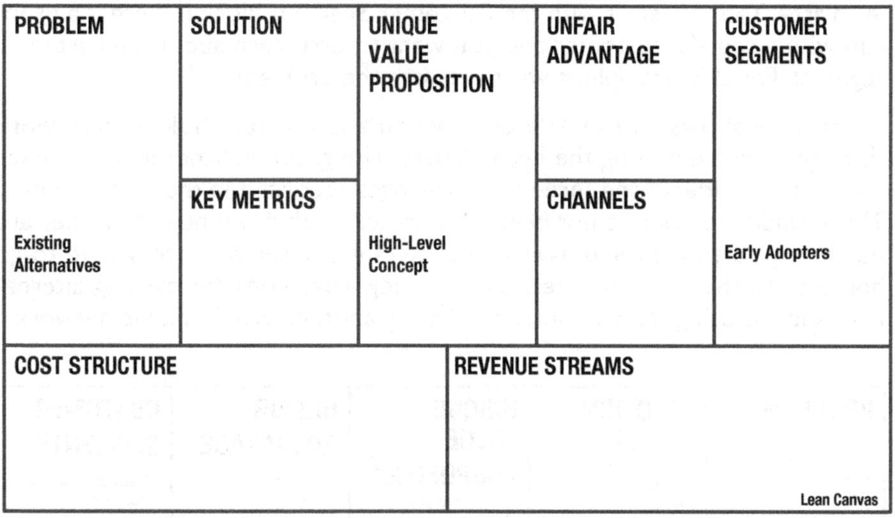

PROBLEM	SOLUTION	UNIQUE VALUE PROPOSITION	UNFAIR ADVANTAGE	CUSTOMER SEGMENTS
	KEY METRICS		CHANNELS	
Existing Alternatives		High-Level Concept		Early Adopters
COST STRUCTURE			REVENUE STREAMS	

Lean Canvas

Figure 13-3. Lean Canvas

The *Unique Value Proposition* block asks how you are different from your competitors. This block also asks for a high-level concept on how your solution fits into the larger picture. Some call this your elevator pitch. The *Unfair Advantage* block consists of the plusses you have over your competitors. The *Revenue Stream* block shows the potential revenue generated. The *Cost Structure* block reveals the expected costs associated with the solution. The *Key Metrics* block includes the metrics that will show progress toward the outcomes being looked for. The *Channels* block focuses on ways to reach the customer segments.

Applying the Lean Canvas

This section provides you with an example of working with the Lean Canvas. The PO and those who have an investment stake (sales, marketing, and so on) in solving the problem may be collaboratively involved in building the Lean Canvas. Once built, the canvas should be shared during the Reveal stage to determine if the idea is high priority enough to move forward with.

Work on the Lean Canvas typically starts by identifying the problems you have in an area. You may start with the Customer Segment block if there is a problem with a specific customer and you want to first learn about the customer segment. For this example, it will start with the problem.

Figure 13-4 shows an example of how you and the stakeholders may work through a problem using the Lean Canvas. The group collaborative discusses the problems, identifying three top challenges recorded in the *Problem* block. This includes customers not being able to access their money when they are out, losing customers, and having customers get upset when they have to go home or to the bank to access their money. They consider existing alternatives such as using the computer or sharing another bank's mobile network.

PROBLEM	SOLUTION	UNIQUE VALUE PROPOSITION	UNFAIR ADVANTAGE	CUSTOMER SEGMENTS
Customers can't access their money during the day when they are out	Build a Mobile application for Banking Customers to get access to their money	Have high security banking	Large Customer Base	Existing Banking Customers
Losing Customers		Can access from wherever you are	High Customer Satisfaction	New Banking Customers
Customers get upset since they have to go home if they need banking access	**KEY METRICS**		**CHANNELS**	
	Sign-up for Mobile Account	**High Level Concept**	Radio Commercials	
Existing Alternatives			Mailing to existing Banking Customers	**Early Adopters**
Use Computer	Mobile Account has profile	Bank from wherever you are knowing your transaction is safe and secure.	Marketing in Banking Office	Gen Y Banking Customers
Competitors mobile Banking network	Transfer activity has occurred			

COST STRUCTURE	REVENUE STREAMS
Servers to host mobile application	Reduce customer attrition and associated revenue to avoid losing 24000 customers/yr. for $14,400,000 loss
Integration tools with current banking applications	Potential increase in gaining 36,000 new customers/yr. for $21,600,000 gain
Developer Costs	$36,000,000/yr. benefit
Customer Awareness marketing	Lean Canvas

Figure 13-4. Lean Canvas in action

From there, the team explores the *Customer Segments* block and realizes that the problems impact many of the existing customers and are a barrier to getting new customers. The team identifies the Gen Y customers as early adopters since they tend to be willing to adopt new solutions, particularly mobile-related solutions, more quickly. They consider their *Unfair Advantage* block and recall that they have a large customer base with historically high customer satisfaction.

Agile Pit Stop   When considering your customer segment, it is important to identify early adopters as they are often more willing to use early versions and provide feedback.

The team decides to consider their *Unique Value Proposition* block and recognizes that security protocols have made banking secure and the pervasive access using ATMs and computers has made it special for their customers. The team collaboratively crafts a simple elevator pitch of how they want the bank to be perceived: "Bank from wherever you are knowing your transaction is safe and secure."

The team decides that the solution should be to build a mobile application for their customers. They work on key metrics to help them better grasp if progress is being made once the mobile application is released. The team collaboratively considers the *Channels* block to determine where they can make their customers aware of the new mobile application.

They conclude by walking through the high-level *Cost Structure* block, which includes servers, integration tools, development time, and marketing. Finally, they consider the *Revenue Streams* block, where revenue can be made with new customers or avoided by reducing customer attrition.

LEAN CANVAS EXERCISE

Think of an idea that is either waiting to be considered or has already come to fruition. Find at least one other person to work with you. Start with a Lean Canvas template and apply each block to the idea in the order of the example above: Problem, Customer Segment, Unfair Advantage, Unique Value Proposition, Solution, Key Metrics, Channels, Cost Structure, and Revenue Streams. Explain the idea to two other people. What was the feedback and what did you learn?

Customer Value Canvas

Just as the Business Model Canvas is an adaptation toward leaner business plans, the Lean Canvas is an adaptation of the Business Model Canvas to solve more immediate problems. The Customer Value Canvas is a change of the Lean Canvas with a singular focus of being customer-value-driven (CVD) and incorporating elements of value (CoD, feedback loops, personas, and so on).

The Customer Value Canvas is an actionable way to document and evaluate an idea based on the first step in learning customer value. It was adapted to focus on ideas to determine their value and align with a discovery mindset (sometimes referred to as the Discovery Canvas). It is, for this reason, why this canvas is a good approach for the enterprise idea pipeline. The Agile culture behind the enterprise idea pipeline is meant to support the immediate evaluation of meaningful and concise ideas as they come in.

The Customer Value Canvas is a one-page, straightforward way to map business elements to a proposed idea specifically focused on getting to customer value. It gets established during the Record stage. It is particularly useful within the context of the enterprise idea pipeline as ideas are meant to evolve. The Customer Value Canvas is meant to pivot as new information is learned (for example, challenged assumptions, feedback from experiments, iterations, increments, and demonstrations).

Here is a walkthrough of the blocks in the Customer Value Canvas illustrated in Figure 13-5. The *Opportunity* block is where you state the problem you are trying to solve or the new idea you want to explore. This block also asks you to consider existing alternatives in case an existing or partial solution is currently available in-house or on the market. The *Customer Personas* block contains the customer or user groups you are targeting.

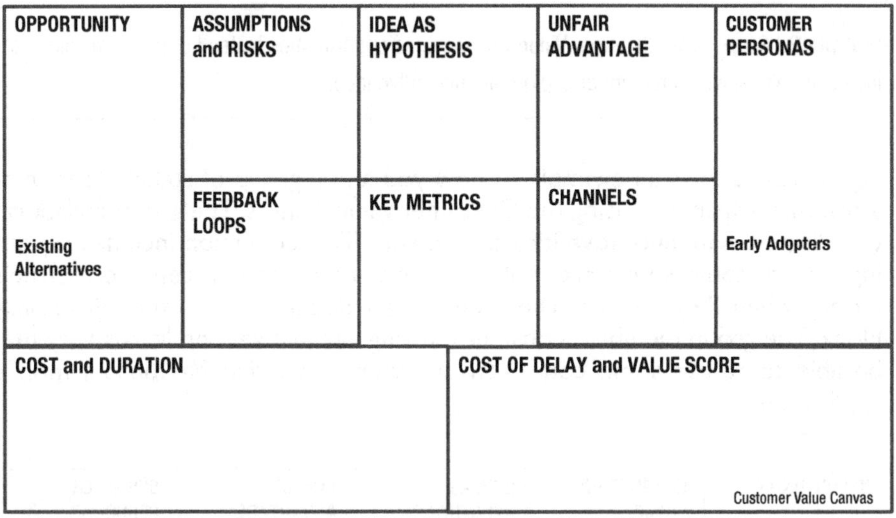

OPPORTUNITY	ASSUMPTIONS and RISKS	IDEA AS HYPOTHESIS	UNFAIR ADVANTAGE	CUSTOMER PERSONAS
	FEEDBACK LOOPS	KEY METRICS	CHANNELS	
Existing Alternatives				Early Adopters
COST and DURATION		COST OF DELAY and VALUE SCORE		
				Customer Value Canvas

Figure 13-5. Customer Value Canvas

The *Idea as Hypothesis* block asks you to create a hypothesis that affirms you are approaching your idea in a more scientific and data driven manner. The *Assumptions and Risks* block asks you to include assumptions and risks you identified as they relate to the idea when calculating CoD and duration. The *Feedback Loops* block includes the ways you plan to capture feedback to validate you are moving in the direction of customer value.

The *Unfair Advantage* block tells you what advantages you have over your competitors. The *Channels* block shows ways to reach the customer personas. The *Cost of Delay and Value Score* block includes the type of cost of delay (CoD), the CoD per week, and the CoD divided by duration (CD3) as the value score. The *Cost and Duration* block shows the expected costs associated with the solution, including an estimate for dream duration. The *Key Metrics* block contains the metrics that show progress toward the desired outcomes and the results once released.

Applying the Customer Value Canvas

This section provides you with an example of working with the Customer Value Canvas. The PO and those who have an investment stake (that is, the product owner constellation) in evolving the idea should collaboratively build the Customer Value Canvas in the Record stage. Once built, it should be shared during the Reveal stage to determine if it is high priority enough to move forward.

■ **Agile Pit Stop** The Customer Value Canvas uses opportunities instead of problems since the idea can be to solve a problem or explore an innovative idea.

Figure 13-6 shows an example of how you and a group of stakeholders may work through an idea using the Customer Value Canvas. The group collaborative discusses an innovative idea or problem. This discussion includes capturing new customers who are mobile-centric and those that can't access their money when they are out. These details get documented in the *Opportunity* block. The group members consider existing alternatives and learns they may be able to re-use some code from another group that has built a mobile application.

OPPORTUNITY	ASSUMPTIONS & RISKS	IDEA AS HYPOTHESIS	UNFAIR ADVANTAGE	CUSTOMER PERSONAS
Capture new customers who are mobile centric Customers can't access their money when they are out	24K Mobile Customers Lost/yr. 36K New Mobile Customers/yr. Security protocols work on mobile	The mobile app will increase sales by 30% for mobile users in the next 3 months	Large Customer Base High Customer Satisfaction Strong security Protocols	Erin the Senior Citizen Sunny the Gen X-er
	FEEDBACK LOOPS	**KEY METRICS**	**CHANNELS**	
Existing Alternatives Reuse Mobile locator app code	Buy a Feature in Story Map Customer Demos Beta	Participants for Beta Sign-up for Mobile Account Transfer activity has occurred	Radio Commercials Mailing to existing Banking Customers Marketing in Banking Office	**Early Adopters** David the Gen Y-er

COST & DURATION	COST OF DELAY & VALUE SCORE
Servers to host mobile application Integration tools with current banking applications Customer Awareness marketing Development Team – 6 weeks dream duration	Protect Revenue – Avoid customer attrition - $276,923/wk. Increase Revenue – Gain new customers - $415,385/wk. Total CoD - $692,308/wk. Value Score (CD3) = $692.308/6 wks. = 115K Customer Value Canvas

Figure 13-6. Customer Value Canvas in action

From there, the team explores the *Customer Personas* block. The team realizes that while *Erin the Senior Citizen* may benefit from a mobile app, *Sunny the Gen X-er* will be the primary persona of the idea. The team identifies the *David the Gen Y-er* persona as an example of early adopters since they tend to be willing to adopt new ideas, particularly mobile-related ones, more quickly. They consider their *Unfair Advantage* block and realize that they have a large customer base with historically high customer satisfaction along with strong security protocols.

In the *Idea as Hypothesis* block, the team crafts the idea using a hypothesis format. They consider their costs and duration of the work in the *Cost and Duration* block, which includes servers, integration tools, marketing, and a dream duration for development time. Then the *Cost of Delay and Value Score* block is visited where the cost of delay is established and the value score is calculated using CD3. Because there is very limited data and information at this point in the idea life cycle, they document the assumptions being made and known risks in the *Assumptions and Risks* block.

The Feedback Loops block is added to include customer input and feedback during the Refine stage and throughout the Realize stage. The team works on key metrics to understand if progress is being made while building the mobile application and once it is released. The team collaboratively thinks through the *Channels* block, determining where they can make their customers aware of the new mobile application.

CUSTOMER VALUE CANVAS EXERCISE

Think of an idea that is either waiting to be considered or has already been realized. Find at least one other person to work with you. Start with a Customer Value Canvas template and apply each section to the idea in the order of the example above: Opportunity, Customer Personas, Idea as Hypothesis, Assumptions and Risks, Feedback Loops, Unfair Advantage, Channels, Key Metrics, Cost and Duration, and Cost of Delay and Value Score. Explain the idea to two other people. What was the feedback and what did you learn?

The Living and Pivoting Canvas

When using any of the canvases discussed in this chapter, you should consider them all living. They should live as long as the idea is deemed valuable and should be archived when it is clear that it will not float high enough in the Reveal pool to merit attention.

The idea on the canvas is the manifestation of an actual working product or service as it flows through the enterprise idea pipeline. The canvas is the record for the idea and, therefore, should evolve as the idea evolves. A canvas is meant to be updated as new information changes the idea.

For the Lean Canvas and Customer Value Canvas, the canvas should be updated as you work through each part of the 5R or 6R model, assuming the idea continues to be valuable. It should be a snapshot in time for where the idea is to date. However, it is not meant to be a status report of the idea but should reference where more information can be found.

Are You Painting Your Canvas of Ideas?

Just as the Business Model Canvas is an adaptation toward leaner business plans, the Lean Canvas is an adaptation of the Business Model Canvas to solve more immediate problems. The Customer Value Canvas changes the Lean Canvas for a singular focus of being customer-value-driven and working with the elements of value (CoD, feedback loops, personas, and so on). I strongly recommend that you experiment with the Lean Canvas and Customer Value Canvas to gain personal experience with each one.

What colors are you using to paint your canvas? If you are either using a heavy document like a business plan or providing very little information to make a qualified and quantified decision on what to work on next, consider adapting to a canvas approach. Try it once. Adapt it to fit your needs if you find it helps.

For additional material, I suggest the following:

- *Business Model Generation: A Handbook for Visionaries, Game Changers, and Challengers* by Alexander Osterwalder and Yves Pigneur, Jon Wiley and Sons, 2010

- *Running Lean: Iterate from Plan A to a Plan That Works* by Ash Maurya, O'Reilly Media, 2012

Incorporating Customer Feedback

It's not about achieving Agile for Agile's sake. It's about delivering customer value and achieving better business outcomes.

—Mario Moreira

The most important ingredient in understanding customer value is precious customer feedback. A customer-value-driven (CVD) enterprise is a company that optimizes for what the customer finds as valuable and adapts until this outcome is met. As you look to build a CVD engine within your enterprise, the customers and, specifically, their feedback are the "driver" that steers the engine of customer value.

Gaining customer feedback along the delivery axis is crucial, from the Record stage to the Reveal stage to the Refine stage to the Realize stage to the Release stage and, finally, to the Reflect stage. Feedback should be collected more than once, and it should always be incorporated. It must be collected, considered, sorted, merged, and applied toward customer value on a continuous basis.

© Mario E. Moreira 2017
M. E. Moreira, *The Agile Enterprise*, DOI 10.1007/978-1-4842-2391-8_14

As a reminder, who is a customer? A customer is someone who has a choice of what to buy and a choice of where to buy it. A customer is someone external to the company and pays money to help you stay in business by purchasing your product. Consequently, engaging the customer is of utmost importance. When talking about customer feedback in this chapter, we are referring to people who are outside of the company who have the choice of buying your product and, hence, providing revenue to the company.

Throughout this chapter, I will discuss incorporating feedback loops along your delivery axis, constructing personas, embedding personas, and creating a customer feedback vision. By doing these things, you can more systematically understand your customers and engage them during many meaningful moments to receive their precious feedback.

Customer Feedback Loops

Feedback loops are specific points along the idea pipeline where the output received from one activity is used as input in the next activity. In the case of building an idea, feedback from a customer who has attended a demo is used as input in the next planning session to adapt the direction for the product or idea.

Agile Pit Stop   There are two types of feedback loops. Verification ensures you are building the product right, and validation ensures you are building the right product.

Feedback is the result of an activity and can be termed as testing an idea. There are two primary types of testing: verification and validation. Verification testing provides you feedback to help determine whether you are building the product right and that it works as designed. If the button is supposed to take you to a new location, verification testing will check it and provide feedback on whether it does or not. The testers in most verification testing are employees internal to the company.

Validation testing provides you feedback to determine if you are building the right product and are satisfying the needs of customer. If the user story says to build a button, then validation testing would ask the customers if they are satisfied with the button, providing the enterprise with customer feedback to understand if the product is adequate or if a change is needed. In this case, the testers in validation testing are meant to be customers who are external to the company. Customer feedback loops are, therefore, a type of validation test to ensure you are meeting the needs of customers.

Customers delight in seeing working product in action and the inspect-and-adapt approach allows customers to consider and adjust their needs until they are transformed into a valuable working product. Feedback loops should be considered all along the delivery axis of the idea pipeline, as illustrated in Figure 14-1. The outcome of each customer feedback loop informs future decisions and product direction. As a note of caution, a non-disclosure agreement (NDA) may be needed with external customers prior to sharing ideas as part of any feedback loop.

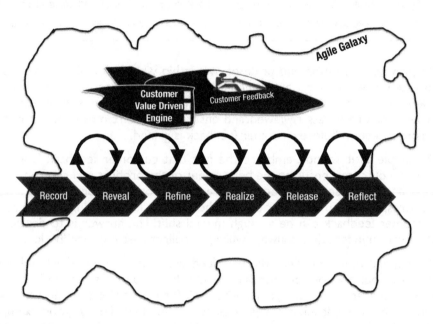

Figure 14-1. Feedback along the delivery axis

Mindset behind Customer Feedback Loops

The concept of learning what the customer considers valuable is an important mindset in the journey to customer value. This learning allows you to shed the dangerous attitude of pretend or arrogant certainty and allows you to explore what the customer needs. The best approach is to incorporate the concept of learning through feedback to identify what is customer value. This is a discovery method of gaining incremental information through customer feedback loops and taking what you learn to continuously adapt toward customer value.

The goal is to have as many customer feedback loops as feasible. This can be challenging and, in some Agile efforts, the result is few if any customer feedback loops. Customer feedback can be an uncomfortable endeavor in that it can frustrate those who've invested time into a building a product. It requires a mature and willing mindset to collect, consider, sort, merge, and apply the feedback to get closer to customer value.

■ **Agile Pit Stop**   Establishing customer feedback loops consists of part mindset and part practice. You need to believe in the importance of customer feedback to achieve customer value.

To prevent frustration and pride of ownership when a lot of time has been invested in working on a product, apply short iterations or periodic time-frames where demonstrations occur more regularly. This limits the investment of time before it gets reviewed and ensures you don't move too far in the wrong direction before customer feedback is gained.

As simple as it sounds, embrace the fact that customer feedback is a very positive outcome, ensuring the betterment of the product and company success. If you are used to a process where you sub-optimize for following a plan over responding to customer change, then responding to change by accepting customer feedback can be a tough mental shift. The answer is to develop a discovery mindset that is always willing to collect customer feedback.

Also, spend time identifying the best feedback loops for the effort and construct a sound vision for customer feedback. As you consider the best customer feedback loops for your effort, look for places along the delivery axis where getting feedback is of high importance and low effort. A good example is the Web-based sprint review or demo. Customers can observe the demo in a low-effort manner from the privacy of their office or home.

Types of Customer Feedback Loops

There are many types of customer feedback loops that can be applied as the idea travels through the enterprise idea pipeline. The most common customer feedback loop is the sprint review or demo where customers view the working product developed to date. As illustrated in Figure 14-2, there is a list of customer feedback loops with details that you should consider applying to build a stronger path toward customer value.

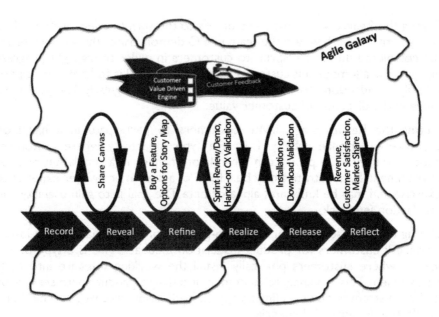

Figure 14-2. Various customer feedback loops through the delivery axis

During the Reveal stage, share the idea on a Lean Canvas or Customer Value Canvas with customers. Then walk through the idea with customers to see if the idea's manifestation is what they had in mind or if it is something that they would find valuable. The goal is to understand if you are moving in the direction of customer value.

During the Refine stage, play the "Buy a Feature" game referenced in Chapter 12 to help POs choose the features to include in an upcoming release that would be most valuable. In this game, the players (customers) use play money to buy and negotiate for features they find most valuable. The goal is to understand what customer value looks like to customers.

During the Refine stage, bring in customers to review the user story map prior to cutting an increment. Highlight the backbone and process in order to validate the customers' experience path. Then walk through the options to gauge their level of interest and to see if some options are more compelling than others. The goal is to move in the direction of customer value.

■ **Agile Pit Stop**   Customer feedback loops can be applied along the delivery axis from five stages: Reveal to Refine to Realize to Release and, finally, to Reflect to help you move toward customer value.

During the Realize stage, invite customers to the sprint review or demo. This is a type of feedback where the team or PO demonstrates the working product completed during the sprint to customers in order to highlight progress and gain the all-important customer feedback. The goal is to have demos periodically so adaptions to customer value can occur regularly. The goal is to move in the direction of customer value.

During the Realize stage, invite customers to participate in a hands-on customer-experience activity. This is a type of activity where customers experiment with the product in a hands-on manner in a simulation or pilot environment. Such activities may be a form of a customer or user experience exercise and may be known as alpha or beta. The goal is to gain usability and satisfaction feedback.

During the Release stage, for those on-premise products that require installation, ask customers for product-installation feedback. This is a type of validation where customers physically install the working software into their environment. This can apply to customers installing a product onto servers or mobile customers downloading an app. In both cases, receiving technical and satisfaction feedback is beneficial.

During the Reflect stage, the idea has made its way to the public. This is a time to collect an array of feedback: how well it is doing in the market, how many customers have paid for the product, if the deliverable is satisfactory to customers, if the product is being used as advertised, and more. Primarily, the goal is to capture revenue data, market share data, and customer satisfaction data to ascertain if it is perceived as valuable to customers.

As you look at possible feedback loops, the question is not about having a lot. The question is about having feedback loops at points where they can help you understand customer value. Some feedback loops may return less feedback value than the effort it takes to establish them. Look for the "high feedback value, low effort to establish" feedback loops first.

FEEDBACK LOOPS EXERCISE

Consider the product that you are working on today. What customer feedback loops do you currently employ? What additional feedback loops along the delivery axis can you add to allow you to adapt toward customer value?

Building Customer Personas

When you are building a product, how well do you know your customers? Can you visualize who they are? Do you understand their motivations? Do you have user stories for all of the customer types that may use your product? By knowing who your personas are for the product that represents your idea, you can answer yes to these questions.

Personas represent specific users for your product or service and act as examples for the types of users who would interact with it. Most products have several personas that use the product in different ways. Examples of three personas for a banking product are Erin the Senior Citizen, Sunny the Gen X-er, and David the Gen Y-er.

- *Erin the Senior Citizen* represents customers who use very basic user interface functionality to conduct straightforward tasks. They primarily use a computer or work with tellers to conduct their business. They are primarily motivated to check balances and extend their investments.

- *Sunny the Gen X-er* represents customers who need more complex interface functionality to handle sophisticated tasks. They are technically savvy on the computer and less so on the mobile phone. They are primarily motivated to do more banking on the phone to take advantages of opportunities.

- *David the Gen Y-er* represents customers who can work on both simple and complex interface functionality. They are technically savvy on the mobile phone. They are relatively new to investment and are motivated to understand investment practices and for ways to invest their money.

All three customer personas use the product differently, and diverse features are designed for their respective needs. Personas are a powerful way to guide your decisions about functionality and ensure that you are, in fact, building functionality to help each persona. Personas are a key ingredient in the way user stories can be presented. Including the persona in a user story description provides you the *point of view* (POV) and defines who the user story is for. Typical information in a persona includes the following:

- Fictional name with function

- Demographics: age, gender, education, and family status

- Background, responsibilities, and experience in story form

- Motivations that drive their ideas and behavior

- Pain points that show the areas of frustrations that impact them

- The goals or job to be done

- A quote that sums up what matters most to the persona

- Casual picture representing that user group

I recommend that you establish a persona for each persona type. This description typically portrays a fictitious person who represents a real role. Writing a persona as a fictitious person with a name makes the persona easier to imagine and relate to as illustrated in Figure 14-3.

Sunny the Gen X-er

"I need to easily gain access to my bank account and the ability to quickly make transactions on my phone."

- Banking customer.

- Female in mid-40s, married with children.

- MBA with Bachelors in finance.

- Has a busy life focused on commercial real estate. Has a regular and business account.

- Technically savvy on the computer and less so on the mobile phone.

- Has been a loyal customer for 10 years.

- Motivated to do more banking on the mobile phone, particularly on the business account.

- Pain point includes she is missing opportunities by not having her bank accounts readily available through her mobile device.

- Job to be done are to transfer funds, do online banking, and grow her balances with stock trades.

- Tends to work from home office or on the go.

Figure 14-3. Example of a persona

Typically, the product owner constructs a persona. Personas should be initially considered as early as the Record stage, should be drafted in the Refine stage, and should be shared with the team so team members better understand whom they are building the idea for. Afterward, the personas should be posted in the Agile team or work room where refining, grooming, planning, and other Agile team events occur. They should also be shared with those stakeholders involved with prioritizing the work in the Reveal stage.

■ **Agile Pit Stop**   *Jobs to be done* shift your focus from the product and to the job that product can do for the customer. It isn't a calendar. Its job is to remind you of appointments.

Consider establishing personas for your products so that you can understand the customer point of view when evolving the idea from the Reveal stage to the Reflect stage and build a product that better aligns with customer needs.

PERSONA EXERCISE

Consider one of your products or ideas. Identify at least two different persona types that may use that product. Using a format similar to Figure 14-3, draft those two personas including a fictional name, demographics, background, motivations, pain points, jobs to be done, a quote, and a casual picture. Share the personas with at least two other people, explain them, and get feedback for improvement.

Personas of Today and Tomorrow

Customer value comes in two parts. The first is understanding the customer of today via personas. This is having the pulse of the customer and the marketplace as you continually receive and adapt to customer feedback. It takes a creative, yet disciplined, focus on what you think the customer needs and where you think the customer marketplace is going.

The second is understanding the customer of tomorrow. This can be crafted in the persona called *Customer 2.0*, which is the customer of tomorrow, and looks to find out what you think they want and what they don't yet know they want (unknown unknown) to help with future product direction.

■ **Agile Pit Stop**   Customer 2.0 is the customer of tomorrow that you are aiming for.

An example of an unknown unknown is the large smartphone. Who would have guessed that, as the market was moving to smaller and smaller flip phones, customers would move to larger phones? An example of a known is customers wanting their apps better integrated. During the Refine stage, you may establish a part of your idea or backlog of work to integration work. Customer 2.0 can be aligned with the future perspective of a product vision and help you adapt personnel and tools toward that vision.

Customer 2.0 is a unique type of persona known as the "future customer." While it may be hard to identify people that fit into this persona, you can look for people who are trendsetters searching for the cutting-edge technology or products. While Customer 2.0 is focused on the future, your primary focus should be on the needs of the customer of today with a secondary focus on the needs of the customer of tomorrow. Immediate customer feedback should drive a majority of your decisions.

Using Personas from Record to Reflect

Personas can have a significant benefit along the delivery axis to ensure what is being delivered is of value to the customer. The main benefit is that anyone associated with the idea will better understand the customers and users, which helps guide better decisions about the functionality. In order to effectively apply the intent of the persona, you must embed the concept of personas all along your delivery axis, as illustrated in Figure 14-4.

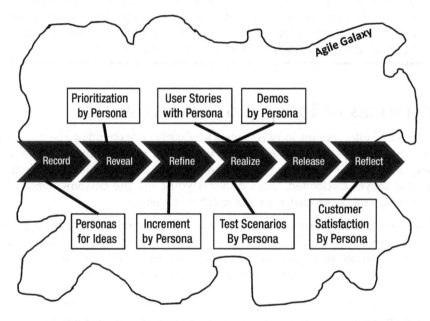

Figure 14-4. Using personas along the delivery axis

As early as the Record stage, personas should be considered to gain an understanding of whom the idea is meant for. If you use any of the canvases discussed in Chapter 13, there is a specific block for personas (that is, customer segment).

In the Reveal stage, personas could be used to help drive prioritization decisions. Particularly for existing products, there may be a specific persona that needs significant attention, which helps drive prioritization. For example, if the mobile interface is currently complex and geared to David the Gen Y-er (as early adopter) but you need to adapt it to Sunny the Gen X-er, knowing the Gen X-er persona can help with Sunny's experience.

In the Refine stage, a specific persona may be used as the reason to cut a first increment of the idea. When you consider the user or customer experience, is there a specific persona that you are targeting? For example, David the Gen Y-er may have a different customer experience or pathway through the mobile interface than Sunny the Gen X-er.

In the Realize stage, personas should be part of the user story construct. This ensures that a persona is written into the user story. It also helps teams understand who the requirement is being written for. For example, Erin the Senior Citizen may require a simpler mobile interface than Sunny the Gen X-er.

In the Realize stage, testers can create acceptance tests and test cases that support the way specific personas might use the product. For example, the test case of how David the Gen Y-er may might use the mobile interface is different from the test case of how Sunny the Gen X-er might use the interface.

■ **Agile Pit Stop**   Ensure you gain feedback from the right persona because feedback from the wrong persona can lead you down the wrong path.

In the Realize stage, based on personas, the product owner knows whom to invite to the reviews or demos to gain the best feedback. This is particularly important as the feedback from one persona can give you bad feedback if the feature is meant for another persona. For example, feedback from David the Gen Y-er will give very negative feedback about functionality meant for Erin the Senior Citizen. In fact, for every feedback loop of any kind, you need to consider the right persona group(s) to invite.

In the Reflect stage, when you collect revenue data, market share data, and customer satisfaction data, it can be beneficial to attempt to understand what personas the data are coming from. If, for example, you learn that 90% of your revenue is coming from Sunny the Gen X-er, then during future prioritization decisions in the Reveal stage, this information can be factored into what gets built.

Customer Feedback Vision

The composite of thinking through and establishing a serious feedback approach for ideas, along with feedback loops and personas, is something I term as the Customer Feedback Vision. Unfortunately, serious thinking and applying feedback loops are missing from many product teams professing to be Agile. Most customer feedback in Agile is limited to the demo and often customers are not in attendance. Customer feedback is the guide for customer value and should be taken far more seriously.

The goal of the vision is having a place to capture the thinking behind applying customer feedback. This simple vision includes building personas, establishing feedback sessions, identifying the companies, and finding ways to motivate the customers to attend the feedback sessions, as illustrated in Figure 14-5.

CUSTOMER PERSONAS	TARGET COMPANIES	FEEDBACK LOOPS	MOTIVATION
Erin the Senior Citizen - bankers who use very basic user interface products to conduct straight-forward tasks.	*Acme Corp – 50,000 customers, seasonal*	*Reveal – Feedback from review of canvas*	*Offer a chance to be a member of the customer advisory board*
Sunny theGen X-er - bankers who need more complex interface products to handle sophisticated tasks.	*Burns Industries – 10K potential customers* *Spacely Sprockets 10K robots and 1K employees, seasonal*	*Refine – Feedback from review of story map* *Realize – Feedback from Sprint review – every sprint*	*Offer a $25 gift card to attend a feedback session* *Offer a early insight into new development*
David the Gen Y-er - bankers who can work on all interface products and are technically savvy on the mobile phone.	*Gringotts – 1K goblins and 5K customers*	*Reflect – Feedback from market – revenue, satisfaction, market share*	*Offer the chance to be a leading voice in the way the idea gets built*
			Customer Feedback Vision

Figure 14-5. Example of a Customer Feedback Vision

This vision should be owned by the Product Owner and live with the product. Once established, the vision should be shared with the team so that everyone is aware of the vision and the importance of the validation activities. The Customer Value Canvas can be used as a starter home since feedback loops and persona blocks are included. If you currently don't have a place for formulating and establishing a feedback vision, then the Customer Feedback Vision should be used.

Are Feedback Loops Leading to Customer Value?

As you look to build a customer-value-driven (CVD) engine within your enterprise, the customer or, more specifically, customer feedback, is the "driver" that steers the engine of customer value. A CVD enterprise optimizes for what the customer finds as valuable and adapts until it meets this outcome. This means gaining customer feedback all along the delivery axis is crucial. Feedback must be collected, considered, sorted, merged, and applied to guide you to what the customer finds as value.

In pursuit of customer value, implementing effective feedback loops form the backbone for a CVD engine. Establishing personas help you and all those involved to gain a strong understanding of whom you are building for. Embedding personas along the delivery axis ensures that the right customer(s) is being focused on. Remember, you can get feedback from the wrong persona, which can lead you away from customer value. Knowing what persona(s) you are focused on will provide a stronger focus toward delivering customer value. Packaging your feedback approach into a Customer Feedback Vision can help you consider feedback elements leading to more meaningful customer feedback.

For additional material, I suggest the following:

- *VFQ Feedback* by Emergn Limited, Emergn Limited Publishing, 2014

- *Buyer Personas: How to Gain Insight into your Customers Expectations, Align your Marketing Strategies, and Win More Business* by Adele Revella, Wiley, 2015

Establishing Your Requirements Tree

To know if the highest-value ideas are being worked on, you need to recognize the parent/child relationships from idea to user stories.

—Mario Moreira

Requirement is a nebulous term. It can mean something large like a corporate strategy or something tiny like a task. People often throw around the word *requirement* without a strong sense of the type of requirement it refers to or the level it belongs to. Are people talking about a user story, a business requirement, a technical requirement, a strategy, an idea, or a task?

The fact is that companies have all levels of requirements. However, the levels of requirements are not always clear to employees or management. I'm not suggesting that the levels have to be the same across an enterprise, but they should be known at a product team level. This lack of clarity should not be left up to chance, and I suggest that you take the effort to understand what your requirements tree might look like.

© Mario E. Moreira 2017
M. E. Moreira, *The Agile Enterprise*, DOI 10.1007/978-1-4842-2391-8_15

Requirements Tree

I often recommend that a company or product team understand their requirements lineage, which I term a *requirements tree*. It is a structure that represents the relative hierarchy among various requirements elements within your enterprise. The *idea* that has been discussed in previous chapters is a key requirements element that is at the larger end of the requirements element spectrum. User stories are found at the smaller end of the requirements element spectrum. Since requirements drive the work within an enterprise, it is good to know if you are working on the highest-value requirements or random requirements that made their way in through the secret and often unevaluated backdoor. Can you trace the lineage of user stories and tasks to the high value idea they represent?

What are the various requirements elements? There is no industry standard group of requirements elements, and they can vary from enterprise to enterprise. The point is to understand what yours might look like. I like to start with corporate strategy and end with tasks, as illustrated in Figure 15-1.

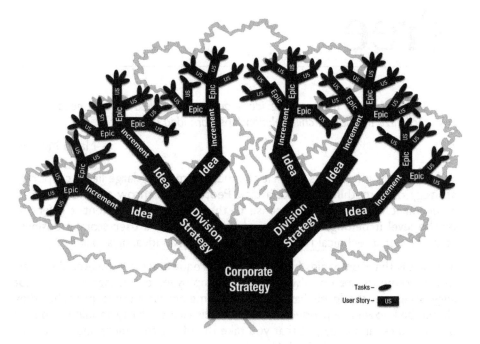

Figure 15-1. Example of a requirements tree

Once you establish the levels of your requirements tree, it is important to craft a definition to describe each level. Using the requirements levels from Figure 15-1, here is how I describe each level. A corporate strategy includes high-level goals and direction set for the enterprise. A division strategy focuses on goals and direction for a division. An idea is a value-driven and outcome-based opportunity. An increment is an end-to-end slice of the idea to validate the value of an idea. An epic is a function, feature, or large user story. A user story is a requirement that fits into a sprint or can be completed in days, is non-compound, and is for one persona. A task is a very small unit of work that has a tangible result of incrementally building the user story.

■ **Agile Pit Stop**   A requirements tree allows you to understand the level of requirements being discussed, traceability among requirements, and education needed for the team on levels.

You may notice that instead of putting the corporate strategy on top, I place it on the bottom. I do this to represent the corporate strategy as the trunk of the tree because it should provide guidance for how the smaller requirements elements (such as ideas, increments, epics, user stories, and tasks) should grow. While your strategy may adapt over time based on customer feedback and where your market place is headed, it should guide the type of work you may consider in the short run.

This version of the requirements tree as illustrated in 15-1:

Corporate strategy to division strategy to ideas to increments to epics to user stories to tasks

Other versions of a requirements tree may be as follows:

Business vision to business objectives to business requirements to technical requirements to tasks

Corporate objectives to features to use cases to user requirements to tasks

The key to your requirements tree is for you to establish one that makes sense for the type of work you do. For example, if you only have one division in your company, a division strategy isn't necessary. Those that may consider creating a requirements tree are a combination of executives, product owners, and team members. Once crafted, the tree should be shared with everyone.

REQUIREMENTS TREE STRUCTURE EXERCISE

Consider your organization. Can you define the relative hierarchy of requirements from the largest requirements element down to the smallest? Consider working with another person or two. Attempt to illustrate it. Is there any difference of opinion or confusion as to how it may be structured?

Attributes of Requirements Elements

Having a requirements tree benefits you in several ways. First, the tree helps you understand the relationships of the various requirements elements from the largest requirement (corporate strategy) to the smallest requirement (task). Second, the tree helps management and employees understand what level of requirement is being discussed. Third, it helps you understand if you are missing a requirements level. While it can be reasonable to miss a level, you should be aware of it to determine if a discussion is necessary.

As you think about the ideas that flow through your organization and how to decompose them into user stories and tasks, it is important to know what your requirements tree might look like and the attributes the requirements elements should have. This may include the following:

- All requirements elements should be customer-value focused.

- Other than corporate strategy, all other requirements elements should have a parent (the epic is the parent of the user story) unless unneeded (some user stories won't have tasks).

- For every parent, there are typically two or more children requirements elements (an idea is made up of six epics).

- Not all children need to be completed in order for the parent requirements element to satisfy the customer need (five of the eight user stories of the epic may satisfy the customer).

Within an enterprise, different divisions, groups, and teams can have different requirements trees. The exception is that the more dependencies and collaboration among teams, groups, and divisions, the more mutually beneficial it is to have a shared and common requirements tree.

Navigating the Requirements Tree

There are at least three key benefits to having a requirements tree. First, it can help you understand the level of the requirement being discussed. This may be more important than initially realized. If someone is talking about a requirement at the user-story level vs. the idea level, the discussion can derail very quickly. At the idea level, it may be more of a divergent conversation where people are considering options, while, at the user story level, it may be more of a convergent discussion where people are attempting to pin down details because it will be worked on very soon.

■ **Agile Pit Stop**   Understanding the traceability helps you know if work is coming from an idea or getting inserted through the backdoor from another source.

Second, a requirements tree can help you understand if tasks, user stories, and epics are traceable to an idea. Understanding the traceability of work can help you know if the work that is considered of customer value is indeed being worked on. It can also help you ascertain if some user stories are getting inserted through the backdoor from another source, instead of coming from the idea. This can explain why key user stories are not getting completed. It is reasonable to have requirements come from other places, but there should be accountable awareness that it is occurring.

Third, having a requirements tree can help you educate the team, management, and particularly new staff on the levels of requirement types, who participates at each level, and what Agile concepts and practices may be used at each level. Figure 15-2 illustrates an example of the requirements tree in action and how you might decompose from the corporate strategy level up to the task level.

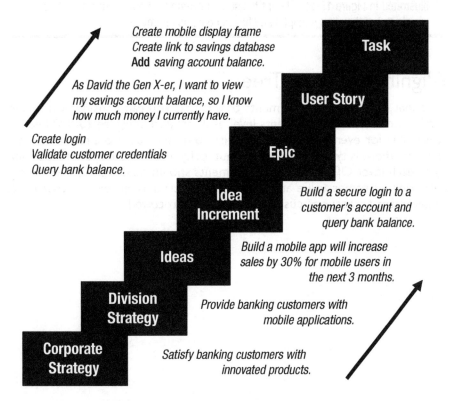

Figure 15-2. Working example of navigating the requirements tree

In this example, I start with the corporate strategy, which may be to *satisfy banking customers with innovated products*. From there, a division strategy will consider the corporate strategy and apply it to *provide banking customers with mobile applications*. Then an idea may be to *build a mobile app that will increase sales by 30% for mobile users in the next three months*.

An increment of the idea may be a thin slice to *build a secure login to a customer's account and query bank balance*. From there, epics may be to *create login*, *validate customer credentials*, and *query bank balance*. Using the query bank balance epic, a user story may be as follows: *As David the Gen X-er, I want to view my savings account balance, so I know how much money I currently have*. Tasks could be to *create mobile display frame*, *create link to savings database*, and *add saving account balance*.

REQUIREMENTS TREE NAVIGATION EXERCISE

Working with another person or two, think about your requirements tree. For each requirements element level, document what the requirement might look like (as illustrated in Figure 15-2). Attempt to use real examples. Share your tree with a few people. Ask if they find it helpful and how it could be improved.

Aligning Roles to Tree

A benefit of having a requirements tree is that you can consider who might participate at each requirements level, as illustrated in Figure 15-3. While it is reasonable for everyone in an enterprise to have input into a requirement at any level, there is typically a bounded authority as to who has the responsibility at each level. Of course, all requirements should be driven by the focus of delivering customer value and not arrogant certainty, so expect changes to requirement to occur as customer feedback is received.

Figure 15-3. Role alignment to requirements tree

For example, who has the bounded authority over the strategy, who has the authority over an increment of an idea, and who has the authority over the user stories? For a corporate strategy, senior management may make the decision to consider top strategies. For considering increments of an idea, the product owner may make the decision but include input from the team and customers. At the user-story level, the team makes the decision on how to craft and self-organize around them.

How might your roles align with your requirements tree? Keep in mind that anyone can contribute an idea, but only the senior management or product owners can make the priority call.

REQUIREMENTS TREE NAVIGATION EXERCISE

Working with another person or two, think about your requirements tree. For each requirements element level, who may provide input and who may have authority? Create a diagram similar to Figure 15-3. Share it with a few people. Ask if they find it helpful and how it could be improved.

Aligning Agile to Tree

Another benefit of having a requirements tree is that you can consider what Agile concepts and practices may be suited at each requirements level, as illustrated in Figure 15-4. While it is reasonable to experiment with many of the Agile concepts and practices that may work at various requirements levels, it can be beneficial to have a starter set and then adapt as you learn what works well or what the feasible options are. For example, it may be reasonable to start with use cases to help you cut increments and then advance to story mapping once there is experience with it.

Figure 15-4. Example of Agile concepts and practices used at each requirements level

Following Figure 15-4, executives may use a vision statement to share goals with the company at an all-hands. The divisions use a Business Model Canvas to discuss where they've been, where they plan to go, and how they plan to support the vision. Ideas come through the enterprise idea pipeline via a Customer Value Canvas that include a cost of delay (CoD) and value score.

To understand if the idea has value, the idea is decomposed using story mapping and an end-to-end, thin slice of the idea carved out. Epics and user stories that come from the increment are added to the backlog and groomed. Use cases are used to flesh out the epics. User stories are written in canonical form and have a corresponding unit test. Tasks are then written following an incremental development mindset to incrementally build the user story.

As part of the Agile concepts and practices, feedback loops discussed in Chapter 14 should be considered for each requirements level to validate the direction toward customer value. Find the Agile concepts and practices to help you decompose the work from strategy to task that work best for you.

REQUIREMENTS TREE PRACTICES EXERCISE

Working with another person or two, think about your requirements tree. For each requirements element level, what Agile concepts and practices can best help you collaborate and grasp the requirements elements at that level? Create a diagram similar to Figure 15-4. Share it with a few people. Ask if they find it helpful and how it could be improved.

What Does Your Requirements Tree Look Like?

The term *requirement* can be quite nebulous as it can mean requirements at many different levels. Do you mean corporate strategy, user story, feature, idea, or something else? I suggest that you do not assume everyone understands the requirements levels in your enterprise or product team. Instead, establish a common requirements tree so people have a baseline of common terms. This doesn't mean the terms and levels are locked in, but instead they will be something you mature and adapt over time. A requirements tree provides lineage from user stories and tasks to ensure that high value ideas are being worked on.

I have found that it can be beneficial to create a requirements tree diagram that includes all three aspects (requirements elements example, roles, and Agile concepts and practices). This can be an effective one-pager similar to a canvas to provide both transparency and guidance on how requirements are related and how people work together in the enterprise to create customer value.

Decomposing Ideas with Story Mapping

Story mapping points you at options that help validate customer value.

—Chapter co-author JP Beaudry

When you have determined that an idea is the highest-priority item to work on next, it is time to consider how you may validate its value to the customer. In the spirit of the Agile mindset, instead of attempting to build the full idea (that is, big batch), you should look at a way to build a portion of the idea to gain customer feedback. This is where decomposition comes into play and where user story mapping can help.

In this chapter, you will learn why big ideas should be decomposed and executed via smaller increments. Using the short form known as "story mapping," you will see why it is an excellent tool for that purpose. You will understand the basics of doing story mapping, and you will see how story mapping and the artifacts it generates can fit in and interrelate with other tools in your Agile galaxy and along your journey to build and deliver customer value.

© Mario E. Moreira 2017
M. E. Moreira, *The Agile Enterprise*, DOI 10.1007/978-1-4842-2391-8_16

Why Decompose Ideas

Decomposing big, bold business ideas means slicing smaller increments that have customer value. It is a critical activity performed by Lean and Agile organizations. It is the core of what happens in the Refine stage of the enterprise idea pipeline, as illustrated in Figure 16-1.

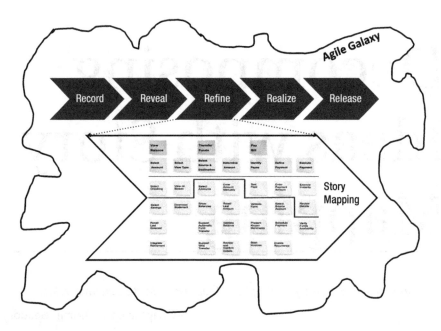

Figure 16-1. Story mapping during the Refine stage

There are many reasons why you would consider bringing your big business ideas to market incrementally. At a high level, the arguments fall in one of two buckets: market reasons and technical reasons.

On the market front, the pace of change in customer tastes and in the availability of competitive products to satisfy those tastes has never been so fast, and it is accelerating. Can you believe that the ubiquitous iPhone is, as of this writing, not yet a teenager? In a world where change is the norm, the past is no longer a reliable predictor of the future. Logical deduction alone cannot identify which products or solutions your customers will adopt. But applying experimental thinking can help you discover them.

From a technical perspective, enterprises that participate in the creative economy never build the same thing twice. Indeed, when something has to be done more than once, it gets automated. Therefore, enterprises are usually solving problems that are new to them. Your own enterprise may be like that. This begs several questions. Do you have the technical capabilities to build the product? Can you do it at the speed that meets customer expectations and at a cost the enterprise can afford and customers can accept?

■ **Agile Pit Stop**   There are two reasons why you want to bring your idea to market incrementally—to better understand market needs and to reduce technical challenges.

Uncertainty surrounding an enterprise's ability to deliver can be just as great as that surrounding market demand. This uncertainty demands a discovery mindset. Experimentation is core to discovery. Because success is not guaranteed, you must have the ability to run multiple experiments. These experiments should be short and inexpensive, yet yield as much information as possible. Experimental thinking is critical to the enterprise. The Refine stage of the enterprise idea pipeline is dedicated to cleverly decomposing big, bold business ideas into smaller increments.

Exploring Story Mapping

In the words of Jeff Patton, the person credited for formalizing the practice, "Story maps solve one of the big problems with using user stories in Agile development—that's losing sight of the big picture." He also calls this problem the "tragedy of the flat backlog."

A story map is a visual representation of the user journey your enterprise seeks to bring to life. It's a summary and reminder of the story you tell one another about what you are building, who you are building it for, what value the users will get, the options you have in satisfying user needs, and so on. Story mapping supports and promotes the conversation. It does not replace it.

A good way to see how story mapping works is to go through a simple example. You'll first see the steps from beginning to end. Later on, you'll get some practical tips on how to execute those steps.

■ **Agile Pit Stop**   Cutting increments of work via story mapping can help determine the value of an idea prior to the whole idea being built.

As an example, let's imagine a bank that has a very basic mobile banking app. Customers can view balances and transfer money between accounts. Now, the bank wants to add bill payment capabilities to the app. How could the bank limit its investment, particularly in software development, to discover whether its customers are interested in such a capability? The story map will make the options clearer. While this example is about augmenting an existing customer experience (the mobile banking experience), the same concepts apply to greenfield initiatives.

Visualize the User Experience Backbone

The first step in story mapping is to describe the flow of the user experience at the highest level. Remember that story mapping primarily focuses on articulating the user experience and not so much on how to bring the user experience to life. In other words, story mapping helps define and organize requirements, and then passes the baton to the team to turn those requirements into products or services.

In the case of the mobile banker, the users in question are the bank's customers. The story map will describe their desired experience. You can think of the basic flow of the user experience as viewing account balances, transferring funds, and paying bills, as illustrated in Figure 16-2. Those big activities represent what is known as the "backbone" of the story map. Each backbone big activity goes on the top of the map.

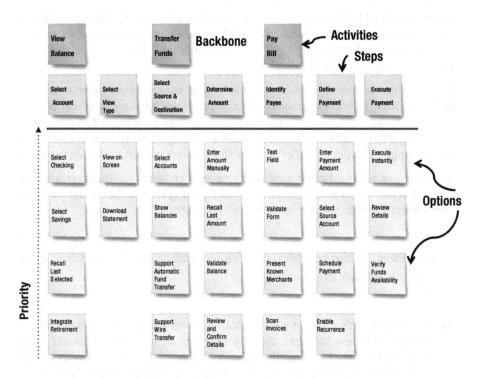

Figure 16-2. Story map for basic mobile app

Determine the Steps

For each backbone big activity, identify the steps that the user undertakes. For example, "View Balance" is a step where a user "Selects an Account" and "Selects a View Type" (screen, statement, and so on). "Transfer Funds" is a step where a user "Selects Source and Destination" and "Determines an Amount."

What about "Pay Bill"? One can imagine steps such as "Identify Payee," "Define the Payment," and "Execute the Payment."

Identifying the Options

So far, the description of the user experience has been very high level and applies to all users. The next tier of the story map becomes much more detailed. For each step, identify different user-facing options that embody it. For the sake of brevity, the remainder of the example will focus solely on the "Pay Bill" backbone element, but the procedure is the same for the entirety of the story map.

What are the different alternatives the bank could offer its customers to "Identify Payee"? One option is for the bank to maintain a list of well-known merchants, credit card companies, and utilities, assuming that doing so would save time for many of its customers. At the other end of the sophistication scale, another option is to provide an empty text field where customers enter name and address of their payee. A variant of that would be to provide a form where fields such as street name, city, and zip code are validated. Another option still is to enable customers to scan paper invoices for payee details. There are likely many other options. Those options are entered under their activity on the story map.

This step is a divergent period with no judgment of the options. You should not yet be concerned with the value, the cost, the feasibility, the completeness, the competitive positioning, or the strategic alignment of the options. That will come later with convergence. For now, you are trying to generate good options. Consider a quiet divergent period so that all options can be considered and no one dominates the conversation.

■ **Agile Pit Stop** High-level walk-through of story mapping: visualizing your backbone, determining the steps, identifying options, prioritizing options, and cutting an increment.

It's time to flesh out the "Define Payment" activity on the story map. One user experience option can be to enter the amount of the payment. Another can be to select the source account of the payment. The goal is to identify as many options as possible. Another option could be the ability to schedule a payment for a later date. Yet another could be the recurrence of payment. The options are only limited by your imagination.

To finish off the example, the "Execute Payment" activity could have options such as immediate trigger, verification of fund availability, pre-submission review of payee and amount details, and so on.

Prioritize the Options

The next step is to prioritize the options in each activity from top to bottom. This is a convergent period where you start to look for those options that may help you gain customer feedback to validate the value of the idea or that can help you determine the technical feasibility.

The criteria for prioritization is context-dependent, but customer value should always play a prominent role. Other criteria can be risk, urgency, and so on. As you can imagine, there is frequently tension between various criteria. You will learn more about prioritization in the "Six Prisms" section and how to have a conversation to navigate that tension in the "Practical Tips for Story Mapping" section.

Cut the Increment

Now answer this question: Across all activities on the map, which options will you deliver to the customer first? Because some options are ambitious and because you have some uncertainty about what the customer truly values, you want to deliver a subset as soon as possible. Delivering all options at once is the textbook definition of a big-batch approach.

The mechanics are simple. Draw a line across the story map through the options. Everything you place above the line is explicitly targeted for your next increment, while everything below is deferred to a subsequent one.

The selection of what goes above the line is where the hard work and magic happen. As previously stated, in traditional or waterfall-style development where all features are released in one go, everything is above the line. But in Agile enterprises, there is a deliberate attempt to bring value to customers as soon as possible. There is also recognition of the limits of our knowledge; what you think has customer value is not validated until it is in the hands of customer. Therefore, the real question is what you move above the line and why.

Let's explore how the bank could make that decision. If the bank is unsure that its clientele wants the online payment feature, it is in its interest to bring to market the simplest (and cheapest) thing that could possibly indicate customer preferences. After all, the bank most assuredly has many other ideas that compete for its finite product development capacity.

After some thought and collaborative discussion by the product owner, team, and a few key stakeholders, they consider a very simple implementation. This includes first selecting a checking account with a view on the screen and then selecting a basic text field for the payee, a payment amount automatically drafted from the ubiquitous checking account, and a review before execution. As illustrated in Figure 16-3 on the story map, those options are moved above the line, while the others are moved below.

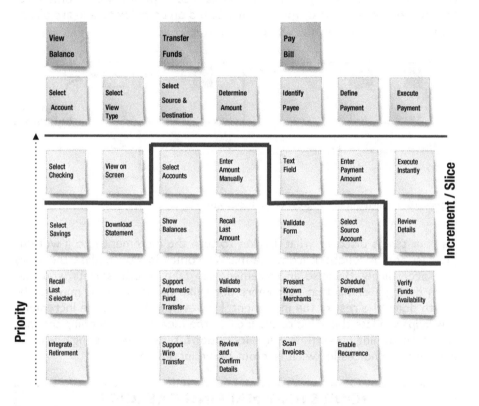

Figure 16-3. Cutting an increment for the mobile banking app

A frequent objection to slicing such a thin increment from a big idea is that the increment doesn't have enough features to satisfy all customers. Remember that the objective of this increment isn't to satisfy all customers. It is rather to see if some customers find the concept useful. If the early adopter, David the Gen Y-er, doesn't find online bill payment useful, then it's possible that no amount of bells and whistles will attract the masses. You can learn more about minimalistic increments, sometimes known as minimally viable product (MVP), by looking up "customer adoption curve" and reading *The Lean Startup* by Eric Ries. This increment could have been crafted differently for many reasons. You will shortly learn about those reasons, also known as prisms.

The Living Story Map

Now that the map is created and an increment sliced, what do you do with it? First, use the story map to track the execution of the defined increment. In many cases, it may take several weeks or sprints to complete an increment. During this time, on the story map, you can indicate which options are waiting, work in progress (WIP), or complete, as illustrated in Figure 16-4. These options tie directly into your requirements tree. Options will become epics and user stories for one or more teams, based on complexity, and are placed into the appropriate product or team backlog.

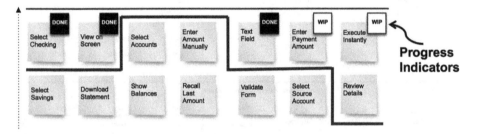

Figure 16-4. Highlighting progress on your story map

As your teams discover what it takes to turn the increment into a working product and as feedback from the market comes in, you update the story map accordingly. Because an increment can take several sprints, you may learn during a demo that customers don't like the idea and it may not be worth doing the rest of the increment. However, if they like the increment, this helps validate the value of the idea. In the meantime, amending the map can mean coming up with new activity options, redefining existing ones, and making new choices for what is in/out of the increment.

YOUR STORY MAPPING EXERCISE

Now it's your turn to do story mapping. Imagine you are hired by a bank to help it structure its mobile payment app. You learn that over 50% of the bank's customers are senior citizens. How could you carve an increment with the persona Erin the Senior Citizen in mind? What options might you provide and what would you work on first?

Six Prisms

To help you consider different ways to carve your thin increment, you can leverage the six-prism technique, as described in *Deliver Early and Often* by Emergn. The six prisms include value, geography, risk, stakeholder, urgency, and necessity. Each prism gives you a different lens to view your story map. The following are details on each prism.

Value asks which piece do customers value most? Instead of waiting to deliver everything, focus on delivering the highest-value piece first. The bank example utilizes this prism. Tools like cost of delay, as discussed in Chapter 12, can help you articulate value.

Geography asks if the product could be launched in just one of the many intended markets. E-commerce vendors that sell in many countries find value in using the geographic prism. If the bank operated a bilingual app in English and Spanish, applying this prism means it would go to market with just one of the two languages. The expense associated with translating into the other language would thus be deferred until the bank's conviction that online bill payment is indeed good business.

■ **Agile Pit Stop**   The six-prism technique allows you to consider different ways to carve your increment considering value, geography, risk, stakeholder, urgency, and necessity.

Risk asks what the biggest risk to this project or its killer assumption is. Applying the risk prism means tackling that first. If the bank were outsourcing its development to a first-time supplier, that relationship would be a risk. Keeping the first deliverable small mitigates the risk because the supplier skills are assessed at the lowest cost possible. Generally speaking, a proof of concept is an embodiment of the risk prism at play.

Stakeholder asks you to think about important stakeholders, whose opinion may have a disproportionate impact on your ability to deliver. This may be a customer in the form of a persona. It may also be an internal stakeholder, such as an executive, who finances your idea. You can learn more about personas in Chapter 14.

Urgency gets you to confront important external deadlines. Has a competitor released a form of mobile that would compel your bank to go to market with a subset of bill payment as soon as possible? Is there a seasonal reason such as Christmas that may urge you to build something earlier? Beware of internal deadlines that can promote unhelpful behaviors.

Necessity asks you to consider the bare minimum you can get away with. Without this minimum, you are not in business at all. For example, our bank could ask clients to send it a text message with their payment instructions and could have its tellers process the payments. This is a very basic way to achieve the concept of "mobile bill payment." Also, necessity can have you building just enough to avoid the fines of missing a regulation deadline.

Practical Tips for Story Mapping

As you consider approaching story mapping, there are a number of helpful tips to get you started. The following are some suggestions meant to maximize the value you get out of applying story mapping.

Streamline: A story map is a model to help focus thinking. It does not represent all the nuances of your application. Don't worry about process flow forks; just serialize them.

Persona: A story map is typically written from the customers' perspective, but sometimes your idea will have multiple user types. That's OK. Just string the various flows side-by-side, taking note of the changing persona. You can learn more about personas in Chapter 14.

Just-in-Time: You are encouraged to resist pre-slicing many increments. You don't need a second increment defined until the capacity to work on it is almost available. Premature slicing is akin to writing a plan. Humans fall in love with the plans they create, which makes them blind to feedback that may suggest the plan needs to be adjusted (in other words, confirmation bias).

Mob Creation: A way to get buy-in is have all types of stakeholders participate in the creation of the story map. Broad participation ensures that you get specialists from all areas. It also avoids triggering the question "Why wasn't I consulted?" in those who weren't represented. This is critical because humans are more vested in the success of the ideas they create than in the ones they are told about.

Diverge, Then Converge: As in many group exercises, you want to hear all the voices during the map creation. One tip is to do ten minutes of silent diverging when the map is first built. A facilitator should frame the story mapping exercise. Then people silently write their ideas for backbone, flow steps, and activity options on sticky notes or a digital tool. Then you facilitate a period of convergence where you identify affinities and remove duplicates.

Living Document: Shortly after an increment is delivered, you need to capture customer feedback. The people who sponsored the work should review that feedback and see if it influences how they want to invest their development capacity going forward. The story map should be updated to reflect the current state of work.

Public Display: Display the story map in an easily accessible public place. It provides transparency for the work and helps others know what the team is focusing on. It also makes an excellent backdrop for a variety of rituals such as planning, grooming, Scrum of Scrums, demos, reviews, and others.

Simplicity: In practice, Jeff Patton recommends building the map "middle-out" and let the activities and steps of the backbone emerge. The big activities are really just a summary of the steps that appear underneath. Smaller maps may not benefit much from this distinction. Only add the complexity if it helps your visualization.

Hypothesis of Value: Last, but perhaps most important, make the hypothesis of the value of the increment clear. When creating a story map, review the hypothesis for the idea and any details written on a canvas or idea pipeline record. If no hypothesis exists, then establish one. See Chapter 10 for how to articulate a hypothesis and Chapter 13 for how to create a canvas. Next, ask yourself whether the increment you have sliced is likely to result in the desired outcome and whether you are ready and able to measure a signal.

Can Story Mapping Help You Build a Better Story?

Decomposing big ideas into smaller increments allows you to better navigate the uncertainty inherent to the work of the creative economy. A useful increment seeks to validate customer value. It will do so quickly by being as small as possible. Incorporating customer feedback reduces the uncertainty surrounding the value of the big idea.

Story mapping helps you validate the hypothesis of customer value as well as the assumptions that underpin that hypothesis. You may find that it is useful during conversations to call out the primary persona. Understanding who the idea is for helps with the customer experience and the types of feedback loops that can strengthen the experiment. Getting all the brains to contribute is one way to manifest more of the collaborative Agile mindset.

Consider exploring story mapping. Which idea is your enterprise thinking about trying next to deliver value to your customers? How could you apply story mapping to deliver value or test critical hypotheses sooner?

For additional material, I suggest the following:

- *VFQ Delivery Early and Often* by Emergn Limited, Emergn Limited Publishing, 2014

- *User Story Mapping: Discover the Whole Story, Build the Right Product* by Jeff Patton, O'Reilly Media, 2014

- *The Lean Startup: How Today's Entrepreneurs Use Continuous Innovation to Create Radically Successful Businesses* by Eric Ries, Crown Business, 2011

Connecting the Idea Pipeline to Backlogs

Connecting ideas at the top to user stories at the bottom helps everyone see the big and connected picture of the work.

—Mario Moreira

One aspect of helping people to see the full picture is the ability to connect the dots from one part of the enterprise to the other. This may not be as easy as it sounds since enterprises are rarely one transparent canvas where you can see the all the moving parts or the full requirements tree in one space.

What you need are people and mechanisms that can help you connect the dots. From a people perspective, you need thinkers, innovators, and leaders. These are people who can grasp both the big view of the world and the tiny, yet important, details that can make an enterprise move forward.

Connecting the dots in an organization is not easy. Aside from seeing both the full picture and the details, everyone involved needs to be able to identify dependencies among problems and information and see patterns and trends. More deeply, they need to be able to identify the root cause of a problem and connect it to a similar root cause in a whole other area.

© Mario E. Moreira 2017
M. E. Moreira, *The Agile Enterprise*, DOI 10.1007/978-1-4842-2391-8_17

Connecting the dots, whether through people, process, or technology, can help you understand how all the pieces of the work are intertwined, what you can do to optimize the flow of the work, and ensure you are actually working on customer value. Mechanisms such as technology and process can help you connect ideas that are valuable to work that will make its way to teams' backlogs.

Connecting to Backlogs

Work comes into the backlog from several sources. The main source should be from the idea increments or feedback from customers. In Chapter 16, the concept of decomposition and the practice of story mapping are shared. When you start a story mapping session, its unclear what the result may be until you cut the first increment. You connect the dots by listening to everyone in a divergent mode and converging to an increment of work.

■ **Agile Pit Stop**   Connecting the ideas in the enterprise idea pipeline to their children (that is, epics and user stories) in the backlog and vice versa helps ensure a smooth flow of customer-value work and traceability from the portfolio level to the team level.

There is a lot of storytelling going on during story mapping, where you consider what story the customers are telling as they experience the idea. In making storytelling a collaborative session, we effectively ask participants to listen to multiple options and connect the dots to a meaningful end-to-end slice.

The challenge in connecting the dots between idea and user story is that you start with an idea that can have multiple options and directions. In the middle of a story mapping session, it can be quite nebulous as to how it may end, and it is important to be comfortable with this uncertainty. The end result is a collection of epics and user stories that are added to a backlog(s).

The key is to connect the ideas in the enterprise idea pipeline to their children (that is, epics and user stories) in the backlog and vice versa, as illustrated in Figure 17-1. Connecting ideas helps ensure a smooth flow of customer-value work from the portfolio level to the team level, and it ensures there is traceability from the idea down to user stories and tasks.

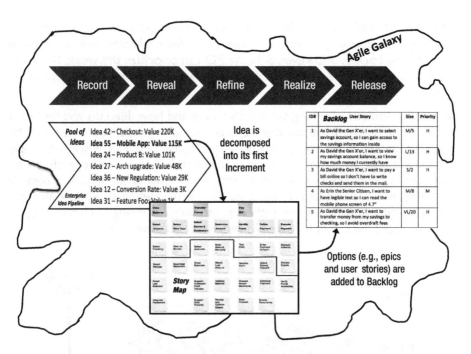

Figure 17-1. Connecting the enterprise idea pipeline to user stories that support the idea

The penultimate backlog is one that virtually supports all levels of requirements elements across your requirements tree. Through the use of filters and tags, you can instantiate any level of requirements you'd like to visualize such as a portfolio view of all ideas (or at least the highest-value ideas), an idea or product view, or a team view. What you really want to highlight is what parts of the idea are actually being worked on. It would be great to be able to click an active idea and instantly see what user stories are actually being worked on that support that idea.

Working with the Backlog

A backlog is effectively a list of prioritized work. Teams in Agile operate from a backlog typically called a product backlog, but may be referred to by other terms. Backlogs can be stand-alone, although I recommend that they be connected to the enterprise idea pipeline of work on the higher end and even a maintenance backlog of work on the lower end.

Product Owners own a backlog. It is their primary tool for collecting and managing requirements. It should be the single source of requirements for both transparency and efficiency reasons. The PO typically adds work items to the backlog and prioritizes them according to the value-based prioritization method he or she chooses to use.

The team should have continuous access to the backlog. In the spirit of self-organizing, anyone may contribute work in the form of epics, user stories, and tasks to the backlog. However, only the PO can prioritize the work. The team should have edit rights to add details to each work element whether epic, user story, or task.

When you look at a backlog, what do you see and how deep do you look? If a backlog is prioritized, you see the requirements elements that are deemed the most important at the top, as illustrated in Figure 17-2. This work is typically the *current work* the team is focusing on, either in a sprint or recently pulled from the backlog. The next set of priority requirements elements are *possible upcoming work*. The reason I say "possible" is that when you apply an Agile mindset, requirements are not locked in and they can change. From there, you have *possible future work* followed by *may-never-get-done work*.

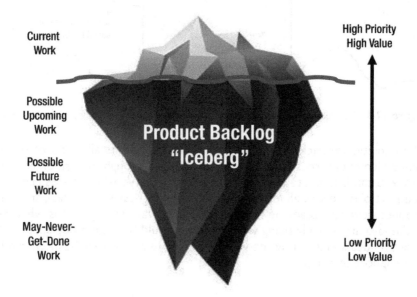

Figure 17-2. Product backlog iceberg

Types of Backlogs

There are many forms of backlogs. They can be in the form of a Kanban board or Scrum board. Traditionally, backlogs are aligned with teams and called product backlogs or team backlogs. These backlogs are usually filled with epics, users stories, and tasks. Agile teams use backlogs to help drive their work. All backlogs in Agile are meant to be prioritized. The following are examples of several backlogs.

▓ **Agile Pit Stop**   Backlogs can be in the form of a Kanban board or Scrum board and may be called an enterprise idea pipeline, product backlog, sprint backlog, or team backlog.

An *enterprise idea pipeline* is form of a backlog. The difference is that the enterprise idea pipeline focuses on the portfolio of ideas as they come into the enterprise, and it tracks progress from the Record stage to the Reflect stage. Stakeholders of value (product owners and chief product owners as well as business, marketing, and senior managers) use this backlog to prioritize by value and drive investment decisions.

A *product backlog* is a backlog of work that revolves around a product, service, or idea. The PO owns it. While anyone can add work on the product backlog, only the PO can prioritize it. Work that comes from decomposing the idea is placed in this backlog if it is product-centric. From there, it is often groomed to add detail and better understand the work. Those user stories that are at the top of the product backlog are of high priority and are ready to be pulled and worked on.

The *sprint backlog* is a backlog of work that fits into a sprint. It represents a subset of user stories that are prioritized high enough to get pulled into the sprint. Those stories that are highest priority and fit the team velocity or amount of work a team can complete within a sprint become the sprint backlog. There is a unique sprint backlog for each sprint. The items in the sprint backlog get pulled from the product backlog during sprint planning. The sprint backlog forms the backbone of the work within a sprint.

The *team backlog* is a backlog of work that is meant for a team. It is beneficial when you have multiple Scrum teams building a product together or if the team is non-product specific. The team backlog represents a view of the work that is geared toward a particular team. During grooming and sprint planning, the team hones the work in their prioritized backlog. From that, the team can establish a sprint backlog of those high-priority stories they will work on within a sprint.

▓ **Agile Pit Stop**   A story map acts as the third dimension to the two-dimensional backlog and provides the customer experience view of the work ahead.

While technically a story map described in Chapter 16 is not a backlog, it does provide a view of the current and future work much like a backlog. More importantly, a story map provides a third dimension to the backlog by providing the customer experience view of the work ahead. It is important when story mapping is being used to connect the idea to the story map to the backlog. The story map used for an idea should continue to live as additional increments are considered and additional options in the form of epics and user stories are generated to populate the backlog.

Attributes of Backlogs

The beauty of a backlog, whether an enterprise idea pipeline or a product backlog is that you can enhance it with attributes that can help you sort and understand the requirements within. Attributes are characteristics that can help you find distinctions among requirements. An example of an attribute is priority. By including an attribute that helps you consider the importance of requirements, you are able to sort the requirements by order of importance, allowing you to focus on the high-priority requirements.

Figure 17-3 illustrates a simple version of a backlog. It includes the identification number, user story, size, priority, source, an indication of progress, and owner of the work. Some people use a paper-based backlog that is laid out on a wall, while most people use an online backlog management tool that often includes a variety of features.

ID#	User Story	Size	Priority	Source	Progress	Owner
1	As David the Gen X-er, I want to select savings account, so I can gain access to the savings information inside.	M/5	H	Customer A	Sprint 1 - done	Ravi and Claire
2	As David the Gen X-er, I want to view my savings account balance, so I know how much money I currently have.	L/13	H	Customer C	Sprint 1 - done	Julie and Mike
3	As David the Gen X-er, I want to pay a bill online so I don't have to write checks and send them in the mail.	S/2	H	Customer A, B, C	Sprint 2 - in-progress	Chris and Alex
4	As Erin the Senior Citizen, I want to have legible text so I can read the mobile phone screen of 4.7".	M/8	M	Strategy	tbd	
5	As David the Gen X-er, I want to transfer money from my savings to checking, so I avoid overdraft fees.	VL/20	H	Customer B	Sprint 2 – in-progress	Staci and Sean

Figure 17-3. Example of a backlog

There are many types of attributes that can be included on your backlog to help you manage the work. These attributes include the following:

- **Requirements Types:** a way to differentiate among requirements types such as ideas, increments, epics, themes, user stories, tasks, and defects.

- **ID:** a way to provide a unique identifier for each requirement.

- **User Story:** a requirement that includes who wants it (personas), what they want, and why they want it.

- **Details:** information learned during grooming and planning including decisions.

- **Acceptance Criteria:** the conditions that satisfy a requirement typically at the user-story level.

- **Source:** the origin of the requirement, such as customer, stakeholder, or strategy.

- **Priority:** a way to differentiate the importance of the requirement, often written as *high/medium/low* or *must have/should have/could have/won't have.*

- **Sizing:** a way to indicate the amount of work involved in a requirement often specified in story points (for example, 1/2/3/5/8/13/20).

- **Complexity:** the factors and risks involved in completing the work written as *high/medium/low.* Can impact the size of the work.

- **Dependencies:** a way to indicate when a requirement is dependent on other requirements or external items.

- **Progress:** the current status of the work. May also include the history of the item.

- **Owners:** the team members who have volunteered to do the work.

BACKLOG ATTRIBUTES EXERCISE

Consider creating a backlog or reflect on your current backlog. What attributes would you include to help you organize and sort through your requirements? Create this backlog similar to the example in Figure 17-3, but with your attributes. Exercise your backlog by adding some actual requirements to the backlog. Explain it to another person. Would they change any of the attributes?

Considering Dependencies

Managing dependencies is a big part of running an enterprise. Similarly, managing requirements is often an activity of managing dependencies. Some work is required in order for other work to complete. Other work may be needed to complete an end-to-end view of the work.

Be aware of lower-value work that may be dependencies. If a high-customer-value user story is the next requirement to get pulled for work, you may learn upon grooming it that it depends on lower-value work getting done first. In this case, either the lower-value work inherits the higher value or you continue to keep it as lower value and create the dependency link.

Importance of Grooming

Grooming or refining is the process of honing user stories to gain a level of detail and get them ready for sprint planning. In relation to customer value, while technical details will be discussed, the key focus in grooming should be the business details on why an epic or user story is needed. When there is a strong understanding of why something is needed and in what business context, the team is able to make more context-specific technical decisions to support the customer need. The business context and reason may be inherited from the story map or idea itself if properly explained.

There are a number of benefits for grooming sessions. Since grooming typically occurs prior to working on the requirement, it allows time for the new work to "sink in" and to mitigate risks, and it gives the PO time to address unanswered questions. It also provides a short window of where the work is headed.

During grooming, the focus should be on the higher-priority work for the simple reason that it is better to put effort in the highest-value work and not waste time focusing on lower-value work since you may never get to it.

■ **Agile Pit Stop** The key focus in backlog grooming is to prioritize and rank order the user stories, and then gain more business and technical details of those higher-priority user stories.

The PO is primarily responsible for the grooming event. The PO should invite the full team and include others such as marketing and business leaders who may have business context. Most importantly, the team can ask the PO tough questions regarding specific information and acceptance criteria to gain relevant details about the story.

What does a grooming event look like? It may last a couple of hours when the user stories are reviewed in a priority order. Each story may be focused on for about five to ten minutes with the goal of gaining a better understanding of the work, starting with understanding the business reason for the work. The better you groom the higher-priority items within the backlog, the easier and shorter the sprint planning event will be.

While grooming, you may focus on breaking epics into user stories, ensuring user stories are in canonical form (or a defined form), adding business and technical detail, identifying dependencies, understanding acceptance criteria, identifying unknowns and risks, capturing what is out of scope, and optionally considering sizing (T-shirt sizing of S/M/L or even story points). Finally, you may mark stories ready for sprint planning or ready for work.

How Well Connected Are You to Your Work?

A big part of helping employees see the full picture of customer-value work is the ability to connect the dots from when ideas come in all the way down to the user stories and tasks. This may not be as easy as it seems since enterprises are rarely one transparent, end-to-end requirements canvas where you can see the full requirements tree in one space.

Do you have people, processes, and technologies that can help you "connect the dots" across your requirements landscape? Can you be sure that the ideas of highest customer value are being worked on? Can you see the user stories that help build the increment of an idea? Connecting the ideas to your user stories provide transparency to your work, a view of what work is getting attention, and the assurance that the user stories connected to the highest-value ideas are indeed being worked on.

Collaborating on User Stories

A user story is much more than a written artifact; it is a promise for a continued requirements conversation.

—Mario Moreira

I was tempted to entitle this chapter "Writing User Stories." The reason I decided against it is the work of creating user stories entails much more than just writing. It requires collaboration among the product owner, team, customers, and others; it involves communicating the business meaning behind the story; and it emphasizes how the user story is much more than a written artifact. It is, instead, a promise for a continued conversation.

The Promise for a Conversation

A user story is a piece of user functionality that, when built, can be demonstrated and exercised. A user story has a before-and-after life. Similar to the temporal concept of AD (Anno Domini) and BCE (Before Common Era), the user story has an AD and a BCE. The BCE refers to the journey the idea or problem takes to get to the written user story, and the AD refers to the journey it takes to evolve into a piece of working product or service. In both cases, that journey should be a collaborative one that includes customer feedback. The earlier chapters in this book discussed in detail the collaborative nature of getting from an idea to user story.

© Mario E. Moreira 2017
M. E. Moreira, *The Agile Enterprise*, DOI 10.1007/978-1-4842-2391-8_18

Once the user stories and epics have been identified from the increment of story mapping or other practices that decompose ideas, it is time to write down the user stories. This continues the collaborative process of understanding the user story now that it is written, ergo the saying that the user story or requirement is a promise for a continued conversation.

The concept of the promise for a conversation is to move you away from "throwing the requirement over the wall" since the real value of understanding user stories is in the collaborative conversation along the way. "Throwing over the wall" refers to a practice where one group writes requirements that, when completed, are thrown over the wall to a group that has to build those requirements with little or no discussion, as illustrated in Figure 18-1.

Figure 18-1. "Over the wall" approach to requirements

A more robust approach is to have those who build the requirements be involved in the decomposition and grooming process to collaboratively flesh out the requirements in a collaborative manner, as illustrated in Figure 18-2. This is a mindset shift that recognizes that first-hand and shared information benefits the team with an outcome that is more aligned with customer value. Having team members involved in story mapping or the practice of decomposing ideas provides the team with insight into the customer experience and how you got to a thin-slice, end-to-end flow of the idea.

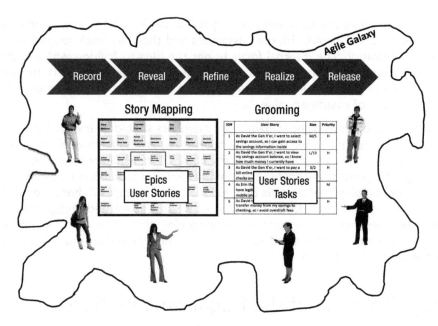

Figure 18-2. Collaborative conversational approach to requirements

Once the epics and user stories are visible from the first increment of story mapping, further refinement of epics and user stories can occur, as discussed in Chapter 17. This should continue through sprint planning or the next level of planning to better understand the work ahead. The collaborative process utilizes the brainpower of the whole team whereby each member may contribute to the understanding of the requirement to better shape a working solution based on the customer needs.

Collaboratively Engaging the Team

In an Agile world, writing down requirements provides a focal point where you can have collaborative conversations between the business and engineering sides. Whether this is between the PO and team or the customer and tester, the importance is that a shared understanding begins and continues. This discussion initiates the learning between the business and engineering sides where the engineering side better understands the customer value of the requirement and the business side better understands the options that can suit the customer needs.

■ **Agile Pit Stop**   The collaborative conversation includes internal people who bring the idea to fruition and external people who provide feedback to move in the direction of customer feedback.

The collaborative conversation goes beyond those internal to the enterprise. As discussed in Chapter 14, the customers and their feedback loops add to the collaboration. The internal focus brings the idea to fruition with healthy conversations to understand the customer needs. The external focus involves customers to gain their important feedback to determine if you are moving in the direction of customer value.

There are debates as to how many team members should be involved in story mapping or grooming user stories. My answer has always been all of them. For grooming user stories, this is the team. Having the whole team collaborate through the process eliminates the need of sharing second-hand information. For story mapping, the caveat is that you may do it in stages if there are more than ten people involved. The reason is to keep it active and engaging while allowing everyone to participate. For grooming and sprint planning, having the whole team collaborate ensures a greater understanding and applies the brainpower of everyone.

Top Branches of the Requirements Tree

User stories are a form of requirements. The challenge with the word *requirements* is that it may indicate requirements at many levels and sizes, such as user requirements, technical requirements, and business objectives. Because of the possibility for confusion, you need to be aware of your requirements tree discussed in Chapter 15. You need to determine where any particular requirement belongs by virtue of its scope and size in a hierarchy of requirements. Figure 18-3 illustrates user stories that live in a requirements tree that starts with corporate strategy and then has the levels of idea, increment, epic, user story, and task.

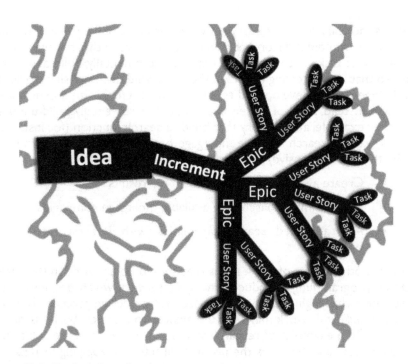

Figure 18-3. Top branches of a requirements tree

Since this chapter of the book continues the journey of the idea now being decomposed to user stories, a more detailed definition of *epic, user story*, and *task* as they relate to building new ideas follows.

An *epic* is the parent of multiple user stories and is roughly equivalent to a function, feature, or very large user story that encapsulates a large piece of functionality. Epics are typically written by the PO but may be contributed by other stakeholders or may result from a story mapping or other decomposition session. They should be decomposed into user stories before being introduced into a sprint.

A *user story* is the equivalent of a business or user requirement and is collected and managed by the PO. Stories provide user functionality that represents value to the customer. It should be non-compound and have one persona. A user story should be able to be built within a sprint. The next section discusses user stories at length.

A *task* is the child of a user story—a very small unit of work—and is equivalent to an incremental decomposition of the user story that the team defines. The intent of tasks is to allow the team to incrementally build and test the story so that not all testing occurs at the end. Avoid decomposing stories into stand-alone design, develop, and test tasks, which emphasize a mini-waterfall approach. Instead, tasks of a user story should incrementally build upon each other. For example, a user story that builds a search function (for instance: As a user, I want to search available mortgage options so I can determine which will be the least expensive) can be decomposed into the following:

- Create a static Web page to hold my results

- Build a simple search with available mortgage companies

- Add advanced search capabilities with interest rate options

There are other types of work items that should be captured in the backlog. Extreme programming introduced the *spike solution,* which provides a focus on solving a challenging technical, architectural, or design problem. Known as a *research spike,* this work may seek the answer to a critical business or technical issue. Two examples of research spikes are "What database solution will the team use?" and "What is the product direction in applying forums?" The answers serve to support subsequent epics and user stories.

User Stories

Within an Agile context, user stories are the primary currency used to determine what needs to be built by the team that represents customer value. User stories describe functionality that will be valuable to a customer and user (in other words, persona). User stories are the primary topic discussed in grooming and sprint planning. The intent of a user story isn't to specify every detail of the need but to provide enough business and technical detail to have a healthy and collaborative conversation about the story.

■ **Agile Pit Stop**   The user story is the basic building block for a piece of functionality that needs to be built. It is the primary currency for the team to understand customer value.

The product owner is responsible for eliciting user stories from customers and stakeholders and identifying them in decomposition exercises such as story mapping. Many others, however, may contribute user stories to the PO, including the team and the sales and marketing departments. The PO collects and adds user stories into the backlog. Those user stories that are rank-ordered highest within the backlog get selected and built within a sprint or are the next to be pulled. The attempt is to build user story functionality within a sprint or approximately a week time box.

User Story Canonical Form

There are many ways to write a user story. The *canonical form* is one example of a requirements language construct that is geared toward Agile and customer value. This brief statement expresses a user story as *who* wants something, *what* that person wants, and *why* he or she wants it. The canonical form transcends process and works just as well for any methodology or process. There are three key elements of a user story in canonical form: the persona, the action, and the business benefit.

The *persona* represents a particular user, as discussed in Chapter 14. Examples include Erin the Senior Citizen, who uses basic user interface functionality for straightforward tasks; Sunny the Gen X-er, who needs more complex interface functionality for sophisticated banking tasks; and David the Gen Y-er, who is technically savvy and has simple banking needs.

■ **Agile Pit Stop**   There are three key elements of a user story in canonical form: the persona (who), the action (what is wanted), and the business benefit (why it is wanted).

The *action* represents what the personas would like to do with the product. This will include an outcome they are looking to achieve (for example, create an account) and may include a receiving entity (for instance, get a copy of my statement to read on my mobile phone).

The *business benefit* indicates the value that is gained for the persona. It provides context for the action and helps with testing scenarios. If I said, "As a user, I can create an account" and leave the business benefit empty, why would you think the user wants an account? The answer can lead you to build very different things. If the answer is "to become a member of the site," you might build a MyPage. If the answer is "to make stock trades," you might build a trading application.

When establishing a list of user stories, it is strongly recommended to establish a user story language construct like the canonical form that helps you consistently document the stories, as shown in Figure 18-4.

```
As a <persona>
I want to <action>
so that <business benefit >
```

Figure 18-4. Agile canonical form

The following are examples of user stories in canonical form:

- As Erin the Senior Citizen, I want to create an account so that I can become a member of the site.

- As Sunny the Gen X-er, I want to set up my profile to include my photo so that my distributed team members know what I look like.

- As David the Gen Y-er, I want to search homes so that I know what properties are available in my price range.

The product owner should be educated in writing user stories in the canonical form or whatever form is chosen to articulate user stories. The team should be educated in understanding what to look for in a user story and asking questions regarding the elements of the canonical form to better determine the business need. The PO may also want to educate stakeholders and customers on how to provide their needs in canonical form for consistency and clarity.

It can be very easy to fall in the erroneous habit of writing long user stories. This is often because you want to add more detail to make the user story more meaningful. A better alternative is to write the additional detail into the body or comment section of the user story, depending on what tool you use to capture the user story. For example, it may be as simple as a note card or as sophisticated as a vendor backlog management tool.

USER STORY WRITING EXERCISE

Consider the product or service you are working on. Following the canonical form (As a <persona>, I want to <action> so that <business benefit>), practice writing two user stories to convey a customer need. Explain your best user story to a colleague. Were you able to explain it? What questions did the colleague ask? Did you improve your user story as a result of the questions?

Acceptance Criteria for a User Story

The *acceptance criteria* are an important attribute of a user story. Each user story should have its own unique set of *acceptance criteria*. Acceptance criteria answer the question, "How will I know when I'm done with the story?" They do this by providing functional and nonfunctional information that helps set boundaries for the work and establishes pass/fail criteria for testers to establish the test cases that are used to test a user story.

Ideally, customers provide these criteria when they articulate the user story, but the PO usually writes the criteria, acting as the voice of the customer. If the PO is having problems writing acceptance criteria, team up with QA testers who can draw from their experience to help the PO.

Agile Pit Stop   To write effective acceptance criteria, state the intention, not the solution. In other words, state the "what," not the "how. The team will figure out the how.

To write effective acceptance criteria, state the intention, not the solution. In other words, state the "what," not the "how." For example, it is better to write "The user can choose an account." rather than "The user can select the account from a drop-down menu." The acceptance criteria are independent of implementation details. If the user story is "As Erin the Senior Citizen, I want to create an account so that I can become a member of the site," then the acceptance criteria for a user story may include the following:

- User is presented with an account creation option.
- User must enter an e-mail address and a password.
- The password must follow the security policy.
- Provide user account confirmation within five seconds.
- User lands on the home page after creating the account.

Other Attributes of a User Story

A user story is complemented by several attributes besides the acceptance criteria. These attributes help you describe the scope, ownership, and progress of the story, as illustrated in the story card in Figure 18-5. They may include the following:

- **Comments:** any decisions or details that have an impact on the "how" to build it based on grooming and planning discussions.
- **Size:** a place to include the size, typically in story points.

- **Tasks:** decomposition of the user story into bits of work that represent an incremental build of functionality. They may be nested in a story or linked as individual children records to the user story.

- **Owners:** members of the team working on the story. There should be at least one developer and one QA tester.

- **State:** the status of the work such as *open*, *in progress*, *resolved*, *verified*, and *done*.

User Story : *As a <persona>, I want to <action>, so that I can <business benefit>*		
Comments : _____		
_____		
Size: _____	Owner : _____	State: _____
Acceptance Criteria : _____		
Tasks: _____		
_____		
_____		

Figure 18-5. Holistic view of a user story in story card form

Do User Stories Promote Conversation?

To get to a user story, the journey occurs both before the user story takes shape and after it is written, and it should be collaborative and evolutionary. The written user story is a promise for a conversation that helps the team both understand and shape the outcome to better meet customer value. Ensure you promote the conversation with the team and others.

User stories form the backbone of the work on your team. As you write user stories, consider a requirements language construct such as the canonical form. Including the persona or whom the functionality should be built for helps you understand the point of view of the persona. Including the action helps you understand what needs to be built. The business benefit helps you understand why the functionality is needed. These elements provide clarity for the team to build what the customer wants. The collaborative approach ensures that everyone on the team understands the customer needs so they can better build something the customer wants.

Promoting Agile Budgeting

The key to Agile budgeting is being able to adapt at the speed of the market.

—Mario Moreira

What makes up customer value is changing at a faster and faster pace. Many market leaders have found themselves lagging behind new leaders. Market share from a decade ago may have disappeared and been taken over by new competitors. As markets change and new customer needs emerge, do you have the ability to adapt? Can you adapt your budgeting to the market demand, making people and resources available to capture market share or prevent a reduction to your market share?

It is important to have a budgeting framework that can handle the shifts in the market, turning quickly to the new direction. This takes a combination of looking at your current supply-and-demand system and having the ability to adapt. You also need a budgeting framework that reduces wait states and ensures that the highest-value ideas get to market quickly. While this isn't easy, not doing so will only make your current position in the marketplace more challenging.

■ **Agile Pit Stop**   A great budgeting framework helps you shift to the new direction of the marketplace and customer value, reduce wait states, and reduce time to market.

© Mario E. Moreira 2017
M. E. Moreira, *The Agile Enterprise*, DOI 10.1007/978-1-4842-2391-8_19

From an Agile mindset, you need to apply the Agile principle of "welcome changing requirements." As discussed in Chapter 15, the term *requirements* can mean any level in the requirements tree, from strategy to task and everything in between.

An Agile adoption typically focuses on change to requirements at the team or product level. To truly welcome change, ideas must be welcome at the enterprise level where ideas come in. This means you do not sit on ideas for months or wait for the annual budget cycle. Instead, you welcome change and then determine its level of priority in a methodical way. If the value rises high enough, it is put in position to get pulled into work.

Moving Away from Traditional Budgeting

At its most simple form, a budgeting framework is a means to establish where money gets spent in an enterprise. A good budgeting framework applies a demand system like an idea pipeline where ideas collect. On a regular basis, it assesses the demand based on customer value and enterprise strategy, and then it aligns the supply side to meet the demand.

In many organizations today, budgeting is a yearly affair. Budgeting starts by soliciting ideas, often referred to as projects, that are collected over a period of several months. As illustrated in Figure 19-1, some high-value ideas may have already been in the demand pipeline for up to six months prior to the budgeting cycle. Then the idea waits another three months for the budgeting cycle to identify and prioritize ideas, another month to get approved, and yet another three months waiting to get pulled by a team since their current workload is full for the next three months. That means a high-value idea may wait for upward of 12 months before it gets worked on.

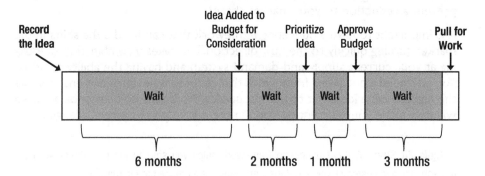

Figure 19-1. Traditional budget process—many wait states

Traditional budgeting frameworks may have many high-value ideas sitting in the pipeline for upward of a year before work begins. If you are familiar with value stream mapping that highlights the wait states in your process, you will find that in a traditional framework, ideas are waiting around during the majority of the process. You literally cannot afford this approach.

If you understand the marketplace well enough, you may realize that a high-value idea a year ago will not have the same level of value now that it had then, and it may completely miss the market window. Additionally, even if you proceed with the idea, you may miss the peak of the total opportunity as a competitor may get there first, resulting in your market share opportunity being much smaller. This is why you need an Agile budgeting framework.

Why Agile Budgeting?

The overall theme of Agile budgeting is for an enterprise to use its money more wisely as it adapts to customer needs and the marketplace. This starts with having an enterprise idea pipeline and stakeholders that readily accept and evaluate ideas as they enter the pool of ideas in the Reveal stage. This effectively eliminates the annual budget process wait states that can make an idea irrelevant and it helps you optimize the flow of getting the idea to market much more quickly, as illustrated in Figure 19-2. In effect, Agile budgeting is an adaptive and continuous budgeting framework.

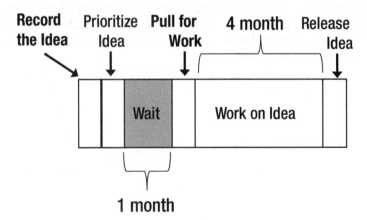

Figure 19-2. Agile budgeting framework—reducing wait time for high-value idea

Figure 19-2 highlights that not only will you get the idea to market up to 12 months earlier than the example in Figure 19-1, you will also much more likely hit the market window and get a bigger market share, resulting in more revenue for your enterprise. Comparing the traditional budgeting process shown in Figure 19-1 to the Agile budgeting framework shown in Figure 19-2, from "Record the Idea" to "Pull for Work," not only will you get the idea to market 12 months earlier, you may also actually deliver the high-value idea six months before even starting the work if using the traditional approach.

Value-Driven Supply and Demand

As you look across your 5R model, the Record and Reveal stages represent your demand side while the Refine, Realize, and Release stages represent your supply side, as illustrated in Figure 19-3. The enterprise idea pipeline is the pool of ideas in a rank order that comprises your demand, and teams comprise the supply of those who can work on ideas.

In a more traditional budgeting framework, a team or division has a fixed budget and supply. If that division or team runs out of high-value work, it pulls lower-value work. If teams are not lightning-bolt shaped (see the following section), then they can only pull the work they are capable of doing.

If no work is coming from the enterprise level, then these teams may create work that is often lower value than what is in the enterprise idea pipeline. The flip side is that if teams have been given their supply of work following a traditional budgeting process, they are often not available for any incoming high-value work from mid-year as their backlog is full from the work given them from the annual budget.

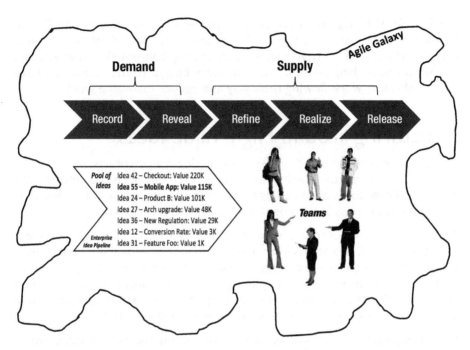

Figure 19-3. Supply (teams) and demand (enterprise idea pipeline)

A more customer-value-based approach is to pair the Agile budgeting framework with the enterprise idea pipeline and lightning-bolt-shaped teams. The advantage is that you can use these concepts as a way to ensure you align the people and teams (in other words, supply) with the most valuable ideas (that is, demand) on a continuous and flexible basis.

Imagine a scenario where the enterprise idea pipeline has a number of very high-value ideas waiting in the pool during the Reveal stage. As part of the Reveal stage, it is discovered that the top idea requires the help from three teams to work on that idea. When you look at the capacity of those teams, the third team is full and cannot pull any more work in.

Now you have two choices. You can ask the third team to evaluate if this new idea is of higher value than their current work and, if so, gracefully wrap up or cut the tail of the work as quickly as possible. Alternatively, if you see that the third team is consistently the bottleneck to pull in high-value work, then maybe it is time to add people to the team or create another team that can fulfill that type of work.

The benefit of having an enterprise idea pipeline is that you can visually see high-value ideas waiting in the pool (demand) and the utilization of teams (supply). The benefit of having an Agile budgeting framework is that you can actually do something about it. You can move budget to the teams that have more high-value work flowing their way and reduce low-value work.

Structuring around High-Value Ideas

The primary theme behind an Agile budgeting framework is to use your money more wisely by enabling effective investment decisions. Investment decisions should focus on matching the highest-customer-value idea (demand) with the earliest possible moment a team can work on it (supply).

A portion of an enterprise's investment will focus on *running* the business activities such as maintaining an enterprise's critical business operations along with maintenance and support. Hopefully, a greater portion is spent on investing in ideas focused on *growing* existing products and services and ideas focused on *transforming* and innovating the business. An Agile budgeting framework considers all three areas (run, grow, and transform).

Your goal should be to have all teams working on the highest-value work. However, it is not unusual to see some teams working on low-value work. Keep in mind that demand, whether in the form of ideas, features, or bug fixes, will typically outstrip supply, which is the teams that do the work. Because there will always be lots of "work," it is important to ensure that the work that your teams are doing is, in fact, of the highest value.

You do not want to wait until the end of the year to realize that a team or whole division is working on primarily low-value work. A traditional budgeting framework has teams work through the annual backlog of ideas as new high-value ideas wait on the bench, as illustrated in Figure 19-4. An Agile budgeting framework gives teams the ability to pull in the highest-value ideas so all teams are working on high-value work.

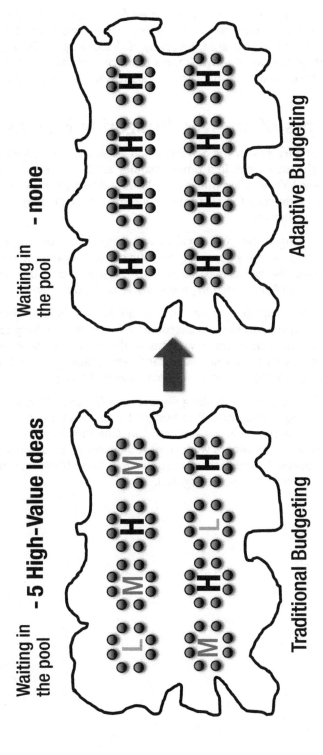

Figure 19-4. Moving from a mix of value work (low, medium, high) to all high-value work

If it is clear that a team or division is the target for a lot of high-value work, then it behooves the enterprise to invest more in those areas by adding more people or teams in that area. Inversely, if the enterprise idea pipeline consistently highlights low-value work for a team or division, it may be time to invest less in those areas or adapt their skills toward the high-value work.

Components of an Agile Budgeting Framework

An Agile budgeting framework is a system that allows you to adjust investment toward high-value work in a timely manner so that high value gets to customers quickly. While called budgeting, Agile budgeting is more than this as it emphasizes optimizing for customer value over management hierarchy and organization structure.

Since enterprises range from very small to very large, how you might implement Agile budgeting will vary according to your context. Given the complexity of an enterprise, the intent is to tailor it to fit your enterprise. Here are the components of an Agile budgeting framework, as illustrated in Figure 19-5.

First and foremost, Agile budgeting requires an Agile mindset where you embrace adapting to the market and customer value, you are willing to adapt your enterprise list of ideas to the new highest-value idea, you apply the Agile values and principles to help you understand why adapting is a very good thing, and you incorporate customer feedback along the way.

Incremental and experimental thinking discussed in Chapter 10 is important in an Agile budgeting framework. You budget for and commit to an increment instead of a whole idea. As discussed in Chapter 2, you cannot be certain an idea is what customers want until you challenge assumptions, take an incremental approach, and gather customer feedback. If the increment is of value, the next increment gets budgeted.

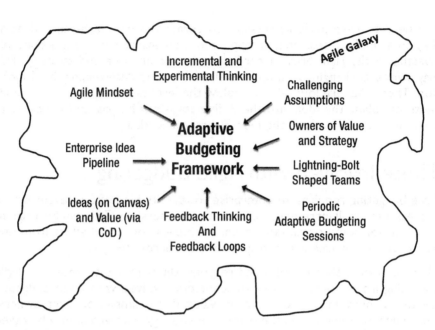

Figure 19-5. Components of an Agile budgeting framework

Feedback thinking as discussed in Chapter 10 and customer feedback loops as discussed in Chapter 14 help with guidance for the Agile budgeting framework. This ensures you validate the increment of the idea with customers to ensure you are moving in the direction of customer value.

You need an enterprise idea pipeline or something like it, as discussed in Chapter 11. It requires methodical discipline that involves capturing the idea in a easy-to-read form such as a canvas, as described in Chapter 13; prioritizing the idea using a value-based method such as cost of delay (CoD) and CoD divided by duration (CD3), both described in Chapter 12; and challenging assumptions of the value, as described in Chapters 2 and 12.

You need to have the key stakeholders as owners of value and strategy. They should be educated on your form of enterprise idea pipeline, value-based methods such as CoD and CD3, and incremental and experimental thinking. They should also understand how to effectively challenge assumptions. In addition, you need to have lightning-bolt-shaped teams that are able to work on several skills and that have experience to work on a variety of work.

You need to have periodic sessions to curate the new high-value ideas as they come in. Each session is an opportunity to ensure you are appropriately investing in the right areas according to customer value and strategy. This may involve challenging assumptions of the idea and determining the disposition. Those that are low value or below the level of having the supply bandwidth of pulling the idea into the Refine stage can be passed for now until such time that it becomes the next highest-value idea.

Those Involved with Agile Budgeting

Agile budgeting requires an enterprise to turn its big upfront, event-driven process into small incremental and continuous sessions. This can be a significant shift for some organizations since it moves concerted effort from one part of the yearly calendar and spreads it out across the year.

There may be a shift of roles and responsibilities in implementing an Agile budgeting framework. The key stakeholders involved with Agile budgeting are the owners and stakeholders of value (for example, product owners) and senior management as the owners of strategy. This group may be called the Agile budgeting team or whatever term suits your enterprise. Avoid any terms with existing baggage.

If there is a portfolio management team, its responsibilities may move away from decision making and instead focus on enabling Agile budgeting by collecting data to gauge customer value and sharing it with the Agile budgeting team. A portfolio management team can help those evaluating an idea and its value by considering strengths, weaknesses, opportunities, and threats (also known as SWOT) as well as focusing on the trade-offs of comparing ideas that may increase revenue, protect revenue, reduce costs, and avoid costs as discussed in Chapter 12.

■ **Agile Pit Stop** An Agile budgeting framework attempts to avoid HiPPO (highest paid person's opinion) for prioritization as this lacks discipline in understanding customer value.

If there is a project management office, the responsibilities may move from ownership of the work to enabling Agile budgeting focusing on dependency management among the ideas. The key take-away is that the decision makers of a customer-value-driven approach, the owners of value, become the drivers of an Agile budgeting framework.

Avoid making a new idea the highest priority because someone says so. An Agile budgeting framework attempts to avoid prioritization based on HiPPO (highest paid person's opinion), as discussed in Chapter 12, where a senior manager makes priority calls based on his or her opinion. This can lead to chaos and a lack of understanding where the higher-value work resides. While the Agile budgeting framework helps you more quickly course-correct toward customer value, it can be prone to chaos if many course changes occur with little discipline in understanding customer value.

In the spirit of ownership and self-organization, as enterprises move responsibility to the level that has the most information typically across the enterprise onto teams, senior management should have more time to evaluate ideas based on value and alignment to strategy.

Lightning-Bolt-Shaped Teams

An Agile budgeting framework can initiate a need for how an enterprise is structured and how employees are educated. Since customer value changes over time, it requires an enterprise and its employees to adapt to that change. The goal is to be able to move the high-value work readily and quickly without extensive reorganizations of the enterprise. The key is to avoid overly rigid and inflexible enterprise structure.

An Agile mindset focuses on optimizing for customer value rather than for the rigidity of enterprise structure. This is why concepts like holocracy, discussed in Chapter 8, can help make enterprise structure more adaptable to customer value. Organizing by team vs. division may provide some insight on how to create an Agile enterprise. Avoid reorganizing arbitrarily when value is focused in another division. Any organization change should be methodical and based on customer value data.

While reorganizing an enterprise can help it align to customer value, another approach is to extend team skills so that you can experiment with and apply the "move work to the team" approach. This advocates an investment in building lightning-bolt-shaped teams willing to learn more. These are teams where each team member has a primary skill, secondary skill, and tertiary skill as it relates to the work.

The shape of a three-pronged lightning bolt has one spike going deep (primary skill) and at least two additional spikes of lesser depth (secondary and tertiary skills), as illustrated in Figure 19-6. The purpose of having various depths of skills is for the team to be able to handle a broader range of work and for team members to be able to step up and fill gaps that other team members may not have or need help with.

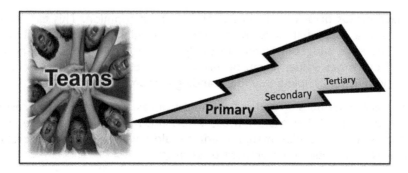

Figure 19-6. Infusing teams with a lightning-bolt set of skills

To create a lightning-bolt-shaped team takes an investment in education to instruct each team member in a secondary and tertiary skill. For example, developers have a primary skill of programming code. As a secondary skill, they learn how to build database schemas and, as a tertiary skill, they learn to write unit tests and run test cases. As another example, developers have a primary skill of programming front-end user interfaces in HTML and JavaScript, a secondary skill programming API routines and protocols, and a tertiary skill writing back-end applications in Ruby and Python.

■ **Agile Pit Stop**   Agile budgeting framework with the enterprise idea pipeline and lightning-bolt-shaped teams provides a way to ensure you align teams (supply) with the most valuable ideas (demand) on a continuous and flexible basis.

The long-term benefit is that if the team members can develop additional skills, there is a greater likelihood that a team can work on a much wider range of ideas while being kept together longer, allowing the organization to gain the benefits of a high-performing team. This can reduce disrupting high-performing teams and increase the ability to build high-quality ideas.

Guidance to Tailor Your Framework

Agile budgeting requires an enterprise to turn its big upfront, event-driven process into a small, incremental, continuous process. This can be a big shift for some organizations. It is best to avoid a big-bang approach when moving to an Agile budgeting framework. If you have an annual budget process that is being used, it is best to pick the next quarter to get started. In this first quarter, allow yourself the three months to experiment with an Agile budgeting framework and tailor it to your enterprise.

Review the "Components of an Agile Budgeting Framework" section and use the time in this first quarter to experiment and set up the framework. Remember, since your enterprise size and complexity is unique, how you might implement Agile budgeting will vary according to your context.

■ **Agile Pit Stop**   It is important to spend a quarter to experiment with the Agile budgeting framework to tailor it for your enterprise and gain some experience with it.

In this first quarter, introduce education for key stakeholders as owners of value and strategy (Agile budgeting team) on what is Agile budgeting, including the Agile mindset focusing on getting to customer value and the Agile values and principles. Conduct a separate session on incremental and experimental thinking with a special focus on challenging assumptions, Cost of Delay (CoD), and CoD divided by duration (CD3). This session should include discussions on feedback thinking and establishing customer feedback loops to validate customer value along the way.

Introduce the enterprise idea pipeline and the way you plan to capture the idea (for example, canvas) and value (for instance, CoD and CD3). Set up your enterprise idea pipeline and decide what you plan to call it within your enterprise context. This setup includes moving your current-and-not-yet-acted-upon ideas to the board that makes up your enterprise idea pipeline.

With a small group, preferably product owners, attempt to calculate a CoD and CD3 value for each idea. Include a list of assumptions used to calculate CoD and CD3. Once you complete this with a subset of ideas (less than 20 ideas), share with the Agile budgeting team.

Set up a working session with the Agile budgeting team to walk through each idea in a rank order according to the CD3 value score. Share your assumptions. Ask the Agile budgeting team to use open-ended questions to challenge assumptions. These may include the following: What led you to that conclusion? What do you think the level of uncertainty is? What is your riskiest assumption? and What information do you need to validate this? This last question is critical and can help you consider the focus of your first increment of an idea and feedback loops to help you validate customer value. This is the time to wrestle with and understand this framework.

As people challenge assumptions or present the value scores, listen for people attempting to get their ideas in their area or division to have higher value scores. This is where the mindset of focusing on customer value becomes important. The objective is to optimize for the greater good of the enterprise and not sub-optimize for a particular division or individual.

■ **Agile Pit Stop**   The tricky part is transitioning from the old budgeting framework to the Agile budgeting framework. Ensure you optimize for the greater good of the enterprise.

After a couple of sessions with the Agile budgeting team, you will have an updated list of rank-ordered ideas according to value where assumptions have been challenged. Now start the ignition of the Agile budgeting framework. Share top ideas with teams that would work on the ideas. This is the transition from the old framework to the Agile budgeting framework. Ask the team(s) when they think they can pull a high-value idea, cut an increment, and begin validating the customer value.

What you may encounter is that the some teams have a backlog of ideas and work that is overflowing. The POs of those teams will need to make value calls as to what is more important—the existing work or the new work. Often you may find that the existing work, while deemed important, has a lower value than the new work. Expect healthy debates.

AGILE BUDGETING FRAMEWORK EXERCISE

Select three of your current-yet-not-acted-upon ideas. Calculate a CoD and CD3 value for each idea. Record the assumptions you used to calculate the CoD and CD3. Once complete, share this with someone who is an owner of value (for example, PO) and explain the value and assumptions. Ask that person to challenge assumptions using open-ended questions. How did the session go?

Cadence for Curating Ideas

Once you have a good handle on your Agile budgeting framework and have tailored it to your enterprise, it is time to begin a periodic cadence for curating the ideas. Identify a schedule to hold the Agile budgeting sessions based on the pace of ideas coming in. While many ideas may come in, a healthy session evaluates just the higher-value ideas, as these are more likely to be worked in the near future.

You need to identify the owners of value and strategy (that is, the Agile budgeting team). You may find there are more people in the session that are necessary. If possible, you need to keep the participants to fewer than 12 who can speak. Otherwise, the session can become unwieldy.

These sessions are an opportunity to ensure you are appropriately investing in the areas according to customer value and strategy. Ideas that are of lesser value can be passed until they become the next highest value. These sessions also provide an opportunity to view the measures that help you maintain a healthy Agile budgeting framework. Agile success measures are discussed in detail in Chapter 20.

Do You Invest in the Highest Value?

An Agile budgeting framework is more than just a budget process. It is a mindset that embraces incremental, experimental, and feedback thinking; lightning-bolt-shaped teams; an enterprise idea pipeline prioritized by customer value; and validated by feedback loops. This enables you to adapt to the changing demands of the customer and marketplace. Equally important is that you can get your idea to market a lot quicker by avoiding the wait states that a traditional annual budgeting process presents.

As markets change and new markets emerge, do you have the ability to adapt quickly toward high-value work? Do you have a flexible budget and investment framework where you can move the highest-value ideas (demand) to teams and resources (supply)? Is your framework optimized to reduce wait states and time to market to get the value to market quickly? While this isn't easy, not doing so can make your position in the marketplace more challenging. Instead, lead with high-value, short-wait states and an Agile budgeting framework to benefit your customers and your business success.

For additional material, I suggest the following:

- *Beyond Budgeting: How Managers Can Break Free from the Annual Performance Trap* by Jeremy Hope and Robin Fraser, Harvard Business Review Press, 2003

- *Implementing Beyond Budgeting: Unlocking the Performance Potential* by Bjarte Bogsnes, Wiley, 2008

Applying Agile Success Measures

With any measures, you either use them or lose them.

—Mario Moreira

Measures and metrics can be challenging because they can be both dangerous and helpful. By dangerous, I mean that if you measure the wrong thing, it can set you in the wrong direction and people can rig the measures if they think they will be used against them. They are helpful when you measure outcomes over output, as successful business outcomes are what you are looking for. They are also helpful for better decision making.

This chapter is not intended to be an inclusive set of Agile measures. It is meant to provide you with enough information to get started in building your measurement framework and use it to determine if you are successfully delivering customer value. Focusing on customer value means that you need metrics that help you gauge if you are moving in the direction of customer value. It may also mean that many of your current metrics may not be of value or certainly have a lesser value. Also, you should only keep those metrics that you actually use for decision making and navigation.

© Mario E. Moreira 2017

M. E. Moreira, *The Agile Enterprise*, DOI 10.1007/978-1-4842-2391-8_20

Outcomes Matter

The primary goal of Agile measures is to help you become more aligned with delivering customer value. This is why outcome-based measures are much more aligned with Agile than output measures. Output measures focus on how much you delivered, while outcome measures focus on the results of what you deliver. It is the results that matter.

Outcome-based measures are drivers to help you understand business success. You may still need output measures to help you on your way; just ensure that they are relevant to help you determine if you are reaching the outcomes you are looking for.

As discussed in Chapter 3 and illustrated in Figure 3-3, output may count the number of releases while outcome is how many more customers either bought or used the product from release to release. If sales or usage is low even though the number of releases is high, it's the sales or usage that matter. Often people focus on outputs because they tend to be easier to measure or are a carryover from a more traditional mindset.

■ **Agile Pit Stop**   Outcome-based metrics change our perspective from an internal one to a customer or external perspective.

An outcome focus changes your perspective from an internal one to a customer or external perspective. This allows you to better understand what you are aiming for in the customer-value-driven world you need to establish.

Another reason to include the Reflect stage to create a 6R model (as discussed at Chapter 11) is that it is during the Reflect stage when the results or outcomes come to light. This helps you frame the big picture of delivering an idea. It doesn't begin when development starts working on the idea and it doesn't end when it gets delivered.

Value of Metrics

A metric is only as valuable as your ability to digest it and use it to steer your enterprise. Some metrics have a temporary use while others may have a more permanent use. You may observe that although many metrics are created and shared, only a few of them are actually being used for decision making. You have to continually ask what measures can help a team or organization move in the right direction? Before discussing suggested metrics, it is worth having a discussion of the relative value of a metric.

The value of a metric is defined as its usefulness divided by the effort it takes to collect. The dividend implies the metric serves a useful purpose, such as decision making. The divisor implies the metric costs, which are the energy in collecting data and generating the metric. If the usefulness is outweighed by the energy to generate it, then it may not be worth preparing the metric.

■ **Agile Pit Stop**   The value of a metric is defined as its usefulness divided by the effort it takes to collect it. If you are not really using it to navigate your course, retire it.

Some metrics may have a short life cycle, being valuable for only a certain time based on the usefulness they provide. As an example, if an Agile education program commences, it may be of value to collect the number of people educated in Agile. This provides visibility into ensuring the actual number of employees being educated is increasing as desired. However, once you have educated 80% of the target audience, it may no longer be useful to collect this data and keep tracking this metric.

Because the relative value of a metric changes over time, it is beneficial to periodically assess the value being generated. If a current metric no longer provides value, it is time to retire it. If a new one is of value, it may be included if the usefulness outweighs the energy to generate it.

Value of Leading Indicators

Business success is measured in a number of ways. When you think of desired outcomes from a customer perspective, it is more products sold or used, meaning an increase in revenue. Having a customer revenue metric helps you understand whether products or services are being sold.

Capturing revenue is a good starting point. However, because revenue is an outcome metric, it is a *lagging* indicator. To supplement lagging indicators, you need *leading* indicators that provide you visibility into what is currently occurring with the customer and the progress of the idea. This timely visibility is important because it provides input for making better decisions as you move forward. Better decision making with timely data leads to an increased chance of success and more revenue.

■ **Agile Pit Stop**   Revenue is a solid Agile outcome measure since it's about improving business results. However, it is a lagging indicator, so you need leading indicators to provide timely visibility to ensure you are moving in the right direction of customer value.

While customer revenue is an important metric to collect, the question is, what metrics can you put in place to ensure you are moving in the right direction? For every lagging metric, you need to establish at least one leading metric to act as an indicator to provide visibility to gauge if you are moving in the direction of a positive lagging metric (for example, increase in revenue). I call this the *lagging to leading metric path*.

As illustrated in Figure 20-1, the desired outcome is customers' buying/using your idea (that is, product or service). Since this is a lagging metric involving revenue from customers, leading indicators could be the following:

- **Customers attending demos:** a leading metric involving the demos or sprint reviews. You capture how many customers are attending the demo and feedback you are receiving. If customers aren't attending, there is a reduced probability that you'll reach the successful outcome you desire.

- **Customers satisfied with a demo:** a leading metric where you capture customer satisfaction from the functionality viewed in the demo.

- **Customers participating in beta:** a leading metric involving how many customers are willing to exercise an increment of an idea in a beta environment.

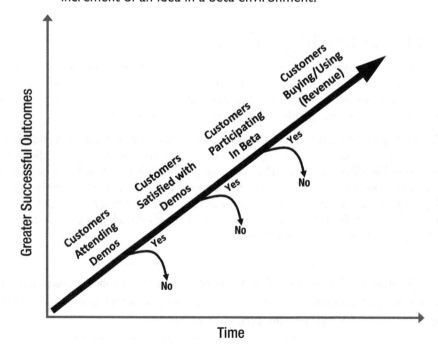

Figure 20-1. Lagging to leading metric path

The value of leading indicators is that they "indicate" if you are moving in the direction of customer value. If no customers are willing to attend a sprint preview of a product, this indicates that maybe the product is not appealing to the customer marketplace. With no customers, you also miss the valuable customer feedback to help you adapt toward customer value.

If customers are reporting negative satisfaction in the sprint review, this indicates that the idea is not appealing to the customer marketplace. Finally, if few customers are willing to participate in the usage of an idea increment in a beta environment, this can indicate little customer interest in your product. The key is building a set of leading indicators to help guide you since no one indicator provides all of the data you need.

LAGGING TO LEADING INDICATOR EXERCISE

Consider what leading indicators you may want to capture if your desired outcome (and lagging metric) is "employees feel ownership of their work" within an Agile context. For example, might you want to capture the number of employees educated in Agile? Might you want to capture the number of employees who feel they are allowed to self-organize around their work? Other thoughts?

Measures for Running the Enterprise

Getting to customer value is a journey. As part of that journey, how do you ensure you are moving in the direction of customer value? The answer is value metrics. To supplement value metrics, a selection of flow, quality, and satisfaction metrics can help triangulate your measures for a holistic view. The key is to establish metrics that you will actively use focused on value or leading indicators to value. The following is a selection that may prove useful.

Value Curve

The value curve is a way to view the value of ideas being worked on vs. those waiting in your pool of ideas. The importance of this metric is to become aware of those high-value ideas (in this case, based on cost of delay) that are waiting and how much low-value work is being worked on that is causing the high-value work to wait, as illustrated in Figure 20-2.

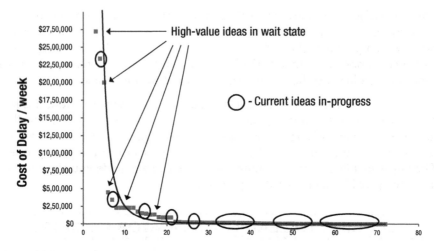

Figure 20-2. Enterprise value curve

It can inform your decision making by providing you awareness of the high-value ideas waiting and aging. When a team pulls for more work, you can ensure that the next highest-value piece of work gets pulled instead of applying the old method, which seems to have resulted in lower-value work coming their way. You can gain more insight of value curves in Chapter 12.

Ideas with CoD and CD3

The ideas with cost of delay (CoD) and CoD divided by duration (CD3) are early indicator value metrics that look at the percentage of ideas that get evaluated with CoD (or designated value score). A complementary metric to add is what percentage of ideas gets evaluated with HiPPO (highest paid person's opinion).

These metrics help you know how serious your enterprise is at applying a value-based practice to the value of ideas. HiPPO inversely looks at how much value priority is driven by a person's opinion. Figure 20-3 illustrates that over time, more CoD and CD3 are being applied and less HiPPO. In mid-January, a CoD education effort occurred, which increased the usage of CoD and CD3. This is a temporary measure. Once you are over 80% at applying CoD and CD3 (using the 80/20 rule), you no longer need to collect this measure. You can gain more insight into CoD and CD3 in Chapter 12.

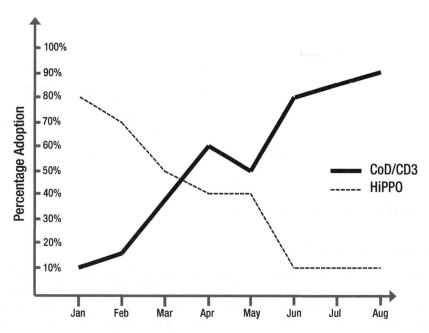

Figure 20-3. CoD/CD3 adoption score

Customers at Demos

The customer-at-demos measure is an early indicator value measure that looks at the number of customers attending demos for a team or product. Captured during the Reveal stage, a low number of customers attending a demo typically indicates either a lack of interest or a lack of actual customer feedback, which are both inhibitors to understanding customer value.

This type of measure can help you understand levels of customer involvement in demos. If you aren't getting much customer involvement in the demos, you are less likely to be moving in the direction of customer value. Looking at Figure 20-4, which product (A or B) is getting more customer involvement in its demos? This is a temporary measure. Using product B as the example, once it is clear that it is getting customer involvement over a few sprints, this measure is no longer needed.

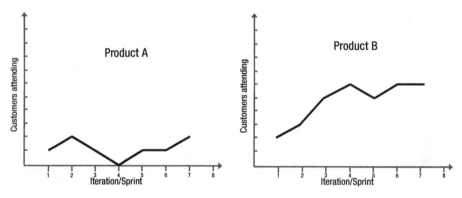

Figure 20-4. Customers attending demos

Customer Satisfaction

Customer satisfaction is a way to gauge if a company's products and services meet or surpass customer expectations. The benefit of customer satisfaction is twofold. First, it may be considered a leading indicator of customer revenue, giving you insight into whether you are moving in the right direction. Second, it can focus employees on the importance of fulfilling value to customers. Customer satisfaction is often reported at a cumulative level. It may be measured along various dimensions: usefulness of a product and responsiveness to problems.

As illustrated in Figure 20-5, customer satisfaction surveys should be conducted periodically to provide a gauge of satisfaction of the company's products and identify actions for improvement. Post-purchase satisfaction surveys in the Reflect stage of the 6R model should be utilized to gauge the satisfaction of customers and what specific value the customers found. Because there are many forms of customer satisfaction metrics, consider researching the various forms and identify what is right for you.

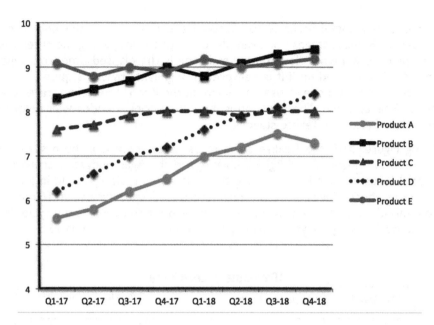

Figure 20-5. Customer satisfaction by product

A key customer satisfaction measure is the net promoter score (NPS). It is an index that measures the willingness of customers to recommend a company's products or services to others. It helps you gauge overall satisfaction with a company's product or service and the customer's loyalty. In answering the question of how likely you are to recommend this product to a friend, you typically select from 1 to 10 where a response of 0 to 6 is known as a detractor, a response of 7 and 8 is passive, and a response of 9 and 10 are the promoters (in other words, those willing to recommend).

End-to-End Lead Time

Often in an enterprise, there are discussions focused on measuring time to market. This visibility provides you the rate in which you are delivering customer value into production. The challenge is that a lot of the discussion focuses on the work during the Realize stage (that is, development). This is known as cycle time. Cycle time focuses on the time an idea begins development work until it is delivered. There tends to be a lot of focus on optimizing the Realize stage without recognizing that there may be much larger improvement opportunities from Record to Refine.

A more meaningful focus is to measure the time across the end-to-end Record to Release stages (for example, concept to cash) along the enterprise idea pipeline known as lead time. Lead time is the elapsed time from when the idea is recorded until it is delivered. It highlights that it is quite possible that there is a lot more elapse time spent in the Record to Refine stages than in the Realize stage. The question is, how long does the idea wait before it gets pulled into the Realize stage?

Using Figure 20-6, the Realize stage takes three months in both scenarios (traditional budgeting and Agile budgeting). In the Agile budgeting scenario, a special focus is placed on reducing the wait states typically found in a more traditional budgeting scenario, reducing the overall cycle time from 16 months to 6 months, a 62.5% improvement for time-to-market even as the cycle time in the Realize stage stays the same (three months) in both scenarios.

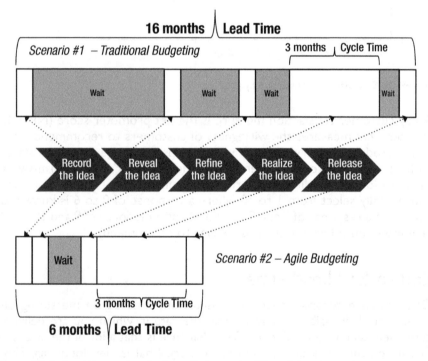

Figure 20-6. Lead time and cycle time relating to the 5R model

When companies first measure their lead time, the length of their end-to-end Record to Release times often surprises them. This is due to learning how long ideas are in wait states. It is advisable to establish a lead-time trend metric, as illustrated in Figure 20-7, at the product, product-line, or enterprise level. A lead-time-trend metric highlights the original length of lead time and the direction where lead time is headed.

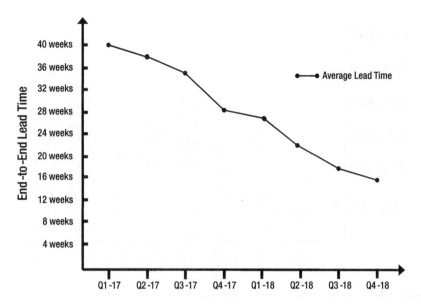

Figure 20-7. Lead-time-trend measure

The goal for the lead-time trend is to identify a pace of change that a customer can absorb. For most websites and retail products, it can be quite rapid and often a faster pace than what is current. In order to set a goal to reduce end-to-end lead time, you should consider leading with education on the incremental thinking and decomposition techniques. You can use lead time as an indicator for revenue. If ideas are taking a long time to get to market, this can have a direct impact on customer revenue.

Customer Revenue

Revenue is a complex term that can be interpreted in many ways. I am referring to net revenue, which is the amount of money a company receives from sales of products and services less negative revenue items such as returned items, refunds, and discounts. Although revenue is a lagging indicator, the benefit of revenue metrics is that they are a key indicator of whether customers find value in the products you are building.

Revenue metrics can be generated at product, product-line, business-unit, or enterprise levels. Revenue can be quarterly, as illustrated in Figure 20-8. Because revenue is a lagging metric, ensure you create a *lagging to leading metric path* so that you have leading indicators to help you gauge your path to an increase in revenue. There are many forms of revenue metrics, so consider researching the various forms and identify what is right for you.

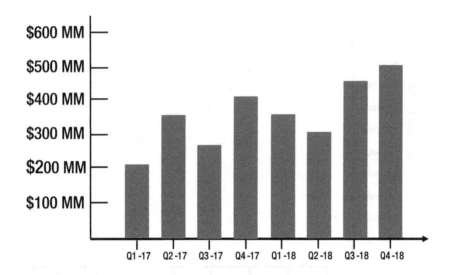

Figure 20-8. Customer revenue from sales measure

Employee Satisfaction

In the spirit of employees matter, employee satisfaction is a way to gauge employees' feeling of contentment within a workplace. Employee feedback allows you to engage in meaningful improvement opportunities. Poor satisfaction can lead to higher attrition rates and low productivity. If employee satisfaction starts decreasing, can it have an impact on customer revenue meaning that employees are less motivated to support the company and less focused on customer value?

Satisfied employees can lead to loyalty and higher productivity. By giving your employees a voice, they can express their interests and concerns. Employee satisfaction surveys can energize and empower employees, provided their results and improvement opportunities are taken seriously. Figure 20-9 illustrates a customer-satisfaction metric using COMETS attributes from Chapter 7 as a framework to gauge employee satisfaction. This example uses a top-box approach where those employees who select 9 or 10 (of 10) are very satisfied with those areas.

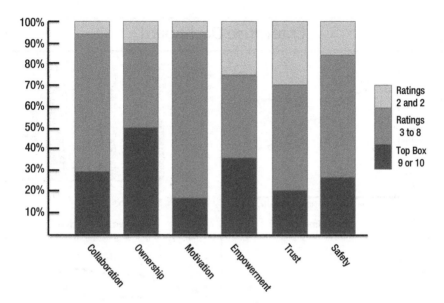

Figure 20-9. Employee-satisfaction metric using COMETS

When commencing an Agile program, it is important to gauge satisfaction. It can help you understand how satisfaction levels change. During an Agile change, while many become more satisfied, some may find their positions of control being reduced and become less satisfied. Because there are many forms of employee-satisfaction metrics, consider researching the various forms and identify what is right for you.

Enterprise Dashboard for Correlation

Once you have a collection of metrics, it is useful to share it collectively in a dashboard. A dashboard is a form of information radiator where you display your key metrics that help you understand where your enterprise is going. It is best to focus on three to six metrics, which should be prioritized by customer value, speed, and satisfaction, as illustrated in Figure 20-10.

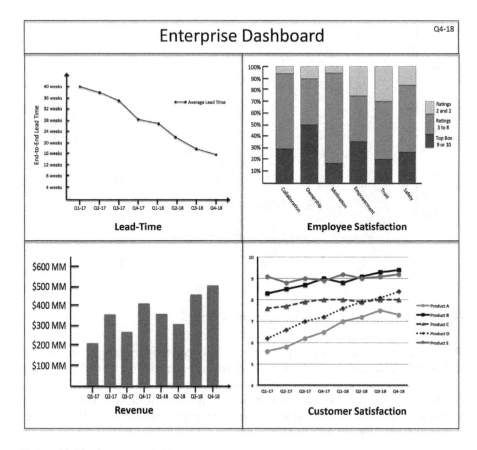

Figure 20-10. Enterprise dashboard

A dashboard provides at least two benefits. The first is that you can view metrics in one place and see them side-by-side, whether on paper or on a screen. The second is that you can correlate them to ensure you are not optimizing for a particular metric inappropriately. An example of sub-optimization is while bringing lead times down, customer satisfaction decreases. Another example is removing all severity 3 and 4 defects for higher quality may inadvertently increase lead times.

In an Agile context, a shared dashboard lends transparency to what is being measured and helps employees understand what is occurring without second-hand interpretation. I strongly encourage you to make your metrics transparent with the help of a dashboard for all to see. Do keep in mind that some metrics are captured at different rates—daily, weekly, per sprint, monthly, quarterly, bi-yearly, and yearly.

What Are Your Measures of Success?

It is important to consider your Agile measures of success. The material in this chapter can give you a jump-start in establishing metrics that give you visibility into aligning with Agile and, more importantly, establishing a direction toward customer value, speed of delivery, and satisfaction. Make sure to consider your lagging and leading metric path and metrics that provide visibility at the enterprise and product levels.

A dashboard provides one place to view key metrics and viewing them side-by-side can ensure you are not optimizing for a particular metric inappropriately. Measures of success are meant to help you determine if you are moving in the right direction of customer value. These metrics should provide insights, help you make decisions, and determine if you should adapt or stay the course.

Reinventing HR for Agile

HR is poised to reinvent its role to support an Agile world, the future of a value-driven enterprise, and happier, more productive employees.

—Mario Moreira

"Employees matter" is a key principle in Agile, and Human Resources (HR) is there to support employees and build an environment that helps them stay motivated, productive, and thrive. There are opportunities in the HR environment to become more value-added to employees. Much like Agile is looking for more of an incremental approach to building products, HR systems need to become more incremental in the way they approach their work so that they can adapt to the needs of the employees as those needs evolve.

Traditional performance management is often subjective as ranking and rating employees is not always about skills but about how management views a person. Also, there is often a lack of timeliness of feedback. If you wait until December to highlight a problem from June, it isn't for performance management; it's for punishment. I have seen a system where individuals were encouraged to compete with each other at the expense of the team and overall success. Both subjective performance and an individual-only approach are impediments in achieving an Agile mindset.

© Mario E. Moreira 2017

M. E. Moreira, *The Agile Enterprise*, DOI 10.1007/978-1-4842-2391-8_21

HR teams are poised, should they be willing, to take a leadership role in Agile and move to the next generation of a supportive environment for employees. As illustrated in Figure 21-1, this can include promoting Agile and the discovery mindset, experimenting with motivation, exploring self-management, fostering servant leadership, getting closer to the customer, facilitating Open Space, incorporating gamification, supporting the shift toward Agile roles, moving to team-based performance, moving toward continuous employee feedback, and hiring Agile-minded employees.

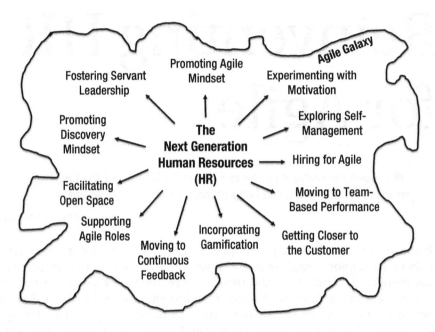

Figure 21-1. Moving HR to the next generation

HR as Promoters of Agile

As you move your enterprise toward an Agile mindset where employees matter, there should be a shift where HR becomes a coach and mentor for employees. While there will still be senior team members and managers to grow teams, HR can provide the bigger view of employee needs, looking for patterns as they build enterprise employee programs.

HR must be continuously in touch with employees through a number of vehicles such as 1:1s to help grow and coach individuals to Open Space Technology activities where dozens to hundreds of employees share their thoughts and ideas to support their well-being. HR can be the coach for advancing self-management and servant leadership within a company.

Promoting the Agile and Discovery Mindset

HR can promote new programs within an Agile framework and mindset. By applying the discovery mindset including incremental thinking, experimental thinking, divergent and convergent thinking, feedback thinking, and design thinking, as discussed in Chapter 10, HR is in a position to support a transformation toward Agile and the discovery mindset.

Agile Pit Stop   HR can promote the education of the Agile and discovery mindset and include it in orientation programs as new employees are brought in.

HR can promote the education surrounding the elements of an Agile and discovery mindset. This education can be brought in as one of the early orientation programs as new employees are brought in. HR can team up with Agile coaches to determine the right level of education and how Agile knowledge can be periodically built over time via education and experience.

Experimenting with Motivation

HR can become leaders, innovators, and promoters of experimentation within their companies in regards to HR practices. What is becoming clearer is that traditional HR practices and programs have less of an appeal to the younger population of employees and traditional performance management systems haven't been particularly successful in motivating individuals.

Business thinkers, like Daniel Pink in his book *Drive*, emphasize intrinsic motivation factors over extrinsic factors. Pink argues that the use of reward and punishment is antiquated. He proposes that you adapt your thinking to include autonomy, mastery, and purpose. It is important for HR leadership members to experiment with and experience this new way of thinking so that they can identify what sorts of motivation will raise employees' happiness and morale and bring more productivity to the enterprise.

Since there should be a strong focus on employees in an Agile-focused enterprise, applying a discovery mindset in HR can set the tone for the behaviors that you are looking for in employees. HR may include employees in their experiments for what works best in an enterprise. Will 360-degree performance reviews work? What type of questions should you ask when hiring for an Agile mindset? Do team-based performance goals continue to motivate an individual team member?

Exploring Self-Management

Self-management is a relatively new concept and effectively asks you to think of operating without management. It asks you to take bounded authority to the level where those who have the most information make all of the decisions for a particular space.

■ **Agile Pit Stop**   HR can both experiment with self-management within their own groups and help an enterprise explore and remove impediments to achieving self-management.

The more predominant alternative to self-management is the traditional management structure where top-down hierarchical decision making occurs. Within a self-managed enterprise, there are few management levels and employees are happy, as they are both self-directed and empowered to make decisions. Self-management also leads to optimizing the flow of delivery and improvements as the bureaucracy of a traditional management structure is effectively eliminated because waiting for top-down decisions from people who have less knowledge no longer occurs.

Since self-management has a very real and direct impact on how an enterprise operates, it should be an area where HR can have a strong role. This starts with HR's learning how self-management works. HR can set the tone for experimenting with self-management. It can explore self-management within its own HR group and then help management and teams expand boundaries and remove the system impediments from achieving self-management. A good resource for self-management is the Morningstar Self-Management Institute.

Fostering Servant Leadership

Providing management with a servant leadership mindset can result in stronger relationships between leaders and their teams and direct reports, which can lead to higher degrees of loyalty and productivity. Servant leadership focuses on servicing your employees first. Instead of being in front and giving directives to your team, you are leading from behind, sharing ownership of what needs to be done with integrity.

In their book *Servant Leadership*, Robert K. Greenleaf and Larry C. Spears share ten attributes of servant leadership: listening, empathy, healing, awareness, persuasion, conceptualization, foresight, stewardship, commitment to grow people, and building community. This forms the basis for education that can be given to an enterprise's leaders.

■ **Agile Pit Stop**   HR should attempt to identify servant leaders in the company since those that exhibit servant leadership often go unrecognized and choose to give credit to others.

In his book *Turn Your Ship Around*, L. David Marquet emphasizes that true leadership is about giving control instead of taking control. This helps improve morale and performance, and it reduces retention. The information in this book can be used as an example for true servant leadership.

By learning and experimenting with servant leadership, HR will be poised to embrace and promote servant leadership within its enterprise. HR should also attempt to identify the servant leaders since those that exhibit servant leadership often go unrecognized and avoid the limelight by choosing to put the light on their team members. To gauge if you are a servant leader, ask yourself, "Am I serving others or myself first?"

FOSTERING SERVANT LEADERSHIP EXERCISE

Identify several managers. Prepare a session on the ten attributes of servant leadership (listening, empathy, healing, awareness, persuasion, conceptualization, foresight, stewardship, commitment to grow people, and building community). Facilitate a session with the managers and describe and discuss servant leadership with them. Primarily focus on listening to the managers' responses (both positive and negative) to each of the attributes.

Getting Closer to the Customer

As part of the shift toward customer value, HR can promote the two-degrees-of-customer-separation technique that emphasizes the relationship between the customer and company employees, as discussed in Chapter 2. The goal is for HR to have witnessed the products the teams are building and meet the customers those products are meant for by attending demos or sprint reviews and visiting customers who are using products from the company.

The benefit of HR's having a customer view can help in two ways. First, HR has first-hand experience in how teams are working with customers and gaining customer insight. Second, HR can use this experience to better understand the needs for the employees in the company. HR can then better promote how you lead by learning what a customer wants using discovery, experimentation, increments, and feedback while avoiding certainty in thinking that you know what a customer wants.

Facilitating Open Space

Open Space Technology (also known as Open Space) is a method that enables self-organizing groups focused on complex themes or problems in a short period of time. Open Space is a way to initiate what is termed as *unconferences*, which avoids a lot of upfront planning. For HR, the theme or problem is how to create a better performance excellence or employee well-being system.

■ **Agile Pit Stop**   Open Space is an approach for unconferences to avoid a lot of upfront planning and to allow participants to self-organize around topics they select.

An Open Space agenda is emergent as a number of topics may be addressed and surface during the start of the session. You can share a theme and ask for topics or problems around that theme. Attendees then gather around the topics they feel are a priority and provide thoughts, ideas, and solutions to those topics. In learning Agile and Open Space methods, HR can act as facilitators for Open Space sessions and support teams who may want to take advantage of this method. To learn more, I suggest you read *Open Space Technology: A User's Guide* by Harrison Owen. Also, to see Open Space Technology in action, consider reading Chapter 22.

Incorporating Gamification

Gamification adapts game concepts to non-gaming situations in order to engage employees and motivate them to improve their performance and behavior. It rewards employees for completing performance levels with points, badges, privileges, and sometimes monetary incentives. While initially an extrinsic motivator, it is a way for the enterprise to reward those who embrace Agile and the focus on customer value.

The key to gamification is that it must be driven by a clear business objective. Within the context of Agile, the goal of gamification is to encourage employees to become Agile champions and achieve an Agile culture. Gamification can be deployed to engage employees in Agile educational elements. Although it may start with training, you eventually would like employees acting as Agile champions to give back to their community. If you use gamification, ensure the achievement is real, it helps employees with their work, and is aligned with objectives of the enterprise.

Supporting the Shift toward Agile Roles

In an Agile world, what used to be primary roles in a traditional workplace will shift when moving to an Agile workplace. An example is that Product Owners (PO) become the owners of value and decision making for their products. There is less of a need for project managers and more of a need for the emerging roles of ScrumMasters, facilitators, and coaches.

■ **Agile Pit Stop**   HR needs to know the Agile roles well enough to explain the roles and offer support for those who change their roles.

Middle managers, who may have been the solicitors of the work, will find their roles change as the work is now coming from the backlogs via the PO. Middle managers, who might be challenged by the new culture that Agile brings, are the same folks who traditionally conduct performance reviews. Because you are moving from a hierarchical world to a flatter world, this can be particularly disconcerting for some managers.

HR is well positioned to be the support for those whose roles are shifting. HR needs to understand the Agile roles well enough to explain the roles and offer support for those who change their roles. For a better understanding of the evolving Agile roles, consider reading Chapter 8.

Writing Goals in Canonical Form

There can be many ways to describe performance goals. It can be advantageous to draft them in as objective a manner as possible. HR may suggest the user story canonical form to specify the performance goal.

As discussed in Chapter 18, the canonical form is a language construct used to document user stories. This includes the "who" or role ("As a") you are playing, the "what" or your action ("I will"), and the "why" or business benefit ("so that"). Applying the canonical form may help in describing your goal more objectively and effectively, as illustrated in Figure 21-2.

> As a Scrum Team member, **I will** size the work using story points with the team during Sprint Planning, **so that** we gain team buy-in to support the velocity for the sprint and complexity of each story.
>
> As a Scrum Master, **I will** exemplify servant leadership attributes **so that** I can help my team become self-organized.
>
> As a Product Owner, **I will** continuously groom and prioritize the Product Backlog **so that** the Scrum Team has a list of user stories to work on.
>
> As an Agile Coach, **I will** coach and mentor the product team **so that** the they can adopt the Agile mindset.

Figure 21-2. Performance goals in canonical form

Once you have the performance goal written in this form, you can decompose the goal-based user story to the tangible tasks. You may consider this as another interesting way to use the canonical form.

An alternate and promising approach to performance goals is Objectives and Key Results, also known as OKRs. The objective is the outcome that is sought, written in a qualitative, time-bound, and actionable manner. The key results are quantitative, written with three-to-five specific and measurable statements that help you know if you have met your objective.

OKRs should be cascaded from the enterprise to the division to the team and individual level, getting refined at each level to support the level above. In order to allow people to be innovative, it is recommended that only two-thirds of the OKRs be completed within a time period. To learn more about OKRs, consider reading either *Objectives and Key Results* by Paul R. Niven and Ben Lamorte or *Radical Focus* by Christina Wodtke.

Moving to Team-Based Performance

Because Agile focuses on the team, the performance goals and the evaluation should be team-based. In traditional performance review models, upward of 100% of the goals are individual-based. Employees with individual goals conduct themselves toward the greatest potential for individual reward and security. This is why individual goals are in polar opposition to the Agile team mindset. HR can help the enterprise move to team-based goals, which can only be accomplished by no longer incentivizing individuals to choose their success over team success.

It may be difficult to move to team-based objectives immediately for a number of reasons. The performance management system may not be functionally able to accommodate common goals across multiple people (the team), or you may want to maintain an individual-based component to the objectives, so the specific percentages across objectives may need to be applied. You may want to take an incremental approach toward team-based performance. If you think aiming for 100% team-based objectives is too difficult, start with 50%. This will at least provide some incentive for individuals to work successfully as a team.

Moving from Annual Performance Reviews

Some companies are moving away from the annual performance review approach and instead applying more frequent conversations. They are also moving away from forced rankings as this supports an individual-based performance system. The challenge with an annual cycle is that it rewards and punishes employees based on past performance with less focus on newer improvement and growth.

HR can help an enterprise move away from traditional annual or biannual performance reviews. A good first step is to transform your performance reviews into a weekly or bi-weekly discussion between manager and employees with a more continuous and collaborative approach in discussing objectives, challenges, progress, and learning. The goal behind this is that employees should never be surprised by a performance review because there should be continuous feedback from their manager.

Agile Pit Stop   HR can help an enterprise move away from the annual performance review and move toward a continuous feedback model.

These sessions should be low-key and replace the "big-bang" performance reviews. There should be an effort from both management and employees to be transparent to avoid surprises when ratings or compensation matters are discussed. Ultimately, the performance review process should move away from the stodgy, often negative and intrusive event and evolve into a continuous and collaborative discussion on progress and employee needs.

Gaining Insight into Employee Progress

When moving to the empowering environment that Agile brings to teams, the manager role will have less insight into what an employee is doing. The manager must learn that discussions of performance should occur in a continuous and collaborative manner, focusing on progress and learning.

The challenges are twofold. First, the employee is not taking work orders from the manager any longer; instead, the work should be driven from the backlog. Second, the manager actually does have less visibility into what the employee is doing since the employee is committed to the team. How does a manager gain first-hand information?

During the daily Scrum, the manager may quietly listen to the progress the team members share during this brief session. During the sprint review, the manager can quietly view employees' progress by seeing what is being demonstrated. The word *quietly* bears emphasis. Agile practices are not for the manager's benefit, but rather for building customer value and making progress.

Hiring for Agile-Minded Employees

When hiring for Agile-minded employees, focus on how intrinsically motivated they are. While extrinsic motivators exist such as expecting to be well paid or paid equivalent to peers, once you move beyond the basics, you should look for employees who are intrinsically motivated by the work.

This may not be so easy. Some employees look at work as just a job. What I mean by this is that the intrinsic motivators of these employees are enjoying home life, hobbies, and their friends, and they have few intrinsic motivators at work. This is not a judgment but rather something to be aware of.

Other employees look at work as their career. While they may have intrinsic motivators at home, they have equal intrinsic motivators at work to improve their competency in their job. They take pride in producing a quality product, and they have a cause to make everyone on their team better.

If you are willing to build a culture where employees matter, having intrinsically motivated employees can help you achieve this. The question is, what does HR look for when hiring intrinsically motivated employees? Look for thoughts around autonomy, mastery, and purpose. Ask them the following questions:

- What things are you learning on your own?
- What is the last article you read?
- What are you curious about?
- What are your goals in mastering skills?
- What do you think about autonomy in your work?
- What role does a customer play in building products?
- What are some ways to promote collaboration?

In general, look for things where the interviewees can expand on what they value at work, what brings them meaning, how they describe progress at work, and what drives them to build mastery. You can learn more about intrinsic and extrinsic motivation in Chapter 7.

Are You Adapting toward Excellence?

HR is poised to play a whole new role in an Agile world and in enterprises focused on delivering customer value. The annual review of traditional performance management is out of touch with today's ever-changing employee needs. "Employees matter" is a key principle in Agile, and HR can support employees and build the next-generation HR environment that adapts to employee needs.

Through a combination of promoting Agile and the discovery mindset, experimenting with ways to motivate employees and self-management, fostering servant leadership, getting closer to the customer, facilitating Open Space, incorporating gamification, supporting the shift toward Agile roles, moving to team-based performance, moving away from annual performance reviews to continuous feedback, and hiring for Agile-minded employees, HR can help employees stay motivated, productive, and thrive. The question is how will you adapt your enterprise toward the next generation of performance excellence and human resources?

For additional material, I suggest the following:

- *Drive: The Surprising Truth about What Motivates Us* by Daniel H. Pink, Riverhead Books, 2011

- *Turn your Ship Around!: A True Story of Turning Followers into Leaders* by L. David Marquet, Portfolio, 2013

- *Objectives and Key Results: Driving Focus, Alignment, and Engagement with OKRs* by Paul R. Niven and Ben Lamorte, Wiley, 2016

- *Radical Focus: Achieving Your Most Important Goals with Objective and Key Results* by Christina Wodtke, Boxes and Arrows, 2016

- Morningstar Self-Management Institute, www.self-managementinstitute.org/about/what-is-self-management

- *Open Space Technology: A User's Guide* by Harrison Owen, Berrett-Koehler Publishers, 2008

Sharing an Agile Enterprise Story

Storytelling in Agile is a great way to open up a window into how Agile can operate and where you could be in the not-so-distant future.

—Mario Moreira

Once upon a time, there was a company called OnHigh, which was doing Agile. Well, employees weren't really sure what they were doing, but they were at least following the mechanics of an Agile method. After a couple of years, they were seeing some improvements but not really achieving the outcomes they were looking for. They thought Agile would give them an edge and much more business success.

There were a few enthusiastic and passionate Agilists on some of the teams who kept trying to move the needle toward exploring Agile beyond the mechanics because they were finding that their teams were getting stuck on the mechanics. They proposed exploring the Agile values and principles because they realized that they pretty much jumped into the mechanics of a process without really embracing the values and principles. This helped move the needle a little bit. What they learned was that while most employees responded positively to the principles, some weren't ready to embrace them, particularly the managers who attended those sessions.

© Mario E. Moreira 2017

M. E. Moreira, *The Agile Enterprise*, DOI 10.1007/978-1-4842-2391-8_22

An Agile principle that some people got stuck on was "welcoming changing requirements, even late in development." Some interpreted "welcoming" as being forced to make the change. After explaining that "welcoming" provides you with the opportunity to hear new ideas and then methodically determine their priority on when and if to do them, most employees firmly agreed with this principle. There was still more to discuss.

Initiating an Open Space Unconference

They decided to use Open Space Technology in an attempt to identify the common Agile-related challenges in delivering customer value. There was a call-out to teams doing Agile to join. The facilitator opened up the space by sharing guiding principles and logistics (Figure 22-1).

Figure 22-1. Executing an Open Space session

Participants posted their topics on the marketplace of ideas. There were enough ideas posted that three break-out timeframes where conducted. At the start of the first break out, participants self-organized around the topic that interested them. Participants could use the Law of Two Feet to move from topic to topic according to their level of interest.

At the end of the timeframe, the facilitator shared the "Evening News." After three such rounds, the facilitator's notes were gathered and the session was closed. The report summary was prepared, as illustrated in Figure 22-2.

Getting to Agile and Customer Value - Report Summary

- Not everyone was participating in the Agile change particularly most of management
- Realization that an annual planning cycle left many great ideas in a holding pattern for upwards of a year (until the next planning cycle)
- There were no measure of value and no effective means of prioritizing the work, so all were treated equally
- Many of the ideas were built as big bang projects. While an iterative method was being applied, teams felt that they had to build it all
- There were very few customer feedback loops and some of the ones they had, the feedback really wasn't being incorporated very effectively
- Few really understood their customers well, who they were, what motivated them, and how they used the company's products
- While Product Owners were being deployed, most of the priority was still being driven by managers
- A lot of focus on shortening the development cycle and very little on the end-to-end lead times
- Reorganizing teams so often to move teams to the work resulted in teams constantly having to reform
- Employees on teams felt that they had very little control over their work
- There was too much certainty upfront on what customers wanted which was surprising since it didn't feel like much was known about the customer
- There was little Agile education to give people a common understanding of what Agile is (and isn't)
- Budgets and projects seemed to be set for the year so when higher value work came in, there was often no budget and team for it
- With 100% utilization of people, there was no time to form bonds in an Agile community or for innovation.
- Still being measured based on cost and schedule with no focus on value or flow of work
- Very little connection between the company strategy and the work the teams were doing

Figure 22-2. Report summary from Open Space session

This led to a fairly clear conclusion. If the enterprise wanted to gain the business benefits that Agile can bring, it must get serious about a cultural transformation toward Agile. The good news is that there was a senior leader who wanted to become the Agile sponsor. The Agile sponsor allocated money to build a small team of Agile coaches. She brought in one Agile consultant who had enterprise Agile experience and promoted three Agile champions from within the company who were willing to grow further. These coaches called themselves the Agile Advantage Team.

The Increments of an Agile journey

The two principles that drove the Agile Advantage Team were focused on being customer-value-driven and employee-focused. They used these principles as a litmus test for all of the adoption activities they considered. Did the activity move the needle toward customer value and empower employees?

Since the team was small, they took an incremental approach toward adopting Agile. This way, they learned from the results of each increment before they moved ahead, very similar to the Agile approach taken to incrementally build a product. As illustrated in Figure 22-3, they used an adoption approach focusing on learning, growing, accelerating, transforming, and finally sustaining the Agile adoption.

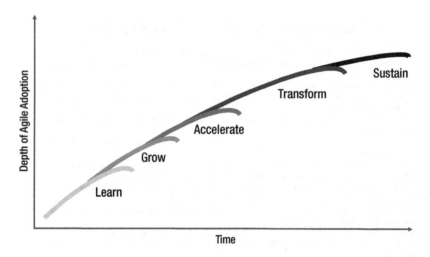

Figure 22-3. Incremental approach toward an Agile adoption

Learn

"Learn" primarily focused on understanding the enterprise's focus on value, learning about the people (that is, employees), and offering learning (in other words, Agile education), as illustrated in Figure 22-4. This started with a baseline to understand where the enterprise was from an Agile perspective. It incorporated details from the Open Space report summary and was extended to include interviews from key leaders to gauge the enterprise's focus on customer value and employee engagement.

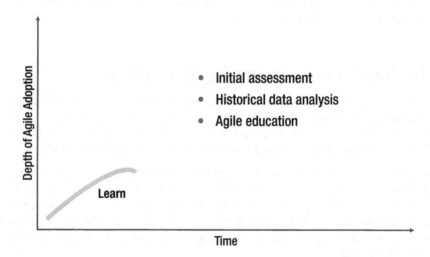

Figure 22-4. Learning about value and the employees while offering education

Value-based questions focused on how value is measured today and how that value is validated along the way with customer feedback. It also included base-lining existing data such as how long it takes to deliver an idea from the moment it is recorded to when it is released. To learn about the people, employee-based questions focused on levels of collaboration, ownership, motivation, enthusiasm, trust, and safety, with a particular focus on self-organizing teams.

As the coaches were learning about the enterprise, they were providing Agile education primarily focused on readying the minds of those who expressed an interest in Agile. This involved an Agile 101 session of Agile values and principles, what a customer-value-driven enterprise looks like, and an understanding of what the current Agile galaxy looks like for their enterprise (see Chapter 4 for more details).

The results of this increment highlighted that there was little focus on customer value throughout the enterprise. There were a few spots where both Agile and self-organizing teams were understood. Also, lead times for delivering customer value were very long, averaging about 28 months.

Grow

"Grow" is where things got interesting. "Grow" focuses on education and experimentation, as illustrated in Figure 22-5. The assessment provided enough telling data that the company knew that it needed to respond more quickly to the marketplace. The Agile Advantage Team coaches opted to work from a pull model where they would initially provide coaching to teams that were asking for Agile help. They thought that the teams that were showing enthusiasm for Agile were more likely to put more effort into owning their Agile change. Coaching focused on helping teams begin experiments in bounded authority and self-organizing around the work.

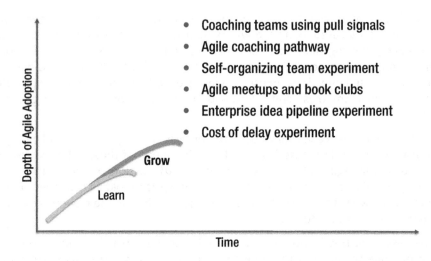

Figure 22-5. Growing knowledge of Agile through coaching, education, and experimentation

The Agile Advantage Team coaches also began their own education program focused on helping the enterprise increase customer value through delivering early and often, optimizing the end-to-end flow for faster delivery, enhancing quality through fast feedback loops, increasing employee motivation and ownership, understanding coaching, and learning ways to promote change. They did this in the form of an Agile coaching pathway of education where there were at least 18 Agile and Value, Flow, Quality (VFQ) topics covered over a period of similar weeks. It seemed like a long period, but learning is best achieved over time and enterprise transformation is serious business.

Following the pull model, the Agile Advantage Team coaches initiated periodic Agile meet-ups within the company. All employees could join and it included a specific Agile topic for the first half and a Lean Coffee approach for the second half, where attendees decide the agenda. This helped coaches understand the topics of interest that fed into the Agile adoption effort.

The biggest focus in "Grow" was experimenting with an enterprise idea pipeline model. This involved establishing an enterprise portfolio of ideas and applying a cost of delay (CoD) to understand priority and order of magnitude differences among ideas. This provided visibility to leadership on low-value work being done at the expense of high-value work waiting in the pipeline. Education and experimentation with leadership and chief product owners occurred around a customer-value-driven model so it could be tailored to the specifics of this enterprise. This formed the beginning of a continuous Agile budgeting framework.

Accelerate

Feedback from the "Grow" increment was quite positive. Teams liked that the education wasn't just focused on process but covered concepts of value, discovery, flow, experimentation, and quality. "Grow" also made it evident that there was more demand for Agile education and coaching. The experiments in "Grow" were not always successful, but the learning helped adapt the use of the idea pipeline and cost of delay. "Accelerate" expanded coaching and experimentation, as illustrated in Figure 22-6.

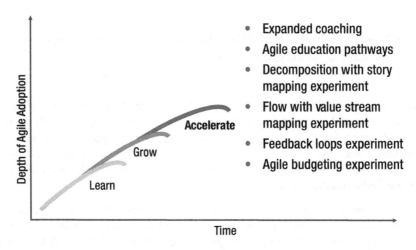

Figure 22-6. Accelerating the Agile adoption through expanded coaching and more

The pull signals led the Agile Advantage Team coaches to expand coaching with teams and leadership. They also experimented with a more formal education program that focused on employees and teams that wanted further education, again using a pull system. They did this in the form of an Agile practitioner pathway (APP) where there were at least eight topics covered over a period of similar weeks. The topics included the discovery mindset, increasing customer value through delivering early and often, optimizing the end-to-end flow for faster delivery, and enhancing quality through fast feedback loops (for example, VFQ). These pathways used work-based education where, after learning a topic, the cohorts applied the knowledge to their own teams for greater learning, which also advanced the adoption.

The coaches began experiments with story mapping for those engaged teams to improve decomposition and cut increments that bridged the gap between idea at the enterprise level and user stories at the team level. This helped employees better understand the requirements tree from strategy to ideas to increments to epics and user stories. In addition, since the historical data highlighted that many high-value ideas would wait for long periods of time before they got worked on, a value stream mapping experiment was initiated on several product lines to understand the process efficiency. Efforts were then made to eliminate bottlenecks and reduce wait states.

■ **Agile Pit Stop** Experiments in the early stages of your Agile transformation are a good way to find out what works for you and your enterprise.

It became evident that in order to align with customer value, customer feedback was needed along the way. A few of the teams wanted to experiment with customer feedback loops. The coaches were happy to support this experiment applying the customer feedback vision practice (see Chapter 14) to better understand customer personas and where feedback loops may provide the highest-value feedback.

Since there was a decision to continue with the enterprise idea pipeline and cost of delay experiment for the next six months, it was felt that it was prudent to experiment with Agile budgeting (see Chapter 19) to allow a more effective means of aligning to high-value ideas (that is, demand) and adapting supply to meet this demand. Leadership and finance became part of the group that learned and began experimenting with this concept.

Transform

Feedback from "Accelerate" was positive so the enterprise committed to "Transform." This focused on three increments, as illustrated in Figure 22-7. The first focused on role evolution, scaling coaching, and education for product owners who lead with value, HR engagement, and commitment to Agile across the enterprise. The second focused on leadership education, dependencies across the work, and measures of success. The third focused on scaling education, influencing outside vendors to apply Agile and assessing our state of Agile.

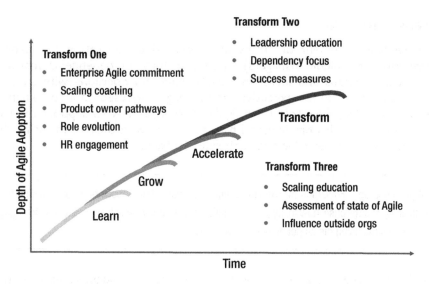

Figure 22-7. Transforming in three stages

Transform One

The first increment of "Transform" started with many teams committing to Agile (bottom-up) and leadership committing to Agile (top-down). This provided a good overall balance of commitment although it was also stated that no one would be forced to become Agile.

Now that there were many people keen on applying Agile, there was a need to scale the coaching. The Agile sponsor agreed to add four more coaches to the Agile Advantage Team. The coaching positions were filled with two external hires and two internal Agile champions. They were educated in a pattern similar to the Agile coaching pathway.

Education was focused on those that had the responsibility of driving customer value, which included product owners and product managers. The product owner pathway focused strongly on understanding the customer with personas, identifying value with cost of delay, challenging assumptions, and establishing customer feedback loops.

Also included was a focus on role evolution as the coaches, management, and teams realized that some roles were already changing (for example, needing product owners, moving from project managers to ScrumMasters, and evolving management's role). HR realized that it had a role to play in role evolution and the Agile adoption effort in general. HR took part in understanding the elements of embracing employees focused on building trust, learning more about intrinsic motivation, promoting collaboration, and so on. HR also started to realize the importance of building a learning enterprise so it started taking part in understanding the discovery mindset and participating in experiments.

Transform Two

The second increment of "Transform" focused on education for leaders (executives and middle managers), a particular focus on dependency management across teams and ideas, and establishing and operating with success measures. Education for executives and managers focused on a combination of understanding their role in an Agile enterprise, how to support the use of an enterprise idea pipeline, and how to engage with their teams using the language of customer value and capturing feedback.

■ **Agile Pit Stop**   Education for executives and managers should focus on understanding their role in an Agile enterprise, how to support the use of an enterprise idea pipeline, and how to engage with their teams using the language of customer value.

As the enterprise idea pipeline was used, it became evident as early as the Record through Refine stages that some of the ideas required effort from multiple teams. This led to promoting lightning-bolt-shaped teams so that a team could work in more than one area. It also led to restructuring some teams to include a more cross-functional set of skills that reduced dependencies on other teams. This started with experiments in both areas with executives and managers adapting as they learned what worked better to reduce cross-team dependencies.

As management played a role in optimizing flow by removing impediments, there was a particular focus on the time it took for an idea to go from the Record stage to the Release stage (that is, lead times). In addition, there was a focus on looking for ways to reduce approvals, hand-offs, waiting, and so on. This also included a strong focus by product owners and teams on decomposition and cutting increments of value from the idea.

Finally, there was a spirited discussion focused on measures of success for getting to customer value. Initial discussions focused on the importance of measuring outcomes over output. This continued with a discussion of having leading indicators since outcomes are lagging measures. Primary measures for getting to customer value included value curves, driving with CoD, customers at demos, customer satisfaction, tracking end-to-end lead times, and customer revenue (the outcome measure). Employee satisfaction was also included. An enterprise dashboard was established as a means to correlate and understand progress, to avoid sub-optimization of over measuring, and to improve decision making.

Transform Three

The third increment of "Transform" focused on scaling education, establishing an assessment that focused on an Agile culture, and influencing outside organizations to align with Agile.

Now that there were many people keen on applying Agile, there was a need to scale the delivery of the education. Since there were a number of local Agile champions within the company, they were leveraged to help co-deliver the Agile practitioner pathway. Most were very enthusiastic as it was their way of giving back to the Agile community. A large number of employees were educated in a relatively short period of time.

As the transformation continued, there was a focus on assessing the Agile culture to gain an understanding if the Agile adoption was leading to a transformation. The Agile Cultural Assessment Survey (see Chapter 5) was used to gauge the current level of the Agile mindset in the enterprise. This was combined with the success measures on the enterprise dashboard (see Chapter 20) to correlate Agile cultural alignment with customer focus. Due to the focus on removing impediments and cutting increments of value, lead times were reduced from the original 28 months down to three months.

It was learned that some of the impediments that were slowing the enterprise was the way outside companies delivered to OnHigh. Often, when something was provided, it would have to be reworked in order to integrate the amount of feedback that was gathered. This led to educating vendors on the Agile mindset and the incremental cadence expected in their work. It also included experimenting with how to work with vendors in less of a time-and-material approach and more of an inspect-and-adapt and incremental approach. This helped further reduce the end-to-end lead times.

Sustain

Transitioning to "Sustain" doesn't mean you are done focusing on Agile. However, the culture was focused on identifying, validating, and delivering customer value and on teams self-organizing around the work. "Sustain" effectively lasts indefinitely, with peaks and troughs of effort depending on the shifting needs of the enterprise and leadership changes.

As leadership and employees change, there is a continued focus on education and coaching. While levels of coaching support are often less than previous increments, a continued focus on Agile concepts, practices, and mindset remain in place. After a few tweaks to the Agile Cultural Assessment Survey previously mentioned, it was decided that it would be used during the "Sustain" period at least for the next year.

There was also a focus on honing existing concepts and practices as feedback was received on what worked better. This included introducing new concepts and practices focused on bringing higher value to the customer. Figure 22-8 illustrates "Sustain" activities. This will continue for the foreseeable future.

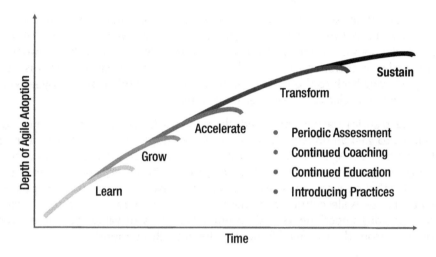

Figure 22-8. Sustaining the Agile transformation

It should be noted that each increment of the Agile adoption that led to an Agile transformation took about six months. Added up, this was more than three years. Transforming an enterprise takes time since it involves a mindset shift and new ways of working. Don't underestimate the effort.

How Will You Write Your Agile Story?

Now it is time for you to write your Agile story. Is your Agile galaxy comprised of a holistic top-to-bottom and end-to-end view of Agile where everyone is engaged? Are you a customer-value-driven enterprise that emphasizes learning customer value through customer feedback? Are your employees given ownership and do they feel like they really matter?

Imagine that your enterprise focuses on the highest-customer-value work. A place where all of the ideas from strategy down to tasks are transparent and visible so everyone knows if their work is aligned with strategy and high-priority ideas. Where employees use 100% of their brain power to self organize around the work and be trusted to build customer value. Where a discovery mindset wins over certainty thinking. Where managers are leaders, leading people with inspiration, vision, and trust. Where customers embrace the products and services being built because they are engaged in the building of the work all along the way. Imagine!

Now it is time for you to imagine your future. Hopefully, this book has provided you with many cutting-edge Agile concepts, mindsets, practices, and techniques to help you adopt Agile throughout your enterprise. It is time for you to write your Agile story. I hope it is one that captures your journey from idea to delivery and from the team level to the executive level. I wish you the best as you imagine and implement your Agile story.

I

Index

© Mario E. Moreira 2017
M. E. Moreira, *The Agile Enterprise*, DOI 10.1007/978-1-4842-2391-8

Get the eBook for only $4.99!

Why limit yourself?

Now you can take the weightless companion with you wherever you go and access your content on your PC, phone, tablet, or reader.

Since you've purchased this print book, we are happy to offer you the eBook for just $4.99.

Convenient and fully searchable, the PDF version enables you to easily find and copy code—or perform examples by quickly toggling between instructions and applications.

To learn more, go to http://www.apress.com/us/shop/companion or contact support@apress.com.

CPI Antony Rowe
Chippenham, UK
2017-03-24 21:58